AMERICAN
MATERIALISM

Why Our Domestic Policies, Our Foreign Policies
and Our Intelligence Assessments Often Fail

JEFF BERGNER

Rambling Ridge Press, LLC
416 Wilderness Drive
Locust Grove, Virginia 22508

Bergner, Jeffrey T.
American Materialism: Why Our Domestic Policies, Our Foreign Policies and Our Intelligence Assessments Often Fail

ISBN 978-0-9890402-6-6 Hardcover
ISBN 978-0-9890402-7-3 Softcover

1. Materialism 2. Progressivism 3. Marxism 4. American Foreign Policy 5. Intelligence Policy

Printed in the United States of America.

For my grandchildren

We live in an age of science and of abounding accumulation of material things. These did not create our Declaration. Our Declaration created them. The things of the spirit come first. Unless we cling to that, all our material prosperity, overwhelming though it may appear, will turn to a barren scepter in our grasp. If we are to maintain the great heritage which has been bequeathed to us, we must be like-minded as the fathers who created it. We must not sink into a pagan materialism.

CALVIN COOLIDGE, JULY 5, 1926

PREFACE

This book has been roughly 45 years in the making. In 1978 I was a newly hired staff assistant to Senator Richard Lugar of Indiana. Senator Lugar was a member of the last Senate delegation to Iran before the abdication of the Shah in January of 1979. I followed events in Iran closely.

One morning after the Shah's hasty departure I ran into a mid-level CIA acquaintance. I asked him "How did you guys get Iran so wrong?" After all, Iran was not just another Middle East nation but, with Israel, our closest ally in the region. "How did you miss the collapse of the Shah's regime and the rise of his soon-to-be successor the Ayatollah Khomeini?"

His answer was fascinating. He said that American intelligence was very good at tracking tangible things that could be counted. The Shah had so many hundred thousand troops, so many thousand tanks, and so many thousand SAVAK (secret police) agents. There appeared to be nothing on the horizon which could seriously challenge him. My acquaintance said that American intelligence tended to overlook non-material, "soft" factors including religious belief.

As I went about my subsequent work as chief of staff for Senator Lugar, staff director of the Senate Foreign Relations Committee, government relations consultant, adjunct professor of national security policy at Georgetown University, and Assistant Secretary of State, I saw this same tendency play out again and again in many different contexts. Everywhere the notion of economic/material determinism seemed to inform American policymaking and analysis.

This book aims to document the pervasive American belief in economic or material causation, which achieved a new salience with the progressive movement in America. It argues that while economic causation is important, an over-reliance on this too-narrow view of human motivation leads to both policy and intelligence failures. Finally, it suggests that a fuller, more nuanced view of social causation will lead to policy and analytical improvements.

Lake of the Woods, Virginia

CONTENTS

INTRODUCTION

EXPLAINING SOCIAL CHANGE

E xplaining social change seems at once too easy and too hard.

It is too easy because there are many causal factors—an unlimited number really—which can be seized upon and proposed with at least superficial plausibility. Explaining the decline and fall of Rome is of course the textbook case. Even before Rome fell, but was merely declining, Roman authors proposed villains in the story, including in some cases Christians. Augustine was quick to defend Christians against this charge. In modern times philosophers like Montesquieu, historians like Edward Gibbon, sociologists like Max Weber and a host of other critics seeking to draw moral lessons from Rome's collapse have waded into the debate.[1]

The same is true of any other social event. Why did the Protestant Reformation occur? Why the Industrial Revolution? Why the American Civil War? Why has today's Democratic Party moved to the left? Not all explanations stand up equally well to scrutiny, and it is the task of historians, social scientists and other critics to evaluate and judge the claims which are made.

Explaining social change seems too hard for the very same reason. There are always many potential causal factors and, harder yet, it seems that valid explanations often require more than one factor to understand complex events properly.[2] This creates a second order problem of how to weigh these factors.[3]

11

Despite best efforts, it seems likely that experts will continue to disagree not only about specific causes, but even about the types or categories of causation which are useful.[4] While some kinds of explanations go in and out of fashion, so long as freedom of inquiry is permitted it seems unlikely we will see the kind of consensus which characterizes the physical sciences.[5] The most that can be hoped for, as social philosopher R. M. MacIver has proposed, is that continuing interpretive efforts will gradually bring us closer to the truth. Even this is not so clear.[6]

Despite the many theoretical questions involved, however, there are times when a working resolution is required. This is when we choose to *act*. At such times, when we seek not only to understand social change but to bring it about (with apologies to Marx), we inevitably act upon some belief—explicit or implicit—in the efficacy of one or more causes and not others.[7] Such is the case when we adopt domestic or foreign policies. Action requires setting aside the complexities of social change causation and acting upon some notion, well understood or not, of how to bring about change.[8]

Among the types of causes to which social change can be attributed, there is a rough and ready divide between what we might call material and ideal causes. Material causes focus on changing the economic condition of people or nations and expecting behavioral changes to follow. Ideal causes are those which speak to the ideas, attitudes or sentiments which people hold, on the premise that if these can be changed, behavioral changes will follow. These types of causation are not so easily divorced in theory, in which both material and ideal causes are often present.[9] But to act is to choose.

The argument of this book is twofold. The first is that many of our current domestic policies and programs, many of our foreign policy tools and many key assessments of our intelligence community are predicated fully on material or economic premises. I will refer to this as economic determinism. Second, these premises often are not well understood by our policymakers themselves; they seem to policymakers quite natural and persuasive, often even to suggest there is no other reasonable basis on which to act.[10] But in diminishing or even ignoring non-economic, ideal factors which often motivate human beings, they miss important truths. And thus they often fail. In this book I will show in detail how this works.

Chapters One through Three address the distinction between material and ideal causes and the bias of the American commercial republic in favor of material causation. Chapter One confronts the strongest exponents of material determinism—Marx and Engels—with Deirdre McCloskey's comprehensive study of what she calls the "great enrichment." It concludes there is an important—though by no means exclusive—role for ideas as the source of social change.

Chapter Two addresses the dilemma which Marx and Engels left to communists who aim to effect social change. It argues that practicing Marxists (of which Lenin and Mao are the best but not the only examples) maintained the notion of material determinism rhetorically, but threw that notion overboard in their actions. They were not in this way very good Marxists.

Chapter Three argues that today's economic determinists are not to be found among so-called Marxist regimes at all. They are found in modern commercial republics like America. This is where the notion of economic man, and a rough and ready economic determinism, find their strongest advocates today.

There is a long tradition of criticism directed at classical liberalism for a tendency to reduce human relations to an economic basis. Today this critical tradition is best illustrated by the work of Patrick Deneen.[11] There is some truth to this, but not as much as these critics suggest. This book understands classical liberalism in a different and more nuanced way. It argues that classical liberalism was conscious of the limits of economics, the importance of human virtue and the need for limited government.

In these ways modern progressivism is not simply a latter-day version of classical liberalism. Progressivism, as its authors stated often and without equivocation, is very different than classical liberalism. Progressivism is better understood as a hostile takeover of classical liberalism than as its present-day cousin. This can be seen in its apotheosis of progress and the necessity with which it unfolds, its economic interpretation of history, and its eager reliance on government to enforce its preferences. It is not the purpose of this book to defend this argument in detail, but rather to demonstrate today's policy failures which result from an over-reliance on the notion of economic causation.

Chapters Four through Six consider America's public policy programs which, while well-intentioned, often fail. Why after many decades of federal programs is there still widespread poverty? Why after the expenditure of hundreds of billions of dollars are crime up, educational performance down, and suicide, depression, and drug addiction up? Why after expenditures of hundreds of billions of dollars is there still worldwide poverty and rampant kleptocratic governance? Why after the expenditure of hundreds of billions of dollars do our intelligence assessments—despite massive collection of useful information—often miss transformational changes? These policies may be well-intentioned, but their over-reliance on economic determinism condemns them to partial success at best.

Chapter Seven offers an array of suggestions about ways in which our domestic policies, foreign policies and intelligence assessments might address these shortcomings and help to make them more effective in achieving their hoped-for results.

THEORY

ONE

MARX ON ECONOMIC DETERMINISM

It has always seemed quite natural to assume that our thoughts can not only apprehend both the natural and social worlds, but can also change them. One assumes, for example, that a band of primitive hunters could identify both its prey and its enemies—not apparently but actually—and organize to attack them—again, not apparently but actually.

This is not to say all human thoughts correctly apprehend reality. Some may be mistaken, even systematically mistaken as a result of cognitive biases (confirmation bias, etc.) or logical fallacies. Nor is it to say there are no limits to human thought which human beings frequently come up against, such as making accurate predictions about the distant future. But confidence in the ability to think freely and correctly about the natural and social worlds, and to bring about change based on these thoughts, has provided a sense of at least limited control over our world.

One exception concerns the claims of theologies with a transcendent God. Here we may find the claim that there is something in our lives or our characters which will systematically mislead us. If we do not follow the teachings of a transcendent God we will misapprehend reality at its deepest level. "I am the way, the truth" or "the fear of God is the beginning of wisdom" represent such claims. In such cases our thinking is radically distorted, so it is said, because we have not taken into our understanding and our practice the ideas of God and his teachings.

That a material cause should distort our thinking is an unusual claim, to say the least. Yet this expansive claim is just what Karl Marx and Frederick Engels assert: if we do not understand that our thoughts about the social world, and especially the success of our actions, are dependent on the underlying economic mode of production and the social classes which grow up around it, we will invariably be misled. Worse yet, the illusion of our ability to think freely about the social world masks unknown but very real tendencies which support the most powerful groups in society. Marx and Engels assert that our social lives and our consciousness can be understood correctly only through the lens of a specific kind of economic thinking which they call historical materialism. Despite efforts by Marxist revisionists to explain away the limits which Marx and Engels put on the production of ideas, their words are straightforward. And despite similar efforts to justify a degree of "voluntarism" in Marxism, Marx is very clear that thinking which is not in alignment with the prevailing economic mode of production cannot lead to significant social change. And by the way, this is one, but not the only way in which Marxism takes on the quality of a secular religion.

MARX, ENGELS AND
HISTORICAL MATERIALISM

Marx and Engels did not begin as historical materialists. Marx began as a philosopher. No longer drawn to his presumed career in jurisprudence, Marx became deeply attracted to philosophy. His doctoral dissertation (written between 1841 and 1843) addressed "The Difference Between Democritean and Epicurean Philosophy of Nature." In it one sees an early concern about the relation of ideas and reality. But one will not find a single word to suggest that Democritus or Epicurus must be understood in the context of the economy of the ancient Greek slave state.

Likewise, in a letter to Arnold Ruge in September of 1843, Marx's revolutionary tendencies were clearly expressed in his call for a "ruthless criticism of everything existing." He speaks of reforming human thinking whether it appears in religion (which Ludwig Feuerbach had already more or less accomplished) or in politics. Marx's own focus is on reforming the way in which human beings think about politics, and Marx appears here as a political revolutionary. There is no word to be found, however, about the way in which politics (or thinking about politics) is itself dependent upon the economic means of production.

This begins to change after 1843 in Marx's *Critique of Hegel's Philosophy of Right* and in Marx and Engels' unpublished manuscript *The German Ideology*.[1] From this point forward Marx and Engels elaborated upon their theory of historical materialism for the remainder of their lives.

What happened? Marx ceased being a philosopher and became an economist. In postulating an order of causation based on material factors, Marx focused over time on ever more granular economic matters. This achieved its mature form in Marx's *The Poverty of Philosophy* and his *Contribution to the Critique of Political Economy*, the latter further elaborated in his three-volume work *Capital*.

What did Marx and Engels mean by their claim that material life shapes human consciousness at its deepest level? They express their thoughts in slightly different ways in various works, but on the whole quite consistently. Perhaps the clearest early statement is found in *The German Ideology*:

> the phantoms formed in the human brain are also, necessarily, sublimates of their material life process, which is empirically verifiable and bound to material premises. Moral life, religion, metaphysics, all the rest of ideology and their corresponding forms of consciousness, thus no longer retain the semblance of independence. They have no history, no development; but men, developing their material production and their material intercourse, alter, along with this, their real existence, their thinking, and the products of their thinking.[2]

Ideas do not necessarily apprehend, much less shape reality; the economics of historical materialism shapes ideas. This thought is restated several years later in *The Manifesto of the Communist Party* in 1848 where Marx and Engels say:

> man's ideas, views and conceptions, in one word, man's conscious-
> ness, change with every change in the conditions of his mate-
> rial existence, in his social relations, and in his social life. What
> else does the history of ideas prove than that intellectual produc-
> tion changes its character in proportion as material production is
> changed? The ruling ideas of each age have ever been the ideas of
> its ruling class.[3]

As Marx would later describe his own intellectual development, he said his studies led him to the following conclusion:

> The mode of production in material life determines the general char-
> acter of the social, political and spiritual processes of life. It is not
> the consciousness of men that determines their existence, but, on
> the contrary, their social existence determines their consciousness.[4]

What are Marx and Engels saying and what are they not saying? Can there be no independence from the economic base of what they elsewhere called the intellectual "superstructure"—politics, religion, philosophy, and spiritual matters generally? This question was addressed by Engels toward the end of his life in a letter to Conrad Schmidt. There Engels says "the material mode of existence is the '*primum agens*,' but the ideological sphere can react back upon it with a secondary effect."[5] He elaborates on this in a letter to Joseph Bloch where he explains that he and Marx never said the economic element is the only determining one, but that the superstructure of ideas "also exercise their influence upon the course of historical struggles."[6]

Engels goes so far as to say that Marx and Engels themselves were partly to blame for the fact that some of their followers laid more stress on the economic side than is due to it, because of the need to combat their opponents who denied the economic basis of history.[7] In further explanation, Engels notes that Marx spent a great deal of time and effort analyzing political events of the day. *The Class Struggles in France, 1848-1850, The Eighteenth Brumaire of Louis Bonaparte* and *The Civil War in France* are good examples, in which Marx carefully demonstrates how political decisions affected the outcome of specific events. Marx's numerous submissions to *The New York Tribune,* for which Marx served as a London correspondent in the 1850's, are also ample testimony to this. Engels says that grasping history by a simple-minded economic theory would be like an equation of only the first degree. History is more complex.

If, however, the intellectual superstructure reacts back on the economic mode of production, and they influence one another reciprocally, this would be no useful theory at all, but only a vacuous circular argument about the many sides of human life. But Engels is careful to say that in the end it is the economic mode of production and its attendant social class conflicts which propel human history at the deepest level. The intellectual superstructure can shape only the particular forms which historical events take, not the essence of that history. England, France and Germany will all move from capitalism to socialism in their particular ways, based on their unique histories, but they will all move from capitalism to socialism.

Two questions arise. First, what evidence did Marx and Engels offer to support their theory of the economic basis of human consciousness? Their evidence, such as it is, consists largely of looking back at human history and interpreting it in light of their theory of class struggle based on the economic mode of production.[8] There is no doubt that these investigations of the past offer novel and often interesting interpretations. They offer fresh perspectives on oft-discussed historical events.[9] Fair enough. But this in itself does not demonstrate that their view is more than one admittedly interesting perspective. Marx and Engels of course intend more than this; they assert their view is the correct interpretation of human history at its deepest level. For this they offer no proof at all.[10] In fairness, Marx and Engels at least attempted to map their theory onto the empirical world—or perhaps vice-versa—which is more than one can say about many of today's theoretical economists. But the proof of their interpretation rests entirely on assertion and anecdotal evidence.

Second, if as Marx and Engels assert, all thought is a "sublimate" of a given material life process, how can Marx and Engels escape this limitation and arrive at the truth of the underlying basis of human history? How can they see their way to the truth, where all previous thought was essentially "conditioned" by its given economic mode of production? Marx and Engels respond that their thinking too derives from the current economic condition within which they work. They say that as the prevailing economic mode of production gives way to a new one, some of the internal contradictions of the decaying system give rise to thinkers who can anticipate what comes next. The owl of Minerva takes flight at dusk. Again, perhaps fair enough. One has seen in each age thinkers who were able to see ahead some ways into the future.

But Marx and Engels are saying more than this. They are saying not simply that they can see the internal contradictions of the current capitalist system, but that they have uncovered the fundamental pattern of history which describes the process of each and every major historical transformation. They are not simply ahead of their time, but somewhat outside of time altogether. They seem uniquely to have been able to see the deepest truth about human history, which no other thinker has seen. What could possibly be the justification for such a claim?

The answer has to do with what Marx and Engels call "science." From the mid-1840's they are at pains to distinguish their work from that which they label "utopian." Utopians like Saint-Simon, Fourier and Owen criticize the failures of the current socio-economic system. They are correct to do so, and they desire to create a better (generally socialist) system in which workers are no longer oppressed. Their intent is admirable but their moralizing, however well-intended, will always be in vain for Marx and Engels because they are merely trying to take ideas in their heads and impose them on social and economic life. The utopians' work in this way is founded only on idealism and hope, and is therefore bound to fail. One cannot will the future into being with ideas in one's head, because transformational change is possible only with a change in the mode of production.

Marx and Engels are at pains to criticize their fellow socialists. What Marx and Engels say is that socialism will not come to pass because they wish for it—though they do—but because they have examined empirically the economic facts of the capitalist mode of production and understand through the lens of historical materialism that capitalism is fated to give way to socialism. Marx and Engels, so they say, do not engage in idle speculation and willfulness, but in science.[11]

What do Marx and Engels understand as science? By the mid-nineteenth century science was widely advanced as a virtue. The idea of science had moved beyond the small number of its practitioners to seize hold of the popular imagination. To be scientific was to be in the vanguard of thought.[12] When Marx and Engels ceased being philosophers and became economists their work became "scientific." Historical materialism was a science.

Marx made an early comment that "science would be superfluous if the outward appearance and essence of things directly coincided." This suggests that science reaches a deeper reality—the essence of things—than do common perceptions. It is a highly debatable proposition that a scientific description reaches something more real than does a perception. We do not go wrong with our perceptions, but only when we wrongly build upon them. What is described by science is different and may offer potential understandings and vast uses of the natural world which perceptions cannot. Nevertheless, Marx's formulation clearly expresses the idea that a certain kind of thinking—science—can take us to the essence of things. Marx here sides with Hegel's opposition to Kant, who argued that essences—things in themselves—cannot be known.

This view represents a popularized version of what science actually does. It is by no means as careful as Newton's statement "hypotheses non fingo." Newton makes no claim that he has arrived at the essence of anything but has only described accurately how things work. Oddly, it may seem that Marx and Engels are asserting that the science of the bourgeois age takes us to essential truth, which transcends the kind of bourgeois thought that reflects the economic mode of its production. The mantle of essentialism, which has been advanced regularly throughout the history of western philosophy, seems to have been draped upon modern science. How is this possible?

Marx and Engels propose an answer. For them science is not the study of a fixed and unchanging world, such as is described by bourgeois economists. For Marx and Engels this is a kind of science in which temporary realities are described as invariant principles which operate everywhere and always. For Marx and Engels, true science consists in the study of the evolving, changing natural and social worlds. Here is a Hegelian notion of science from which Marx and Engels never depart.

When Charles Darwin published *On the Origin of Species* in 1859, Marx and Engels found not only someone they considered an ally, but a major scientific confirmation of the world's continuing evolution which it is the purpose of science to understand. In a letter to Ferdinand Lasalle in 1861, Marx wrote:

> Darwin's book is very important and serves as a basis in natural science for the class struggle in history. One has to put up with the crude English method of development, of course. Despite all deficiencies not only is the death-blow dealt here for the first time to 'teleology' in the natural sciences, but their rational meaning is empirically explained.[13]

Here is a natural scientific analogy to the empirical investigations of historical materialism. Darwin studied the natural world of animal species empirically. But he did not do only that; he also proposed a general theory of why changes among species occur: random mutation and natural selection. The Marxist analogy to natural selection in the human world was class conflict based on the economic mode of production. Class conflicts in human history play out in different ways—from primitive life to ancient slave states, to feudalism, to capitalism and finally to socialism. This was analogous to the various ways species adapt over time. But however different these social changes were from one another, they all unfolded according to Marx's version of natural selection: the class struggle described by historical materialism. Adaptation among animal species was the natural analogue to underlying conflicts (sometimes called in Hegelian language "contradictions") between social classes formed around the economic mode of production.

But there was a major difference between the evolutionary biology of Darwin (and for that matter of today) and Marx's historical materialism. Darwin offered a coherent theory of the adaptation of species and could point to empirical facts to support his theory. He could also suggest gaps in the historical record which could point evolutionary biologists to where to look for additional confirmation of his theory. But the one thing Darwin could not do—and did not even attempt to do—was to make predictions about the future. He might well suppose that the principle of natural selection was still operative and would work in the future just as it had in the past. What could have changed to affect this in any way? But this would not justify any prediction at all about new species, either their types, their numbers or the moment of their arrival. Evolutionary biology can offer a general principle for the evolution of species, but it cannot make any useful predictions about the future.[14]

Matters were very different for Marx and Engels' brand of historical materialism. Like Darwin, they suggested the future would continue to operate upon the same general theory of class conflict that had operated in past human history.[15] But they also made a very specific prediction about the future, namely, the emergence of socialism from capitalism. This prediction went far beyond anything Darwin ever thought to propose with his theory of natural selection.

On what scientific basis could such a prediction be made? Are we still in the world of empirical investigation, that is, science, or have we left the world of science and entered the world of prophecy? The only grounds on which the inevitable development of socialism could be inferred are an empirical analysis of capitalism that discovers a reason it cannot continue in the future as it has in the past. This Marx attempted in *The Critique of Political Economy* and especially in *Capital.* Marx and Engels purported to see in capitalism a deep internal "contradiction" between its social means of production and the private and uneven fruits of that production, a contradiction that would cause capitalism inevitably to collapse. But what did all this actually demonstrate?

It might well be possible to analyze current economic realities and find therein some basis for a plausible guess about the future. But this is surely not science.[16] That the working class suffered under the economic realities of the mid-to-late nineteenth century is a fair enough observation and Marx describes this suffering with great passion. But that capitalism would ever further immiserate the working class could not be known; it was a guess. And as it turned out it was not a very good guess at that.

It is interesting to note that here Marx adopts a linear view of history akin to that of bourgeois economists. While capitalism will eventually be overturned altogether, in the meantime it seems for Marx able to develop only in a straight line, linear fashion. It can only further immiserate the working class. There seems to be no possible alternative. Until capitalism is overturned altogether it can proceed only incrementally in one direction. Why is no other course conceivable? Why can't capitalism ameliorate its working conditions? Why can't life become a war of all against all? Why can't modern society destroy itself altogether and return to a world that looks like feudal society? Or, more likely (as has in fact occurred) why can't a so-called proletarian revolution turn into a more or less perpetual tyranny?

Indeed, as we shall discuss later in this chapter, Marx and Engels go even further and propose an even less well-grounded notion: not only will capitalism inevitably give rise to socialism, but this will be the final major historical change that will occur. The human world will witness a new, never before seen—at least since primitive times—outcome, namely the end of all social class warfare. This would be tantamount to Darwin suggesting that at some future date natural selection will cease to operate and the natural world will achieve a final stasis. It seems that here Marx and Engels are returning once again to Hegel, whose dialectical process would lead to the end of history when the Absolute Idea was achieved (or achieved itself, if you prefer).

Feuerbach said that the more virtues which humans ascribe to God, the less virtues humans attribute to themselves. Marx and Engels assert that capitalism represents the most complete and universal immiseration of man, a system in which men have entirely alienated their work from themselves. This is a large assertion for which they never offer a grain of evidence. Would it somehow have been less alienating to be a medieval serf? Or worse yet, to be a slave in ancient society whose entire life, not just the objects of his labor were owned by someone else? Feuerbach freed humans from their theological chains by teaching them about the alienation or projection of their human qualities onto God. For Marx and Engels, Feuerbach achieved only a partial, and not the most important part of human liberation. Marx and Engels envision a complete inversion of the alienated qualities of the working class, not merely in their minds but in their material existence. This will achieve a real material freedom for man, apparently a one-time only historical act.

THE ROLE OF IDEAS

Many critics have taken aim at Marx and Engels' notion of historical materialism and the inevitable development of socialism from the so-called contradictions of capitalist society. Some have addressed specifically their claim about the way in which ideas are shaped by the class conflict which grows up around the economic mode of production.[17] But none has done so more effectively than the economic historian Deirdre McCloskey. Even though her work is not addressed specifically to this end, her three volume work on bourgeois dignity, equality and virtues could serve as a counterpoise to Marx's three volumes of *Capital*. Her work serves as one of many possible ways to illustrate the importance of ideas as causal factors in social change.

McCloskey never anywhere says that her work is directed specifically against Marx, who she regards as a seminal economic thinker, calling him "the greatest social scientist of the nineteenth century." She has a target-rich list of both economic and non-economic thinkers at which to aim. What she aims to do is explain what she calls the "great enrichment" of human life which begins in Europe in the seventeenth and eighteenth centuries and reaches full flower in 1800 and afterward. She sees the great enrichment of human life as far and away the most unique and important event in human history since the advent of agriculture. This enrichment has created untold wealth for great numbers of people, in a way scarcely imaginable before its advent.

What is the cause of this great transformation in human life? McCloskey does not identify the great enrichment precisely with the industrial revolution, though the overlap is clear enough. She does not do so because understanding the industrial revolution as the source of our enormous productivity is, in a way, to accept the notion of the primacy of economic technique, which she refuses to do. The problem is not how the industrial revolution created modern riches, but how the industrial revolution as a part of the great enrichment is itself to be explained.[18]

McCloskey leaves no doubt about where to look for this explanation. It is not in material things or in a changed economic mode of production, which only begs the question of their origin. It is rather in changing human ideas and human sentiments—reinforced by a powerful new rhetoric—that the origin of the great enrichment can be found. Consider these statements:

> A big change in the common opinion about markets and innovation, I claim, caused the Industrial Revolution, and then the modern world.

> The cause was not in the first instance an economic/material world— not the rise of this or that class, or the flourishing of this or that trade, or the exploitation of this or that group.

> I argue that depending exclusively on materialism to explain the modern world, whether right-wing economics or left-wing historical materialism, is mistaken.

> I am claiming, in other words, that the historically unique economic growth on the order of a factor of ten or sixteen or higher, and its political and spiritual correlates depend more on ideas than economics.[19]

To which one might say, fine. Here is a set of assertions quite contrary to those of Marx and Engels. Why should we prefer these assertions to those of Marx and Engels? How does McCloskey argue for her position? What is the evidence for her views? She offers two avenues of evidence, one of which is like that of Marx and Engels and one of which is decidedly not. What she shares with Marx and Engels is an empirical examination of early modern western history. Like Marx and Engels, she is an economic historian. In turning her attention to the origins of the modern world, she is able to do what Marx and Engels do not, namely, to demonstrate that changes in the ideas of liberty, equality and dignity significantly pre-dated the industrial revolution and the great enrichment.

There is for Marx and Engels always the problem of showing that if the ideas defending free markets are the reflection of the dominant economic class, why did they arise earlier than that dominant class? We have already touched on this issue, as Marx and Engels suggest that a handful of thinkers can anticipate the breakup of the old order. But Marx and Engels never address the fact that it was not just the anticipation of a small number of thoughtful individuals (such as Marx and Engels saw themselves with the demise of capitalism), but a broad shift of thinking about liberty, equality and the dignity of work. McCloskey documents this in great detail. As an interpreter of the thought of the seventeenth and eighteenth centuries, McCloskey is more extensive, more granular and far more persuasive.

But the stronger reason to prefer McCloskey's account of the priority of ideas as the cause of the great enrichment lies elsewhere. Marx and Engels simply assert the truth of historical materialism, and its value lies in the novelty and striking interpretations this theory can provide. There is no doubt that as an addition to, if not a counter to the "great man" theory of history or the simple listing of political regimes which come and go, Marx and Engels deepened thinking about historical causation. Their historical descriptions were unique and powerful. This, however, is not the same as evidence, but more like the cleverness involved in fitting historical research into a pre-existing framework.

McCloskey, on the contrary, offers a method akin to what doctors in the medical field call "differential diagnosis."[20] When a medical symptom presents itself, it is often one which can have many possible causes. Doctors must find the actual cause if they are to treat the symptom successfully. To do this they follow a process in which they rule out causes in order to find the one likely to be causing the troublesome symptoms. This is very much the same kind of complexity which historians encounter when they seek to explain historical causation. And this is exactly the procedure which McCloskey adopts, and in a very methodical way. In chapter after chapter in her books on bourgeois equality and dignity, she considers each of the many other causes which have been proposed as the engine of the modern world. She considers greed, accumulation, rationality, private property, trade, geography, transport, coal, the mode of production, exploitation, colonialism, imperialism and others and demonstrates that in each case they have been present in many other times and places. She looks for the unique factor which was not present in other times and places in which a great enrichment might have occurred. She aims to rule out the possible, but not actual causes of the great enrichment, just as a doctor does when looking for the actual cause of a symptom. This she finds in the changing ideas and sentiments regarding human equality, liberty and dignity which allowed innovation to take place on a large scale.

This is a process in which Marx and Engels never engaged. In dismissing the priority of human ideas in favor of the given mode of production, they were content with the often sharp insights they produced. They asserted, but never demonstrated, that ideas were the spiritual superstructure of underlying material causes. They could demonstrate that historical materialism was novel and even in part powerful, but not that it was correct—either as a description of the rise of capitalism or any other major historical change.

Here we should pause for a moment to consider what McCloskey is *not* saying, much less trying to demonstrate. That is that economics, or the study of material factors in history, is of no consequence in explaining human actions. To the contrary, as an economic historian McCloskey is sensitive to the influence of those factors:

I do not want to be understood as ignoring constraints, prices, income, geography, climate, class, demography, interests and all the other non-ideational forces elevated to single causes during the age of intellectual materialism, 1890-1980.[21]

She speaks instead of a "dance" between ideas and conditions, and quotes John Stuart Mill approvingly:

> The creed and laws of a people act powerfully on their economical condition, and this again, by its influence on their mental development and social relations, reacts back upon their creed and laws.[22]

If we are back to a "dance" in which ideal and material factors reciprocally influence one another, what have we really learned? Not much that would be of use to anyone seeking to identify the causal factors which initiate social change, and certainly not for anyone seeking an effective basis on which to act.

But we are not. McCloskey makes clear that when it comes to explaining the great enrichment, ideas and sentiments are the indispensable, unique causal factors. What then is the role of economic factors? McCloskey argues—and this will inform our later analysis of public policy—that economic factors are the better, perhaps necessary basis to explain small incremental changes in social life. Economics can explain much, indeed economics is necessary to explain specific and ongoing changes which occur in societies. About this she says:

> Economics did matter in terms of shaping the pattern. It usually does. Exactly who benefitted and exactly what what was produced, and exactly when and where was a matter of economics—a matter of incomes and property and incentives and relative prices. If a historian does not grasp the economics he will not understand the pattern of modern history.[23]

Economics can, and must be used to explain, for example, why Americans burned wood far longer than the wood-poor and coal-rich nations in northwestern Europe. But the great enrichment "did not occur mainly because of the usual economics."[24]

In this way McCloskey envisions a wide role for economics in explaining human choices within historical change which is relatively bounded. McCloskey sees many contemporary economists as "continuists," that is, thinkers who understand social change as a result of continuing incremental processes. For many ordinary historical changes economics works just fine. It would be a grave mistake to ignore economic factors in shaping human choices and in explaining social change. But when continuists aim to explain the extraordinary new development in human history which was the great enrichment, they take their science to a place where it does not work.

The contrast with Marx and Engels is interesting. For Marx and Engels the pattern of political and spiritual life within a social class under a given mode of production is a matter not necessarily determined by, or best understood by economic conditions. This is where there is space for a distinct and unique play of ideas and sentiments—politics, religion, philosophy, and other spiritual matters. The French, for example, have a different way of organizing their lives and of reflecting upon them than do the British or the Germans. But no matter how these spiritual factors are expressed, at bottom they are shaped by the interests of the ruling class which develops around a given economic mode of production. In this view economics takes us to what is the deepest cause of human consciousness as well as the only efficacious way to bring about transformational social change.

With McCloskey it is just the other way around. Economics can account just fine for smaller social realities and social changes which take place in a given milieu. But economics cannot explain the deep transformation of the great enrichment. McCloskey expresses this in the subtitle of *Bourgeois Dignity* which reads *Why Economics Can't Explain the Modern World*. Material factors are very real, but they must not be taken beyond the limits of their usefulness.

McCloskey goes further. She sees in contemporary economics, especially of the mathematical variety, an unfortunate tendency to ignore "soft" causes such as ideas and sentiments in favor of material causes which can be studied quantitatively.[25] Ideas have a role to play not only at the meta-level of the great enrichment, but at the level of narrower but still significant social changes. Here she would include consequential events like the American Declaration of Independence and the ensuing American Constitution.[26]

One might say that much of contemporary economics has been captured by its own methodology, which proceeds on the basis of assumptions which it does not itself defend or perhaps even fully understand. McCloskey mentions especially Paul Samuelson because of his enormous influence on the profession. Economists like Samuelson reduce the motives of men to prudence or rationality in seeking their own ends. This allows economists to explain human behavior in logical and even mathematical ways. But it simply assumes prudence aided by rationality is the only motive of men. Worse yet, such a manner of thinking often tries to resolve all other motives of men into utility maximization (a la Bentham). The method ceases to be a servant but becomes the master. Here too one can see a faint echo of Hegel, for whom the real is the rational and the rational is the real.

This tendency to be captured by method is a great temptation in each of the sciences. What can be known to be true is only what is discovered by an approved methodology. If it is not discovered in this fashion it cannot be true. This understanding is perhaps less characteristic of actual scientists, who usually practice their craft without much concern for philosophical questions which surround it. But what persuasive argument could possibly be made that a method is what constitutes the measure of truth? "There are more things in heaven and earth, Horatio, than are dreamt of in your philosophy."

There is yet another implication of McCloskey's view. For Marx and Engels there may well be differences in the specific ways in which ancient slave societies transitioned to feudalism, feudalism to capitalism and soon enough capitalism to socialism. But lying beneath these different transitions, as it were, is a meta-theory for Marx and Engels, namely, class conflict around the economic mode of production. As we have suggested, there is no evidence offered that this theory is sufficient, much less necessary, to explain all significant social changes. We will say more about this later in this chapter.

For McCloskey there is no assertion that a meta-theory must always and everywhere explain significant social changes. When she discovers that ideas and sentiments are the significant differential that led to the great enrichment, she makes no claim that this must have happened just as it did. It simply happened when and where it did, and in just the way she describes empirically. She points out many times and places in which a great enrichment might have occurred but did not. Both ideal and material factors came together in a way which caused the great enrichment. But McCloskey does not create an over-arching theory which required this to happen in northwest Europe just when it did (except of course that it turned out this way). There were no theoretical or material "contradictions" which created such a moment. Perhaps all that can be said is that it is our great good fortune that it happened when and where it did. We are the happy beneficiaries.

This difference between Marx and Engels and McCloskey creates a significant difference in how to see the future. For Marx and Engels, as we shall soon discuss, the future of capitalism was already determined by its ever-growing contradiction between socialized production and private ownership of the means of production. This is not simply a hope but a foregone scientific conclusion.

For McCloskey there is no such process which necessarily determines the future of capitalism. Here it must be said in fairness that McCloskey has had the benefit of roughly 140 years of history which Marx and Engels, working in the mid-to-late nineteenth century, did not. It is now evident that capitalism has not led to an ever-greater immiseration of the working class. Though there are deep material inequalities among people today, capitalism has raised the standard of living for almost everyone. If Marx were writing today, he could not write what he did in the mid-nineteenth century.

For McCloskey it is quite possible that the critics of bourgeois life during this period of great enrichment might destroy it altogether. These critics which, following Coleridge she calls the "clerisy," are found on both the political left and right. They hold in contempt bourgeois values which they often mistakenly identify as greed or a desire to accumulate thing after thing. They favor other values such as tribalism or nationalism on the right or radical reforms of economic production and distribution on the left.

Nations can reject bourgeois values, as some have, and suffer the fate of a return to pre-capitalist levels of production, such as has occurred in Venezuela or Zimbabwe. There is no guarantee that bourgeois ideas and rhetoric which support the great enrichment will remain dominant, nor is there a guarantee they will not. It depends. It is also possible there is also a kind of middle way in which bourgeois values are more closely constrained, such as we see today in Western Europe. This produces somewhat less efficient but somewhat more equal societies. There is nothing we know that makes any of these outcomes either necessary or impossible. It is certainly fortunate there is nothing that demands a revolutionary end to the innovation which has characterized the great enrichment.

Looking further ahead, Marx and Engels spoke occasionally about the character of socialism that would emerge from the demise of capitalism. They envision a break with all previous history, a view which leaves them precious little empirical basis on which to base their speculations. McCloskey makes no such speculations. Nor does she think that a specific intended result can necessarily be achieved by broad social engineering. As Friedrich Hayek said, it takes considerable hubris to think we can re-engineer a social order which we did not engineer in the first place.[27]

There is another implication in the thought of Marx and Engels. As they look back at the sweep of human history, they see occasional figures who they praise as precursors of socialism. But they find no figures from the past who can really teach them anything. Their vision leads to the dismissal of the past as one long error, perhaps unavoidable, but an error for all of that. In possession of the scientific truth of historical materialism, they see the past as little more than a sad record of imperfection and oppression. One sees this tendency to disregard the past, if not to condemn it outright, very much in evidence among the progressive left today.

In the end, for Marx and Engels ideas have a very limited role to play in creating the future. Ideas cannot bring about socialism; only the destruction of capitalism can do this. Ideas are at best a way for theorists who see the future through the lens of historical materialism to help advance a result which will come about in any event. Marx is, in a way, the economist's economist. Taking from Adam Smith and the bourgeois economists the notion that economics is important, he made it far more important yet, even to the point of its indispensability to understand the deepest springs of human life. McCloskey shows over and over again there is no warrant to do this.

THE FUTURE OF SOCIALISM

Marx and Engels left no doubt about their belief that capitalism would be replaced by socialism. In *Capital* Marx described "these tendencies working with iron necessary toward inevitable results."[28] This self-certainty has perhaps added to the attraction of Marxism for people who like to see themselves on the "winning side" of history. We see echoes of this today among people who describe their own views as consistent with "how the arc of history bends," and with equally little evidence for it.

Marx and Engels spoke occasionally about how, when and where the transition to socialism would occur. About how the transition would occur they were often dogmatic, based not so much on empirical observation as on abstract (Hegelian) theorizing. Their principal assertion was that socialism would emerge from capitalism not in a peaceful evolutionary manner but in a violent revolutionary manner.[29] For a revolution so complete as the creation of socialism, the bourgeois class must be destroyed, not bargained with. Marx asks in *The Poverty of Philosophy*:

> Is it at all surprising that a society founded on the opposition of classes should culminate in brutal *contradiction*, the shock of body against body, as its final *denouement*?[30]

The idea that the bourgeoisie would not go gently into that goodnight was, and still is, a decent supposition, but it is just that—a supposition. It is a supposition derived not from empirical, scientific study but from a not-so-well disguised Hegelian dialectic.

This supposition revealed a deep cleft in the European socialist movement. Many socialists saw a different kind of evolution to socialism, of which we might take the German socialist Eduard Bernstein as the best example.[31] Bernstein did not deny the economic interpretation of history in principle, but saw a different path, and therefore recommended different tactics. Bernstein foresaw the evolution of socialism through the democratic process. Socialist candidates would gain election to the parliaments of Europe, as they had already done in Germany. They would gradually shift parliamentary majorities from the bourgeoisie to representatives of the working class. In this way socialism would take hold of government power and put into effect socialist policies. The end would be the same, but the tactics very different. This cleft between various socialist parties would continue well after the death of Marx and Engels, as we shall see when we consider Lenin.

For Marx and Engels, however, Bernstein's approach was no answer at all. This they called a sham socialism which would provide only the "ideal rights" of democracy but not the very real material rights which the working class so desperately needed. This sham socialism would produce only a modified bourgeois democracy which would fall far short of genuine human emancipation.[32] For Marx and Engels the only way to bring about genuine human emancipation was to destroy the bourgeois state which protected the bourgeoisie's privileged position.

How could such a radical change come about, given the dominance of the bourgeoisie? It could occur only when the numerically superior working class—which Marx and Engels called after an ancient Roman word the "proletariat"—would rise up and destroy the bourgeois state. In this process the proletariat would use the existing state to destroy the bourgeois class once and for all. To achieve this world-transforming event the proletariat would require two conditions. First, the proletariat would have to be driven to violent revolution when its ever-increasing immiseration reached a point where it could no longer be sustained. And secondly, the true interests of the proletariat would have to be made clear to it. This was the role of theorists like Marx and Engels, whose task was to teach the proletariat its true interests and to warn it away from half measures. These theorists would not try to create a socialist society out of their own heads, as it were, but to teach the proletariat its historically determined role.[33]

Thus much about how a transition to socialism would occur. When would it occur? This question offered another difficulty for Marx and Engels, as it required a prediction of the future which could not possibly be based upon empirical analysis. When would capitalism's "contradictions" become so acute that it would be brought down? Though Marx at one point spoke rhetorically of 10 or 20 or 50 years, the best answer they could provide was when the time was "ripe."

Marx and Engels were always pleased to see oppressed workers rise up against their employers or against the bourgeois state, such as occurred in the revolutions of 1848. In that case, however, experience proved that in 1848 both European capitalism and the proletariat were insufficiently developed to enable a successful revolution.[34] Marx analyzed the French Revolution of 1848 in great detail, first in a series of articles which Engels later gathered together as *Class Struggles in France, 1848-1850*. This Engels described as the first detailed examination by Marx which showed the role of social classes which formed around the mode of production. Marx also addressed these questions a bit later in *The Eighteenth Brumaire of Louis Bonaparte*. Each of these accounts is a masterpiece of historical writing, replete with interesting observations and Marx's trenchant, biting sarcasm. But they do not in the end come to any but the implicit conclusion that however the details played out, France was not ready in 1848 for a proletarian revolution.

Marx was, if anything, even more enthusiastic about the brief experiment which was the Paris Commune of 1871. Marx found the sentiments of the revolutionaries much to his liking and he studied the new forms of governance which the revolutionaries put in place. He looked to these reforms, which included a frequent rotation of power and greater equality of pay, for signs of what a post-capitalist society might look like. But again, the collapse of the Paris Commune proved only that the time for a successful socialist revolution was not yet ripe.[35]

What then can we conclude about when socialism would arise from the contradictions of capitalism? Marx offers only one hint and that is not definitive. In *The Poverty of Philosophy* Marx says that if the masses see a given social order as "unjust" this is a sign that that an economic order has outlived its usefulness.[36] This is a sign like that of the death of a canary in a coal mine, though accompanied by no clear date at which a successful proletarian revolution will occur. Engels sums up all that can be said when he says a successful revolution can occur only when certain changes in economic conditions arise, conditions that are not "*invented* by the mind" but discovered in "the existing material facts of production."[37]

In this regard, Marx and Engels often struggled with would-be reformers they called "adventurists" or "terrorists." These reformers aimed to bring about revolution by the force of their own wills, not by looking scientifically at the objective conditions required for a successful revolution. These reformers acted subjectively and not according to a scientific understanding of the objective conditions which are required for a successful revolution. Marx and Engels opposed "subjective" efforts which aimed to make the world conform to ideas in people's heads rather than revolutionists conforming their ideas to what can be truly known about the social world. Marx and Engels opposed "voluntarism" whenever they saw it because such actions—which were often advocated by anarchists—had no hope of success.

Marx and Engels walked a line between caution and adventurism. What all this amounts to in practice is simply this: the proof of the pudding is in the eating.[38] We will know the moment is ripe to destroy the bourgeoisie when it happens, not a moment sooner. Though no admirers of religion, Marx and Engels seem to be in the same boat as those who anticipate the second coming of Jesus. This will definitely occur, perhaps even "soon." But we will know when it happens only when it happens.

Having discussed how and when the destruction of capitalism will occur, let us consider where this will occur. Given the "iron necessity" of capitalism to develop its internal contradictions ever further, it seems logical that the most fully developed capitalist country will be the first to witness its collapse. As a general matter this is more or less what Marx and Engels assert. As the most fully developed capitalist country, England is the place to look. In the first volume of *Capital* Marx says "the country that is most developed only shows, to the less developed, the image of its own future."[39] Other nations can learn from this experience; Marx says that while the general premise is clear, "the birth pangs" of following nations can be lessened.[40]

But if the general premise is clear, Marx and Engels expound upon it in various pragmatic and occasionally inconsistent ways. They often treat England, France and Germany together. They say that while England and France are more fully developed capitalist nations, their head start can be offset to some degree by the superior nature of German theory.

In various letters and other asides Marx and Engels touch on the question of socialism in countries other than the nations of Western Europe. Marx, for example, followed events in North America with great interest and his views are invariably interesting. He was an admirer of Abraham Lincoln and on behalf of the International Workingman's Association sent Lincoln congratulations on his successful re-election in 1864. He pointed to the fact that America had begun its economic evolution in a way very differently than Europe. America had never had a feudal order, but began as a nation in which many Americans owned their own property to a far greater degree than was true of Europe.[41]

His comments bring to mind those of Thomas Jefferson, who also addressed the idea of America developing from an agricultural nation to an urban-based industrial nation. For Jefferson this transition was to be avoided, or at least tempered in the hope of retaining a more or less self-sufficient agricultural populace. For Marx the transition to industrialization in America was inevitable, leading to the gradual disappearance of widely owned private property. Marx saw the impact of the civil war in hastening the development of industrial capitalism in America.[42] He correctly saw that America was rising quickly to the top rank of the world's industrialized nations and thus, he supposed, also to an early crisis of capitalism.

Marx and Engels also spoke about the possibility of Russian socialism, especially after Marx's *Capital* found a relatively receptive audience among Russian socialists. Marx went so far as to speculate that Russia could experience an early socialist revolution, shortening by a great deal its nascent capitalism—but only if socialist revolutions were occurring at the same time in the more advanced European nations. In this way Russia could piggyback on the more advanced nations, presumably shortening the "birth pangs" of socialism.

To make this prediction Marx had to take into account the large peasant class in Russia. The peasant class was of course also oppressed, just as was the newly emerging class of industrial workers. In the general scheme of Marx and Engels' thinking, the peasant class had first to become a class of industrialized workers. This meant they must experience a capitalist revolution before a socialist one. Marx and Engels believed there was no possibility of a peasant class leading a revolution; peasants were too isolated from one another to learn their interests as a class, an awareness possible only for the industrialized urban proletariat. Only if the peasant class were allied with the industrial proletariat could it play a useful role in helping to achieve socialism in Russia.

The overall premise is clear enough. The "contradictions" of capitalism which they invoke characterize only mature capitalist societies. Less developed nations and classes can learn from these nations, they can benefit from their example and they can ally with advanced nations. But it is the advanced capitalist countries which are the driving force behind the prospect of socialism.

Marx and Engels, and especially Marx, were thoughtful analysts of capitalism. In this they certainly count as economists. And they count as significant economic historians with their economic interpretation of history from primitive times to the present. In these ways Marx and Engels undertook a project which was grounded in empirical reality. Their meta-theory of historical materialism, in which social classes form around given economic modes of production, is an attempt to generalize from empirical reality. Economics was for Marx and Engels the master science which was necessary to understand human history.

Marx regarded his theory of social classes organized around the means of production as the first of his three important contributions.[43] We are here on solid, if often mistaken economic ground. The second and third of his contributions, as he saw it, were the necessity of the dictatorship of the proletariat and the abolition of all social classes under socialism. Here we are on different ground altogether. We are no longer on the ground of empirical investigation and the development of theories from this examination. We have entered into the world of prophecy, and prophesy of a sort that cannot be derived from their empirical economic work. Their descriptions of the processes of these future occurrences are entirely different in context and argumentation.

The need for a dictatorship of the proletariat, for example, is derived from no meta-theory of history. It seems more like a corner into which Marx and Engels have backed themselves. The bourgeoisie will not step aside willingly, so the proletariat must turn the force of its political state against it. At their most realistic Marx and Engels do not speak of the entire proletarian class administering the new socialist society—whatever that might mean—but of its representatives which they called (quite accurately, by the way) the dictatorship of the proletariat.

What would such a dictatorship look like? Who would be its members, and how would they be chosen? What policies would it adopt in order to dismantle the bourgeois state, and perhaps more importantly what new policies would set the new classless society in the proper direction? These and many other questions are never really answered. It is perhaps clear that a new equality among people would need to be compelled, at least until the bourgeoisie was destroyed. What kind of force would this be, how determined, and for how long would it need to remain in place? The few hints from the Paris commune do not take Marx and Engels very far in answering these questions.

Despite their grandiose rhetoric, one can almost sense the disappointment of Marx and Engels with such small changes as the Paris Commune put in place. Their policies do not look much different than what could be accomplished by Bernstein and his allies through the democratic process. This seems pretty thin gruel for a world historical revolution such as Marx and Engels preach.

This of course leads to the third of Marx's self-described historical contributions, namely, the abolition of social classes and thus the end of class warfare. Here Marx and Engels descend into utter vagueness. They are careful not to say too much about the classless society of socialism which will be achieved by the dictatorship of the proletariat. This is wise, because such predictions would be nothing but guesswork. When they speak of the socialist future they do so in the least persuasive of ways.

Why will the dictatorship of the proletariat give way to a classless society? This can be presumed only on the basis that the dictators will act on behalf of humanity as opposed to any narrower interests. As we will discuss, this thought is also prominent in progressivism, which assumes that government experts will act for the general good and not form narrow interests of their own. But would it not be every bit as likely that the dictators might see a continuing need for their dictates? Might not the dictators need to maintain a permanent dictatorship in order to prevent any backsliding or the re-emergence of a favored class (a thought we will see prominently in Mao)?

There is only one reason to suppose the dictatorship of the proletariat will disappear and that is neither an empirical one nor a generalization derived from empirical analysis. It derives from the definition of the state as the arm of the bourgeoisie, just as the state has been defined as the arm of the ruling class throughout history. When the bourgeoisie disappears so will the state. If there are no social classes the state will not be necessary to enforce the will of the ruling class and thus the state will "wither away."[44] Voila.

What Marx and Engels do say about the socialist future is found mainly in the *Communist Manifesto*, Marx's *Grundrisse* and Marx's *Critique of the Gotha Program*. These are three different types of writing, one an exhortation, one a general economic analysis and one a specific critique of a socialist platform. In these very different works we see the same underlying thought: Marx and Engels envision society without a state. For them society is the deepest level

of human existence and the state is simply an instrumental creation to maintain the dominance of the ruling class. In a classless society no state compulsion will be required. Society will find a way to order life, but the compulsion
of society, if this is even the right word, will somehow be gentler than the
compulsion of the state. In a stateless society Marx famously says that each
will contribute according to his ability and receive according to his need.[45]
This will occur with no state compulsion at all. There will apparently be no
questions raised in such a society about one of the knottiest of all problems
of politics: who decides, and on what basis, what people are able or unable
to do and what needs are merited?[46]

Engels speaks about this in slightly different language but comes to the
same conclusion. He acknowledges that the social manner of production
under capitalism has produced an unparalleled degree of riches. It has provided sufficient abundance to fulfill the basic material needs of all men for
the first time in history. Capitalism has demonstrated the power of social
production. It has been very successful in producing abundance, though a
"contradiction" with the manner in which this abundance is distributed will
lead to its destruction.

Engels acknowledges there will be a continuing need for some kind of
ordering principle under socialism. Running a railway or any other complex
institution will require some planning and coordination. There will always
remain a need for some organization of a society with a complex process of
social production. Engels sometimes calls this "authority" but how this differs
from the social organization of bourgeois production is hard to say. Engels
says, in a very inadequate attempt to give flesh to this empty notion, that
socialism will be characterized by the administration of things rather than
the administration of people. He never explains the difference, no doubt for
a very good reason: there is none.[47]

Marx said on one occasion that under socialism men will be free "to
hunt in the morning, fish in the afternoon, rear cattle in the evening, criticize after dinner, just as I have a mind."[48] This too presumes, as does Engels,
that the possibility of sufficient abundance to supply all men's material needs

will enable a new and different kind of life. With the struggle over the material necessities of life eliminated, a system of far less compulsion is required. Here we should note the essential materialism of their view. Material scarcity has driven human life up to the present; when scarcity no longer prevails a gentler form of organization, that of administration is possible. As a thoroughly materialist notion, there is of course no thought here that non-economic issues might motivate human beings. Comparisons of distinction between human beings, the desire for power, and a host of other sources of human conflict are dismissed with nary a thought.

With these comments Marx and Engels have left entirely the realm of complex human motivation, not to say common sense. They are certainly no longer pursuing science. It would be difficult to imagine a more fanciful utopian reverie, and on less reasoned grounds than the socialist society of Marx and Engels.

Here Marx and Engels cease being economists and again become philosophers, or perhaps better said, seers. We will have a peaceful, harmonious minimally coercive society managing a complex socialized means of production. It is almost as if this complex society will run itself. Economists, Marx said, are the "scientific representatives" of capitalist society. No economists will be necessary in a classless society.

If this sounds familiar, it should. Men are born free but are currently in chains, chains fashioned by the ruling class. When these chains are broken, men will be free again. This is nothing more or less than the speculations of Rousseau dressed up in fancy German metaphysical garb. Marx and Engels' ordering principle for the classless society of socialism is as vacuous as Rousseau's "general will," a useless notion which is both incomprehensible and unrecognizable, much less able to be brought into existence.[49] Like Rousseau's general will, Marx and Engels' classless society simply defines away the heart of political questions.

We should note two points about this socialist utopia. First, it is clear that Marx and Engels believe that capitalism will produce (though they would not use these words) a *morally better* successor to itself. The theory of historical materialism is not merely a process of the ups and downs in human social life, but—at least at the moment of capitalism's destruction—movement toward what is better. Out of the alienation of man under capitalism will arise the best of all possible outcomes. It is in this way "progressive." From the depths of man's alienation under capitalism will arise the fullest possible human emancipation.

This is very different than Darwin's natural selection. Darwin does not describe evolution as a process which produces what is morally better, except in so far as what has evolved is better able to survive. Later thinkers like Herbert Spencer who follow Darwin add a moral quality which Darwin's evolutionary theory is lacking.[50] What Herbert Spencer provides for the "right," Marx and Engels provide for the "left."

Marx and Engels may envision a better society which will emerge from the ashes of capitalism, but they offer no persuasive evidence that this will be so. Historical betterment is a standard modern view, vastly different from antiquity where evolution almost invariably meant degeneration, not improvement. Ancient theology and philosophy talked of a god or gods who created a material world of descending goodness, each step of which was ever less perfect than they were. From a first principle, the creation of matter was always a descent to what is lower. It is a characteristic modern view, on the contrary, that change does not mean degeneration but progress. One sees this clearly in the Hegelian dialectic in which Marx and Engels embed their materialist conception of history.

The second point we should note is even more radical and, if possible, less well-grounded. Not only is a classless socialist society better—apparently the best of all possible human arrangements—but it will be permanent. Marx and Engels suggest there will be no grounds on which subsequent human evolution will occur. Class conflicts which have driven all previous history will disappear and accordingly significant historical change will disappear as well. We will see the end of history. Is there any conceivable basis, empirical or otherwise, upon which to make such an assertion? On what grounds could it possibly be said that human history will have an "end," much less the one they describe?

Here too we see a significant difference with Darwin, who did not operate under the spell of Hegel. There is nothing in Darwin to suggest that once species have adapted to a certain point, they will adapt no further. On what grounds would natural selection achieve stasis or equilibrium? Are we to envision a perfect, never-to-be-improved set of species? Here Marx and Engels differ radically from the natural science of Darwin which they so much admire.

One is led almost inexorably to suppose that the technology generated by capitalism will come to an end in socialist society. Would there be any incentive to innovate in a socialist society?[51] Moreover, if there were continuing innovations in socialist society might not these become a basis around which new social arrangements would be formed? One could assume an innate human capacity to innovate (which seems actually to be the case), but what has driven innovation under capitalism for Marx and Engels—the tools of ruling class domination—will have disappeared. The only premise on which the serenity, the stasis, the equilibrium of socialist society is based is the absence of significant innovation and radical change going forward. Socialist society will have reached the apex of human existence. History will truly be at an end. We see again the arrogance of Hegel transformed in a material finality.

Is there then a good reason to attempt to overthrow contemporary capitalist society? Are not all the assumed benefits of such a move either obscure or completely unknown? We apparently cannot know all the positive benefits of socialist society until capitalism is overthrown. That there will be such benefits is assumed, stated and fervently proclaimed—but there is not a shard of evidence to suggest this is so. There is certainly no "science" behind all this.

Marx and Engels lay the deepest ills of previous human history at the feet of material causes. In doing so they place the heavy load of human oppression not only upon the ruling classes, but upon the ways material life has shaped human history. But—and this then should not be surprising—the disappearance of conflict over material ends allows for radical human emancipation. Unlike the permanent human "interests" which the framers of the American government postulated, or unlike the innate human sinfulness which Christians preach, the material determination of human history can be lifted off human life. Redemption is possible in this world. For Marx and Engels, the economic interpretation of history is good only under the conditions of material scarcity and its attendant oppression. When these disappear, so too will the need for an economic interpretation of history. When Marx and Engels cross the bar to true socialism, what was once economic analysis becomes pure utopianism.

The full weight of the socialist future for Marx and Engels hangs entirely on one premise: dialectical speculation that the most extreme misery (of workers) must inexorably give way to its complete opposite, full human emancipation. There is literally no other—not any—support for this conception of the future of socialism. It hangs entirely on the gossamer metaphysical thread of a materialized Hegelian dialectic. The only science here is Hegelian "science." Marx and Engels never ceased being Hegelians in terms of how the historical process unfolds. They describe human history in material terms, but it is the dialectical process which characterizes human history's forward motion—until its presumed end in socialism.

TWO

MARXISM IN PRACTICE

LENIN

With Lenin we come to an entirely new place. While the language of Marxism is preserved, the content is very different. To be sure, there remains the goal of revolutionary change from capitalism to socialism. But everything else is different, including the analysis of social classes and especially the role of the proletariat.[1] We see this in many ways, each of which testifies to Lenin's voluntarism and focus on the way in which human wills, operating with *ideas,* are employed to shape the future. In what follows we will not aim at a detailed analysis of Lenin's life and work, which has been set out by many capable authors[2] We will step back and focus on how ideas, not material changes or economic causes, are the driving force of the socialist revolution and the so-called dictatorship of the proletariat.

This has been noted in a slightly different way by Robert Tucker, one of the ablest commentators on Lenin. Tucker suggests that Lenin is best understood as an amalgam of Marxism and a long tradition of Russian radicalism which features an important role for "revolutionary heroism."[3] Revolutionary heroism is demonstrated by individuals, not by economic forces. Lenin constrains this revolutionary tradition with the Marxist notion that such individuals can succeed only if they represent and speak for real underlying socio-economic forces. In this way he criticizes the purely emotional basis of anarchists and other "adventurers." Nevertheless, there remains for Lenin a highly significant role for individuals, as opposed to socio-economic forces, which can be seen both in Lenin's written work and in his role as a revolutionary.

To begin, we see a shift in emphasis between theory and practice, a shift which accentuates the role of practice as a judge of theory. This can be observed in several ways. He speaks directly to this question in *Materialism and Empirio-Criticism*, a long denunciation of then-current trends in German philosophy. He argues that all thought begins in action; it is our practical concerns which drive human thought.[4] Thought then aims to understand objective reality, in order to allow thought to act in accord with reality. It aims, as Lenin says, to turn things-in-themselves into things-for-us.

Thought can grasp what is real, and in *Materialism* Lenin advances a straightforward correspondence theory of truth in which our ideas can be mirror images of reality. Our practice is the impetus to theory, but it is also judge of whether we understand reality correctly or incorrectly.[5] This shares a working similarity with what we call "pragmatism," though for Lenin there is an objective reality which stands behind the success or failure of our actions. Lenin says that our thoughts can come ever closer to a fully disclosed truth, that is, to know reality more fully. But it is always practice which is the judge of the correctness of our thought.

This suggests there is no room for "dogma," as static theories cannot comprehend the ever-changing world of practice. One needs to think anew to address current realities, not employ old theories in a slavish, dogmatic way.[6] This serves as a broad justification for altering or even ignoring portions of Marxist theory in favor of new thinking about how theory can capture and inform current practice.[7]

This concern with practice surprisingly makes a certain type of theory very important—not the theory of Marx, which Lenin agreed with his friend Julius Martov was overbroad—but continual reflection on current realities. One cannot rest content to let Marx do one's own thinking, much less fall back on the notion of an inevitable historical development of socialism. One must use Marx as a guide, not a dogma.

This suggests that the components of theory—ideas and words—can be a powerful source of social change. As Lenin says, "Ideas become a power when they grip the people."[8] Lenin is quite clear about the power of ideas and words to move people, that is, to act as forces for social change. He says that "vulgar evolutionism fails to see that words are action."[9]

An astute reader can no doubt see where all this is heading. It is heading away from economics and toward politics. Broad socio-economic forces have receded into the background, and political decisions have replaced them. Lenin says that the belief that "politics always follows obediently economics" is the view of economists who express the "crude vulgarisms of 'economic materialism.'"[10] Lenin expands on this thought by saying despite the fact that economic interests are decisive (which any good Marxist must say), economic struggle is not the key to achieving socialism. What is key, where the proletariat's "decisive interests" lie, is in radical political action.[11]

Lenin worked out his views on this question in a struggle against what he called "economism." Advocates of economism argued that workers should concern themselves with economic matters like better pay and improved working conditions, not with political revolution.[12] Lenin argued this view was mistaken in two ways. First, economism often counseled inaction on the premise that the transition to socialism was inevitable and need not be compelled. As Baudelaire said, belief in progress is a lazy man's creed. For advocates of economism the revolutionary transition to socialism would occur when conditions were "ripe," which they were not at the present time. In the meantime improved economic conditions would strengthen and not immiserate the position of workers. Some advocates of economism advanced a theory of more or less inevitable "stages" of economic development, which Lenin took as a poor excuse for political inaction.

Second, Lenin believed that workers' movements by themselves would never transcend what he called trade unionism. In focusing on minor palliatives like wages and hours, workers would never come to see the need for a complete overthrow of the capitalist system. They would accordingly never realize their true interests and thus would not achieve true human emancipation. They would be slightly better paid wage slaves.

This limitation of the workers both necessitated and rationalized a Communist Party cadre to educate the workers to their true interests. Lenin is quite clear that the consciousness of the workers does not grow organically with their exploitation. He quotes favorably Karl Kautsky's criticism of the Austrian Social-Democratic Party's program:

> Socialist consciousness is represented as a necessary and direct result of the proletarian class struggle. But this is absolutely untrue. Socialism and the class struggle arise side by side and not one out of the other ... Socialist consciousness is something introduced into the proletarian class struggle from without, and not something that arose within it spontaneously.[13]

Socialist consciousness is said to arise only out of science and the bearers of this science are not found in the proletariat; it was out of the heads of the bourgeois intelligentsia that modern socialism originated. Thus, without education by the Communist Party, Lenin asserts there would be no "awakening of the masses, principally the industrial proletariat."[14]

Much of Lenin's thinking along these lines was tied to the specific situation of Russia in the early twentieth century. While Lenin speculated broadly about the worldwide transition from capitalism to socialism, Russia was by no means on the cutting edge of this theoretical Marxist doctrine. In 1916 Lenin argued in *Imperialism: The Highest Stage of Capitalism* that capitalism had found a way to defer for a time its inevitable collapse. It did so by developing imperialist policies which were not in place during the time Marx wrote, but which had developed rapidly around the turn of the twentieth century. The ruling classes of mature capitalist powers turned to colonization in order to maintain their lease on power. They exploited their colonies, especially the poorest workers in them, just as they exploited their own workers. In doing so,

Lenin had to admit, these powers actually brought some economic benefits to their own workers, thus explaining why capitalism had not yet collapsed.[15]

Lenin described a process in which the concentration of production in a few hands led to a concentration of finance in equally few hands. Advanced capitalist nations were dividing up the entire world among themselves. This Lenin called the "monopoly stage of capitalism."[16] This stage could not be avoided and the mature capitalist powers were fated to fight it out with one another. This Lenin understood as the final, dying stage of capitalism.

None of this high theory, however, had anything to do with Russia, which was neither an advanced capitalist country nor an imperial colonizing power. If there were to be a revolution in Russia, it would have to occur in a very different setting specific to its own unique characteristics. This was where politics would trump economics and in the process display the critical role of a dedicated Communist Party infusing the masses with its ideas.

In Lenin's time Russia was barely a capitalist country at all. It was governed by the tsar along with his bureaucracy and army, and the great mass of peasants lived in an almost feudal manner. There was a small bourgeois class and a small class of urban proletarian workers as well. By far the largest population in Russia, however, was the peasantry. Narodnik revolutionaries had long supported a peasant revolution against tsarist power, but Lenin was consistent in arguing that, although the bulk of the peasant class was poor and oppressed, a peasant-led revolution could not succeed.[17] The urban proletariat was the only truly revolutionary class.[18] Peasants could ally with the proletariat, but despite their numbers, they were too isolated from one another to lead a successful revolution.[19]

Lenin was far less consistent, however, in his view of where Russia stood historically and about whether a bourgeois revolution had or had not occurred in Russia and if so, when. Lenin supported the unsuccessful Russian revolution of 1905. Was this to count as a bourgeois revolution, especially in so far as it had not succeeded in transforming Russia from its semi-feudal status? Lenin seemed to argue that the 1905 revolution was a step toward the rule of the bourgeoisie, and in this sense it was favorable for both the bourgeoisie and the proletariat—even though it had not really created bourgeois rule in Russia.[20] As late as 1915 Lenin still argued that the time was not yet ripe for a socialist revolution.[21] By 1917 he had changed his mind, however, and after the successful Bolshevik takeover, Lenin seemed to suggest a very compact time frame in which the February, 1917 revolution was to count as the bourgeois revolution and the October, 1917 Bolshevik takeover as the transition to a dictatorship of the proletariat.

Defenders of Lenin have tried every which way to find consistency in Lenin's view on this question, but if there is any consistency to be found it is in his continuing pragmatic judgment about what was possible in Russia, and when.[22] Indeed, after the Bolsheviks seized power Lenin went so far as to remark that it was *easier* to achieve a socialist revolution in Russia than in more developed countries.[23] Consistent with what might be called his pragmatic views, he offered the success of the Bolshevik revolution as proof it was possible to have a socialist revolution in a largely peasant country.[24] This was one of several factors that Mao noted carefully about the Russian revolution.

Throughout Lenin's evolving views one finds the notion that different nations at different times require different tactics to achieve a successful socialist revolution. As a theoretical matter, this was consistent with what Marx and Engels professed. But Lenin was far more clearly guided at each step of the way by practical judgments about how political power could be obtained than by any consistency of thought about the "contradictions" of historical materialism.[25]

What Lenin finds most attractive in Marxism is the notion of the dictatorship of the proletariat.[26] Lenin combs through the writings of Marx and Engels to make the argument that this is the key thought of Marxism itself. He says the dictatorship of the proletariat is "the very *essence* of Marx's doctrine."[27]

What exactly is the dictatorship of the proletariat? It is without doubt first and foremost a dictatorship; it is the expression of a "unity of will." How can this unity be achieved? This is not left vague like Rousseau's "general will," nor even as open-ended as Marx and Engels had treated it. It can be achieved only by subordinating the will of many to the will of one.[28] There is nothing "scientific" or theoretically predetermined about it. It is not in the last analysis the expression of abstract socio-economic forces, but the domination of the Russian people by one individual (or committee). This individual may claim to be acting in the interests of the proletariat but there is no way to determine whether this is true or not; it is a matter of the will of the Party. To be successful the dictatorship must rule with an "iron hand" and its methods are likely to include coercion.[29]

We might note that this dictatorship is also called by Lenin a "democracy." How is this possible? Marx and Engels had referred to such a dictatorship in the *Communist Manifesto* of 1848 as a kind of democracy, though they were unclear at the time—as Engels later admitted—just what this meant. It somehow seemed necessary (perhaps useful is a better word) to Lenin to continue to employ this term, which had a very positive resonance across the entire reformist-revolutionary spectrum.

But Lenin's is a very perverse use of the word "democracy," employing it in a way which is more propagandistic than real. The dictatorship of the proletariat is anything but a democracy. Lenin said that a "democratic shell is the best possible shell for capitalism."[30] Such a shell, operating normally by means of parliamentary procedures, Lenin describes as a bourgeois democracy, designed to support the interest of the ruling bourgeois class. This much is understandable. Lenin then proceeds to say that "for the vulgar bourgeoisie the terms dictatorship and democracy are mutually exclusive."[31] So it would seem, and not only for the vulgar. What is Lenin's word salad trying to say?

Lenin argues that a dictatorship can be a democracy if it aims to advance the interests of the mass of people at the expense of the few. But what dictatorship does not make precisely this assertion, namely, that it is acting in the best interests of the whole? There is nothing particularly unique to Lenin, or to Marxism generally, in employing this form of argument. It is simply propagandistic. Gone is any residual meaning of the concept of democracy as a government in which the people chose their governing policies either directly or through elected representatives. In its place is the notion that the dictators know the interests of the people better than the people know their own interests.

Lenin makes no argument that the dictatorship will be benign or that it will require any expression of support or affirmation from the people, as it is the better judge of the people's true interests. To the contrary, Lenin acknowledges that the dictatorship of the proletariat will be a political state, just as was the political state that ruled on behalf of the bourgeoisie. This state will theoretically act in the interests of the proletariat. For Lenin a political state is always the product of irreconcilable class antagonisms.[32] So long as any remnant of the bourgeoisie exists, the dictatorship of the proletariat will necessarily maintain the character of a state; the "special repressive force" of the bourgeois state will be replaced by the "special repressive force" of the proletarian state, that is, a dictatorship acting in the name of the proletariat and peasantry.[33]

The principal task of the dictatorship is to destroy the bourgeoisie, a project which seems very difficult to distinguish from destroying any opposition to the will of the dictatorship. Only when that process comes to an end can the repressive force of the state disappear. The bourgeois state will not wither away; it is the proletarian state, that is, the dictatorship of the proletariat, which will wither away. This is possible only when a fully classless society is achieved, a process which Lenin said in 1918 could go on "for a fairly long period."[34]

Once the bourgeois state has been overthrown and replaced by the dictatorship of the proletariat, what as a practical matter will happen next? What policies will be put in place to promote progress toward the disappearance of the proletarian dictatorship? Here we find the role of the Communist Party and here we find the most fully developed voluntarism of Lenin. Here we find the importance of ideas and of ideal causation front and center. We do not see the importance of raising the economic level of the masses but rather raising the level of their "consciousness." Here we find the prominent role of the Communist Party as educator. As Lenin says of the post-revolutionary period, "the past, although it has been overthrown, has not yet been overcome."[35] The work of education and propaganda which the Communist Party employed in the run-up to the revolution does not come to an end when the revolutionary seizure of power has occurred. There remains an important continuing role for the Communist Party's educational activities.

Lenin had been clear all along, as we have noted, that by itself the proletariat could not achieve consciousness of its true interests. At best it could achieve trade union status. What is required is movement beyond such "primitive democratic" thinking to an understanding of the importance of a truly classless society. This requires instruction from outside. This is the role of the Communist Party, a small group which will serve as a kind of vanguard to shape and guide the thinking of the proletariat.[36]

Old thinking, like old habits, dies hard. To sustain the revolutionary government the Party's educational efforts must continue. When the communist Party has seized control of the bourgeois state—whatever role the proletariat might have played in this outcome—the Party's task of instruction is, if anything, even greater.[37] The Communist Party which controls the government will have certain advantages that it did not have when it was agitating from the outside. But the Party will not confront a fully educated mass which understands the necessity of the new government's policies. The masses, including the proletariat, will continue to harbor notions retained from the long period of its exploitation. This is particularly true of the petit-bourgeois business class and agrarian property owners. As Lenin said, the new regime— even though it announces it is acting on behalf of the masses—will confront a populace as it actually is, not as the regime wishes it to be.[38] A kind of continuing "cultural revolution" (a phrase we will see with Mao) is required, during which period the masses must be brought to understand the world in the same way as the dictators who act on their behalf.

How can this occur? One might suppose that it would occur quite naturally if the policies of the dictatorship were to improve the economic level of the masses and bring forth some of the many promised economic benefits of a classless society.[39] While this would surely be helpful for the success of the dictatorship, it is far from sufficient. What is required is a far broader effort to instruct the masses to secure their support.[40] Consistent with Lenin's general views, economics will not suffice to achieve the goal of socialism. Economic causation is not to be relied upon. What is required is political education. Economic growth or progress is insufficient to produce socialism on its own; education—which might better be called indoctrination than genuine education—is required every step of the way. It is required to bring the masses to support a revolutionary uprising, to understand its results and to sustain it against tendencies to relapse into older class-based notions.

What does the governance of the proletariat look like under these circumstances? Here Lenin moves well beyond Marx, who Lenin said wisely did not try to discover the political forms of the future.[41] Lenin's pre-revolutionary supposition was that governance would be "easy," a sentiment no doubt arrived at by comparing what he took to be the ease of maintaining power compared with acquiring it in the first place.[42] It would be fair to say that Lenin discovered just the opposite; governing churned up many difficult problems on an ongoing basis.

The point here is that Marxist theory had nothing to say about how to address these problems of governance. Lenin repeats the vague, meaningless assertions of Marx and Engels about the difference between governing people and administering things. But he faced the concrete problems of governance faced by any new ruler, problems which had nothing to do with Marxist theory at all.

Lenin describes at great length the practical problems of governing which he encountered.[43] He speaks of the need to create a comprehensive state accounting system to control the production and distribution of goods.[44] Such a centralized system does not spring into existence by itself; it must be created in all its particulars by the Communist Party which runs the dictatorship of the proletariat. What are the steps involved in this and in what order should they be undertaken? How quickly can the nation be moved toward full-fledged socialism? Can agriculture be collectivized at once or must there be a transition period which relies in significant measure on the profit motive? Lenin was to learn about agriculture the hard way—though not as hard as farmers themselves—finally resulting in a step back from socialism with the creation of the "New Economic Policy." Marx and Engels simply did not, could not speak to issues like this. It is for Lenin and his colleagues in the Communist Party to shape the actual policies of their dictatorship and they do so without guidance from Marxist theory. Lenin faced practical problems of governance analogous to those faced by any new political rulers: what are the immediate political aims and how are they to be accomplished?

The same is true about foreign policy problems faced by Lenin and the Communist Party. What is to be done about the major foreign policy issue facing the new Soviet government: should Russia continue to fight against Germany in World War I or should it achieve peace with Germany at more or less any price? This was much disputed among the Communist Party leadership, with costs involved in either course of action. Lenin ultimately prevailed over his colleagues in extricating Russia from the war by giving up claims to a broad swath of territory. There was nothing in historical materialist theory to suggest this course of action; it was adopted as an expedient to preserve the fragile new Soviet government. This was a purely political calculation, not an economic decision shaped by underlying socio-economic causes.

Lenin discovered what should have been obvious all along. The force of nationalism was very strong, and it was not soon to be abolished because Marxist theory demanded it. During World War I most members of the working class in every European nation sided with their own country, as opposed to showing international worker solidarity across national boundaries. Lenin found the petit-bourgeois especially hard to wean away from nationalist sentiments.[45] Lenin finally came to understand that nationalism would remain a vital force for a very long time into the future.[46]

Confronting as he did the immediate problems of governance, Lenin deferred the transition to Marx and Engels' Edenic vision far into the future. He still spoke of a distant time when "formal equality" would give way to true equality and each would contribute according to his ability and receive according to his need. Meanwhile, strict governance from the center would be necessary and "seas of blood" would be required to crush the former exploiters and to bring about a higher consciousness among the masses.[47] The timeline to achieve true communism was pushed ever further into the future, beyond even Lenin's guess in 1905 of fifty years.

Lenin never sketches the slightest reason, much less a plausible one, to think that the dictatorship of the proletariat will evolve to a higher stage of communism. Lenin acknowledges that the dictatorship of the proletariat will make use of the scientific and technical achievements of capitalism, which will require central planning and direction to coordinate.[48] Complex industrial processes which produce the abundance required for socialism will not run themselves. Lenin simply asserts that the end state of all such centralized direction will be one in which no political authority is required. He suggests that if there is no longer an exploiting class, people will observe basic social rules voluntarily.[49] Observing simple fundamental rules of decent human behavior will become a "habit;" coercion will no longer be required.[50] One might suppose that when the entire populace has bowed to the will of the dictatorship—whatever that will might be as it addresses changing world conditions—there will be no need for further coercion. From a state of extreme coercion we will pass miraculously into a society where there is no coercion at all. This is purely idle speculation in no way related to the actual practical decisions which Lenin carried out.

In Lenin's world of revolutionary practice and governance there is no concrete guidance to be obtained from Marx and Engels. The problems he faces must be addressed with ideas in Lenin's head. Reliance on Marx and Engels takes a very different form. All sides in a dispute among revolutionaries look back to Marx and Engels not for actual guidance—because there is none—but as providers of powerful rhetorical support for whatever position they happen to hold. In any dispute each side asks: what would Marx and Engels say? The answer is that they did not say anything relating to disputed topics. There was no practical guidance to be obtained from Marx and Engels—they were deployed as a gospel to defend any and all decisions revolutionaries freely choose. This is much like the way in which the Bible is occasionally used as a weapon to gain support for various political and economic views which parties may hold. Marx and Engels are not looked to for guidance so much as a source of justification.

The future will not be shaped by class conflict around the economic mode of production but by the ideas of the Communist Party which operates the dictatorship of the proletariat. We should be clear: to call this dictatorship one "of the proletariat" does not serve to distinguish it from any other dictatorship. Nor does it make the practical problems of actual governance disappear. Interpreters of Lenin have far too often taken his Marxist rhetoric as the essence of his practice. This is a fundamental mistake. In looking at Lenin's practice one sees nothing terribly new (or Marxist). What one sees is an attempt to address practical problems of governance.

Guidance for addressing political problems can be found in many places throughout human history. To name a few, we might think of Confucius or Machiavelli or the authors of the American Constitution. These sources arguably have as much or more useful guidance for governance as Marx and Engels, whom Lenin acknowledges did not speak in detail about these matters.

When Lenin, for example, aims to steer a course between "left infantilism" and "opportunism," there is really nothing new here. This is simply a different vocabulary that speaks to the ever-present need to steer a course between policies which are too rash and policies which are too cautious. Achieving and maintaining power has always required discarding unfruitful options.

Lenin was a Marxist in that he employed Marxist language and in that he aimed to overturn the power of the then-ruling class. To do so he relied on the force of ideas to change socio-economic realities, not on socio-economic realities to change ideas. The latter notion was consigned to an imaginary future in which a classless society would somehow reshape human thinking. Meanwhile, for Lenin ideas were the galvanizing force of social change. In short, Lenin put politics back where it belongs—as the architectonic human endeavor.

MAO

What is true of Lenin is, if anything, even truer of Mao Tse-tung; turning the peasant class into revolutionaries is everywhere a matter of employing instruction and teaching, that is to say, ideas. As a practical matter, for Mao the Marxist engine of class conflict is not shaped so much by economic forces as by revolutionary ideology which can inform the thinking of oppressed classes.

Mao's thinking is based on his understanding of China as a special revolutionary case. China is a semi-feudal, semi-colonial country for which Marx and Engels' understanding does not apply either simply or directly.[51] In particular, Mao says while there are things to be learned from the Soviet revolution because Russia was also a country with a large peasant class, it cannot serve as a model for China. China cannot slavishly follow the path of the Soviet Union because China is a very different country. Mao says that following the Soviet model without changes would be like "cutting the feet to fit the shoes."[52]

Mao argues that China is a special case in two main ways: it is semi-feudal and semi-colonial. Feudalism and the imperial power which colonized China (Japan) are the two major enemies of the revolution, and one can see in this formulation a very different situation than anything ever described by Marx and Engels. China's circumstance requires that a revolutionary think everything anew from the ground up. A Chinese revolutionary leader who aims to bring socialism to China must think clearly and objectively about the realities of contemporary China, which have very little to do with the realities of nineteenth century European capitalist countries.

As a practical matter, what does this mean? It means first and foremost that the peasants must play a leading role. Mao speaks often about the "leadership of the proletarian class" but this class actually figures very little into Mao's actions. Mao observes that proletarians in China constitute only two to three million workers out of a Chinese population of roughly 450 million. Peasants, however, constitute roughly 90% of the Chinese population and the majority of those are poor peasants who are receptive to ideological indoctrination. For this reason Mao often elides the differences between the peasants and urban proletarians, speaking loosely of an alliance between the two oppressed classes.

Mao's orientation toward the peasants was criticized by Soviet Comintern officials and by members of China's own Communist Party in the 1930's.

Mao ritually acknowledged an important leadership role for the proletariat, but his acknowledgment of the criticism did not change his actions.[53] Party official Li Li-san was deeply concerned about the non-Marxist character of what he called the "peasant mentality" of Mao's focus on the countryside. Mao responded by saying that the revolution in China "will never suffer just because the peasant struggle develops in such a way that the peasants become more powerful than the workers."[54] One would look in vain to find an instance in which Mao based his actions on the urban proletariat so central to Marx and Engels' thinking. In 1939 Mao argued that when led by the Communist Party, the peasants "are the main force of the revolution," which he virtually equates with the "party of the proletariat." He says further that the special situation of China elevates the role of the peasants, where "victory can be won first in the rural areas."[55]

A second result of China's unique circumstance is the priority of political decisions over economics. Mao offers rhetorical support for the Marxist view that the economic base determines the political superstructure. He analyzes the classes in contemporary Chinese society in Marxist terms.[56] But he denounces at some length what he calls the "mechanical materialist conception" in favor of a "dialectical materialist conception." He says "it must be admitted that in certain conditions, such aspects as the relations of production, theory and the superstructure in turn manifest themselves *in the principal and decisive role* [italics mine]."[57] For Mao, who references Lenin approvingly along the same lines, this is decisive. Contemporary China was by no means at a place where imminent changes in the mode of production would bring about a socialist revolution. To the contrary, what was required was a strenuous effort by the Communist Party to instruct the exploited classes, and most importantly the peasants, in a theoretical understanding of their interests. And it was equally important to instruct them on the need to go to war to secure their interests.

Mao's focus from the early years onward reflected what Martin Schram calls an "accent on the human will rather than on objective factors."[58] At no time did Mao act on the notion that objective economic forces were at the base of revolutionary change in China. Revolutionary change was the result of ideology and instruction by the Communist Party. Mao went so far as to say that "the subjective creates the objective."[59] Here too he learned more from Lenin than from Marx. All of this suggests that for Mao the causal agents of change are not economic but political and ideological. Mao said:

> Political work is the lifeline of economic work … Before a brand-new social system can be built on the site of the old, the site must first be swept clean. Old ideas reflecting the old system unavoidably remain in people's heads for a long time. They do not easily give way.[60]

Mao did not attempt to socialize agriculture during the revolutionary period. It was only after power had been seized and the Communist Party had ruled China for several years that Mao and the Central Committee thought the time was right to begin to enforce socialist collectivization of agriculture in the Chinese countryside. Economic conditions follow political power.

Mao's voluntarist orientation was also reflected in his focus on the importance of the army and armed power to achieve political goals. In the late 1920's Mao wrote "the existence of a regular Red Army of adequate strength is a necessary condition for the existence of Red political power."[61] He never deviated from that view. Mao at one point was accused by the Central Committee of attaching "too much importance to military force" at the expense of the revolutionary force of the masses and especially the urban workers.[62] Mao was charged with turning the serious business of revolutionary uprising into a "mere military adventure." Mao was subsequently demoted on the Central Committee on the grounds of "military opportunism."[63]

A decade later Mao explained in more detail his view of the importance of military force. He wrote "In China war is the main form of struggle and the army is the main form of organization."[64] He did not dismiss the importance of organizing the masses, but he made crystal clear that this task was subordinate to the importance of military power:

Other forces such as mass organization and mass struggle are extremely important and indeed indispensable and in no circumstance to be overlooked, but their purpose is to serve the war."[65]

Mao criticized the Communist Party of the early 1920's for failing to understand this reality. He said the Party "did not then understand the supreme importance of armed struggle in China, or seriously prepare for war and organize armed forces, or apply itself to the study of military strategy and tactics.[66] The Party had mistakenly "laid one-sided stress on the mass movement" failing to understand that "experience tells us that China's problems cannot be settled without armed force."[67]

For Mao this was not an abstract armchair doctrine; it was a duty which fell to each and every Party member. Mao criticized Party members who were willing to work only on Party organization and mass movement issues, but who were unwilling to study or participate in war. All Party members must be prepared to go to the front and take up arms at any moment. Mao concludes that "In a word, the whole Party must pay great attention to war, study military matters and prepare itself for fighting."[68]

We have to this point stressed the importance for Mao of imparting revolutionary ideas to the Chinese people in order to bring about social change. We can see this even more clearly in Mao's comments on the role of "culture." Mao speaks as an orthodox Marxist when he says that culture will reflect the underlying economic base of a nation. He argues in some detail that China does not have a unified culture. It has elements of both ancient culture and bourgeois culture, and during the Japanese occupation an imperial culture as well. To the extent that socialism has taken root in various parts of China it also has a partial socialist culture.[69] China will not have a fully socialist culture until China becomes a fully socialist nation. All this sounds like what Mao elsewhere has called "mechanical Marxism." But when it comes to practice, and to the specific condition of China, Mao sees a far more independent role for culture.

Mao asserts that "we stand for active ideological struggle because it is the weapon for ensuring unity within the Party and the revolutionary organizations in the interest of our fight."[70] Active ideological struggle can—and must—take place not only around questions concerning the economic base, but around the cultural superstructure as well. "Revolutionary culture is a powerful weapon for the broad masses of the people."[71] To this end he argues that it is necessary to recruit intellectuals into the revolutionary movement. As a class, intellectuals can be helpful or harmful, depending on their orientation, but revolutionary intellectuals are needed to advance revolutionary culture. After all, Mao says, in China "it was among the intellectuals and young students that Marxist-Leninist ideology was first widely disseminated and accepted."[72]

What exactly is socialist culture? It seems that it is little more than the inculcation by the Party of the ideological struggle itself and the socio-economic ideal of socialism. This suggests the importance of teaching the masses the correct ideological view. Party members themselves can be mistaken about the correct ideological stance at any given moment. Here Mao emulates Lenin when he speaks of "left and right opportunism." Though interpreters often take these terms as if they have a specific Marxist meaning, they are in fact the kinds of mistakes that any political ruler can make in being either too cautious or too rash. Being a right opportunist is being too cautious and being a left opportunist is being too rash.

The importance of "culture" was given special expression in the Great Proletarian Cultural Revolution which Mao initiated in 1966. A full 17 years—almost a generation—after the founding of the People's Republic, Mao thought that members of the Communist Party were displaying tendencies to revert to bourgeois ideas. Apparently the institution of socialism in China was not sufficient to guarantee socialist culture. Mao called on forces outside the Party—mainly youth who came to identify themselves as Red Guards—to combat these tendencies. Culture was apparently not quite so dependent on the economic mode of production as Marx and Engels had imagined.

Indeed, this question has been debated since the early days of the Soviet Union: can a revolution succeed once and for all in creating true socialism or is it necessary to have a more or less "permanent revolution" to ensure the purity of the revolution's goals?[73] Mao was predictably on the voluntarist side of the question, imputing to ideology and the role of ideas generally, the power to shape political and economic realities. He was very much opposed to the notion that purely economic causes were sufficient either to create or to maintain a socialist system. Martin Schram captures this in saying that during the Cultural Revolution, with its apotheosis of Mao and of Mao Thought, "the critical analysis of historical circumstances is almost totally subordinated to the revolutionary will."[74]

For Mao the second major distinguishing feature of China was its semi-imperial character. China had been subject to European imperialism from the 1840's onward, but the imperialism about which Mao spoke was Japanese imperialism. Japan had attacked and occupied portions of northern China in the 1930's. This became Mao's principal concern, exceeding in importance even the socialist revolution. He said that the "contradiction" between China and Japan was the main historical contradiction of the day, more important than the contradiction between feudalism and the masses.[75] A 1935 declaration of the Chinese Communist Party states:

> At this moment when our country and our people are threatened with imminent destruction, the Communist Party once again appeals to all fellow countrymen: whatever the past or present differences of political opinion and of interests among the political parties, whatever the differences of view and of interests among our countrymen in their various walks of life, whatever the past or present hostilities between the various armies, we should all truly awaken to the realization that brothers quarreling at home should join forces against attacks from without.[76]

Why did Mao take this position? It was certainly not dictated by anything in Marxist theory, and in fact some Chinese party members were quite skeptical about it. Mao no doubt took this position in part because of the strong nationalist sentiment that had characterized him since youth. Mao argued that Chinese Marxists who could quote Marx and Engels, but were unfamiliar with Chinese history, were of no use to the revolutionary realities of contemporary China. True Chinese revolutionaries needed to be familiar with the historical greatness of China and its humiliation by imperial powers during the preceding century.

Mao declared flatly that "united front policy [against Japan] *is* class policy and the two are inseparable."[77] He argued specifically that far left communists who argued for purity vis-a-vis other Chinese parties fighting Japan were guilty of an "infantile disorder."[78] Once again Mao uses Marxist terminology to describe what are simply differing tactical views.

It is interesting to note that Mao's view about fighting a foreign power—in this case Japan—was diametrically opposed to Lenin's decision in 1917 to make peace with Germany. To be sure, there were differences between the two situations, but it seems obvious that, despite all pronouncements, there was something very self-serving and practical about both decisions. Each was made with an eye to preserving and expanding the power of the respective communist parties. In the case of Japan, Mao's policies fitted well with the Soviet anti-Japanese position, which again seems dictated not by the class struggle but by the perceived national interest of Russia.

Mao does not disguise this. In addition to his nationalist sentiments, Mao offers a very practical reason for a united front against Japan. He says that whoever can lead the struggle against Japanese imperialism will be seen as the "savior" of the Chinese people.[79] This is particularly true because the peasants and especially the petit-bourgeoisie are strongly moved by nationalist sentiments. Mao's nationalism is both heartfelt and expedient. But it does not derive from Marxist theory.

Here we might note that Mao's nationalism is also evident in the gradual break-up of relations between the Soviet and Chinese Communist Parties in later decades. The Soviet Union had long supported the Chinese Communist Party and Mao expressed his gratitude on many occasions. The immediate cause of the break-up was what Mao called Khrushchev's "revisionism" in denouncing Stalin, and especially Khrushchev's failure to consult with Mao in advance. But looking back it is clear there had been long-standing differences between Mao and the Soviet leadership. Soviet theoreticians had long doubted whether China was "ready" for a Marxist revolution, thus implicitly criticizing Mao. These spokesmen for the Soviet leadership suggested that Mao had not placed sufficient emphasis on urban uprisings and that a peasant-led revolution could not succeed. In this they were of one mind with some of Mao's Chinese critics. At one point Stalin suggested that perhaps China should be split in two, with communists controlling one part and Chiang Kai-shek's forces the other. China scholar Harry Harding has noted it is ironic that Mao adopted a Soviet model of economic development in the early years of the People's Republic, since Mao had succeeded only when he rejected the Soviet mode of urban uprisings in favor of peasant-based warfare.[80]

Mao claimed repeatedly that there was a "unity" between Marxism-Leninism and China's unique characteristics.[81] But just what does this mean? Mao expands on this by saying that it is necessary to "integrate the universal truth of Marxism with the concrete practices of the Chinese revolution." In other words, the universal truth of Marxism must assume a specific national character if it is to be useful in practice.[82] In short, Mao was advocating the sinification of Marxism. In addressing the sixth plenary meeting of the Communist Party in 1938 Mao said:

> Marxism must take on a national form before it can be applied. There is no such thing as abstract Marxism, but only concrete Marxism. What we call concrete Marxism is Marxism that has taken on a national form ... Consequently, the sinification of Marxism— that is to say, making certain that in all of its manifestations it is imbued with Chinese peculiarities—becomes a problem that must be understood and solved.[83]

Here of course we see again the importance of Chinese nationalism. But we see also the clue to the core of Mao's thought. Who is to judge how Marxism should be reconciled with Chinese peculiarities? Who is to say in just what way Chinese peculiarities are to shape Marxism for a practicing Chinese revolutionary? Who is to decide in which ways the so-called abstract truth of Marxism—whatever that may be—are to take on a Chinese form? The answer of course is the Chinese Communist Party, and later in Mao's life "Mao Tse-Tung Thought" itself.

Here we see again Mao's voluntarism and the manner in which politics trumps economics. There are no underlying economic forces at work to instruct a Chinese Marxist how to proceed on any given question. The notion of inevitable worldwide socialism is retained—as a kind of general faith—but every concrete decision must be made on its own terms without guidance from abstract Marxist theory. All decisions which *are* made of course are dressed up in Marxist language so as to seem undoubtedly and theoretically correct, and thus properly somehow "derived" from Marxist theory. But in the end it is the Party, or Mao himself, which makes these decisions. There is nothing fated about them, nor are they dictated by Marxist theory.

Should the Party cooperate with the Kuomintang against Japan? Should the Party spend more or less resources on forming an army or on organizing urban discontent? Is now the time (1954) to move toward collectivized socialist farming or not? How much or little should the Chinese leadership rely on Soviet guidance, guidance which seems always to have its own self-serving quality? These and a thousand other practical questions must be decided without guidance from abstract Marxist theory. They are certainly not guided by the broad economic forces which underlie Marx's theory.

Every practical decision must be made by the Party considering the specific, unique circumstances of the question, that is, the peculiar characteristics of China. As with Lenin, the Party turns out to be the beginning and end of all wisdom. The economic forces of Marxism take a distant back seat to the realities of China at every point in time. Mao' voluntarism, and this is the correct word for it, finds its expression through the dictates of the Party.[84]

In all this we see the priority of the Chinese Communist Party and specifically Mao. We see once again how politics trumps economics; political decisions of the Party shape the economic realities of China, not vice-versa. And to support these decisions the Party cannot rely solely on gentle persuasion or reference to a higher authority. Their enforcement rests on the same power that has usually stood behind political decisions throughout history, that is, armed force. For Mao this is always the army. Whatever else, the leadership of the army must be kept in the hands of the Party. This Mao called "an absolute and inviolable necessity."[85]

Here we might add a few words about Chinese history after Mao's death in 1976. To put it in its simplest form, the fully ideological character of Mao's thought and the chaos caused by the Cultural Revolution were not entirely popular. Mao's death provided an opening to re-consider Mao's views and policies and after a relatively brief struggle, reformers led by Deng Xiaoping came to power. The official ideology of Marxism was not attacked by the reformers, who understood that it provided a broad legitimacy for Party rule. After all, without Marxism upon what basis other than sheer power could a small group of rulers claim legitimacy?

Beneath this rhetorical umbrella, however, enormous changes took place.[86] The economy was opened up, private ownership and production expanded, and ideology was everywhere downplayed. In 1984 Hu Yaobang uttered his famous statement that the goal of the Communist Party was to "make people rich."[87] Talk of class conflict was muted in favor of economic modernization. Part and parcel of the new thinking of the reformers was an increased emphasis on Chinese nationalism. Economic success would make China more powerful and give it a larger role on the world stage. This was called by Deng a "socialist market economy with Chinese characteristics." As we have seen, nationalism played a large role from Mao's earliest days. Under the reformers it assumed an even more prominent role, one more in line with China's rapidly growing economy.

During the past decade we have seen yet another significant transformation in the ideas of China's Party leadership. Under Xi Jinping there has been a partial turn away from the policies of Deng and his immediate successors back to the more political, ideological rule that characterized Mao Tse-tung.

There is of course the obligatory pronouncement that China's "basic system" is socialism. But the current emphasis is not on socialism but on nationalism. In president Xi's important speech on the 100th anniversary of the Chinese Communist Party in 2021, Xi makes this perfectly clear. He speaks of "the rejuvenation of the Chinese nation," "that the Chinese nation is a great nation," and that the goal of Chinese Communist Party leadership is "to achieve lasting greatness for the Chinese nation."[88]

This is a far cry from anything that Marx and Engels ever wrote and goes well beyond any Russian nationalism that Lenin ever expressed. Xi speaks of adapting Marxism "to the Chinese context," and in this he follows Mao. It seems, however, this is not done to justify deviations from pure Marxist historical materialism, as Mao had done, but to utilize China's characteristics as a tool to enhance the greatness of the Chinese nation.

All this is to say, as has one Chinese observer, that today we see "politics in command" and not "economics in command." Xi has made clear that he intends to reduce the openness of the Chinese economy to serve political ends. These include greater centralization, a larger role for the state, reining in successful entrepreneurs and steps to "decouple" the Chinese economy from the western economy. The latter is especially marked since Vladimir Putin's invasion of Ukraine and the resultant western economic sanctions against Russia.

What could justify these steps, which are bound to slow China's rapid economic growth? Xi believes that the political center needs to be strengthened vis-a-vis the centrifugal tendencies of a more open market economy. He seems prepared to sacrifice a degree of economic growth in order to ensure political control of the economic sector. He also believes these steps will protect China in the event of western sanctions which might be levied against China in the event of conflict over Taiwan. As of this writing it remains to be seen how far Xi plans to take these steps. Chinese Party skeptics of this approach are present, but perhaps not in sufficient strength to rein in Xi's initiatives.

Xi is determined to establish what is called "Xi Jinping Thought" in order to elevate himself to the level of Mao and Deng in Chinese history. In doing this he aims to place his thinking beyond any Chinese criticism because like his predecessors his thought is fully appropriate to the needs of the time.

The essentially political, ideological character of Xi's view is clear in one way above all. He calls China's system "socialism with Chinese characteristics." But what are these so-called characteristics? Xi makes the answer abundantly clear; in his speech he says "the leadership of the Party is the defining feature of socialism with Chinese characteristics." Chinese characteristics are whatever the Party says they are. Long gone is any notion of the state withering away. In its place is a permanent Communist Party, backed by the army, whose very existence defines China's policies. Whatever there is of Marxism which remains in practice is difficult to see. What we have in China is a garden variety nation state governed by a permanent self-perpetuating minority. The economic system of this nation will not be determined by economic forces or by class struggle; it will be determined by political fiat in the interest of building a powerful nation. The notion of economic causation has entirely disappeared.

A NOTE ON MARXIST REVISIONISM

Those attracted to Marx's passion for transformational social change have had to come to terms with the fact that his core predictions have not come true. Hardly anyone is an orthodox Marxist in this sense anymore. But admirers of Marx have found much to preserve in his methods, his critique of current society and his hopes for the future. Marxist revisionists comprise a large and varied set of theorists who have employed Marx's language and some of his insights in order to serve new ends.

We will not focus here on these theorists for just that reason—they are theorists and not individuals like Lenin and Mao who aimed to put Marxism into practice. They are often academics who advocate ever new forms of critical theory, literary criticism, cultural criticism and related notions. While aiming to impress their colleagues and perhaps also to alter people's thinking, they rarely advocate, much less engage in revolutionary political transformation like Lenin and Mao.

Nevertheless, because their presence is widespread perhaps a few words about Marxist revisionism would be appropriate. Marxist revisionists arose, as Engels said, "no sooner had Marx died."[89] Their work tends to focus on the intellectual superstructure of ideas and to grant to ideas some of the efficacy which Marx had largely denied to them. They aim to demonstrate that ideas have a certain power to lay bare various forms of oppression. Representatives of Marxist revisionism can be found throughout Europe and America and were especially active in Italy in the early twentieth century.

Marxist revisionism received a new energy and a new center of gravity with the notion of "critical theory" advanced by Max Horkheimer, Theodore Adorno and others who belonged to the so-called Frankfurt School in the 1930's. Horkheimer defined critical theory in a famous 1937 essay on "Traditional and Critical Theory." According to Horkheimer critical theory does not merely theorize about the social world, but aims to change it. He says critical theory aims "to liberate human beings from the circumstances that enslave them." This is akin in form to Marx's 11th thesis on Feuerbach in which Marx says the point of theory is not to understand the world but to change it.

But there is a considerable difference. Horkheimer has generalized Marx's view; Marx's capitalists who oppress the proletariat have been generalized into the far broader but very vague notion of "circumstances" which enslave people. Circumstances can assume a wide variety of forms, some of which may be economic and some of which may not. Poverty, colonialism, patriarchy, gender, race, age, disability, health or any other social distinction is a wide-open field for critical theory. We have obviously come a long way from Marx's economic causation and the economic foundation of the cultural and intellectual superstructure.

Critical theory is so named for two reasons. Its roots reach back to the philosopher Immanuel Kant's use of the word "critique" in his most famous writings. Though critical theory actually has nothing to do with Kant's work, which was entirely theoretical and not at all aimed at social change, the word provides to Marxist revisionists a deep philosophical pedigree. Marx drew on this pedigree himself and gave it a practical twist in his *Contribution to the Critique of Political Economy*.

Second, critical theory flatters itself that it goes deeper than traditional theory. It claims to expose power relationships which lie hidden to traditional theory. This offers critical theory a certain panache as a deeper, more honest account of society and its imperfections than is provided by traditional theory. What is dark, hidden and flawed is advanced as more profound. Whether this is true or not is another matter. Schumpeter makes the reasonable point that "it is not true that he who hates a social system will form a more objectively correct view of it than he who loves it. For love distorts indeed, but hate distorts still more."[90]

What do critical theorists omit from Marx and what do they retain? They usually omit the idea of a historical dialectic working ineluctably behind the scenes, as it were, to achieve a new social synthesis. They doubt that economic classes formed around the capitalist mode of production will be destroyed through revolution. They reject the idea of the proletariat as the principal oppressed class, as well as its leading role in destroying capitalism. They thus find little use for the notion of the dictatorship of the proletariat. And they reject the notion that oppression occurs only when a small minority oppresses an ever more immiserated majority. Majorities can oppress minorities just as easily, if not easier.

That said, what is left of Marxism for critical theorists? First, critics focus on the oppression of one social group by another. This can take many forms. As a general matter, they follow Marx in rejecting the idea that equal legal rights are sufficient to eliminate oppression. Formal legal equality is insufficient to achieve full human emancipation.

Second, they argue that the dominant social group oppresses its victims not only with physical force but with the power of ideas. The dominant group employs thoughts and words to establish and maintain its dominant position. Following Marx, these intellectual tools are referred to as "ideology."

Third, the task of critical theory is to awaken oppressed social classes—and the oppressors themselves—to the ways in which ideology disguises oppression. Oppressed classes can be oppressed without knowing it. Critical theorists aim to overcome "false consciousness"—today often called "becoming woke"—in order to understand the truth of oppression. There is of course nothing novel in the idea of becoming woke; it is a staple of many religions and philosophies throughout history. Becoming woke is simply another name for becoming enlightened or seeing a new vision of truth, a type of self-certainty that has been widely present in past generations.

Fourth, flowing directly from achieving true consciousness (or becoming woke), is the complete disparagement of the past. One does not honor the past; the task is to discard one's past (false) views. The past is nothing but a source of manifold error and oppression. It is as if the woke are the first to think the thoughts which they think. And thus those who are woke offer the first real chance in world history to overcome injustice and oppression.

Finally, the prevailing economic system may or may not be the font of all injustice, as Marx had asserted. Marxist revisionists often suggest other social or psychological bases for oppression. Although capitalism stands as a major source of injustice, it is not the only source; economic causation is but one of many sources of injustice and oppression.

But if economic causation is not the font of all human injustice, *eliminating* human oppression seems to entail an economic solution. It is not sufficient to grant equal legal rights to an oppressed class. Justice requires that an oppressed class must achieve economic parity with its former oppressors. If an ex-colonial nation has a lower per capita income than its former oppressor, justice cannot be achieved until equality has been achieved. If women's salaries are not equal to those of men, this is *ipso facto* proof of continuing oppression. If a racial group has less income or wealth, justice cannot be achieved until economic equality—now often called equity to distinguish it from legal equality—has been achieved.

The only proof that oppression has been fully overcome seems to be economic. This watered-down version of Marxism is consistent with the commercial republics in which revisionists generally live and work. For them, just as for progressives generally, economic or material equality stands as the only possible proof that oppression has ended.

THREE

THE AMERICAN COMMERCIAL REPUBLIC

We have seen in the previous chapter that practicing Marxists, while retaining a rhetorical attachment to Marx and Engels, abandoned the basic tenets of Marxism. Men of practice like Lenin and Mao aimed to create socialist societies; this much they had in common with Marx and Engels. But Marx and Engels were by no means unique in advocating socialism; there were many before and after them who saw socialism as an ideal economic system.

The distinctly unique features of Marxism, however, were abandoned. Gone is the inevitable economic process by which capitalism collapses into socialism. Gone is the class analysis in which the leading role is played by the proletariat. Gone is the way in which thought is shaped by the economic means of production. And most importantly for our purposes, gone is the idea of economic causation as the way in which people's thoughts and actions are to be shaped.

What is retained is mainly the so-called dictatorship of the proletariat, though in a very truncated way. The focus is entirely on the tactical needs of the dictators: how to acquire and maintain power and how to eliminate dissent. All this was, in name only, in the interest of creating an imaginary Eden which would be opposite in every way. Needless to say, never was an actual step taken in the direction of this imaginary goal. As we have suggested, adding the words "of the proletariat" to modify a dictatorship does not serve to distinguish it in any meaningful way from any other dictatorship.

Marxist governments are thus best understood in classical political terms rather than economic ones. Older traditions of thought—political thought which addresses issues of justice and power—better capture the essence of these regimes.[1]

Where then does the priority of economics, and of economic causation, stand? Has the notion of economic causation disappeared along with Marx's other theories? The answer is decidedly not. Surprisingly—or not so surprisingly—this notion flourishes at the center of commercial republics like the United States. It is here that the natural home of economic causation is to be found. It is here that one sees most clearly the central idea that economic changes are the engine to change people's ideas and behavior.

COMMERCIAL REPUBLICS

Philosophers have written about what we might call economic issues from antiquity forward. This was true of Plato, Xenophon and Aristotle, to name a few, among the Greeks. During the medieval period Christians, Jews and Muslims addressed economic issues in light of their theologies. Questions concerning the legitimacy of charging interest on loans or discovering the "just price" for goods and services are but two examples.

Prior to the development of broad markets, however, in which land, labor and capital gained some independence and could be employed more flexibly and abstractly—a broad world of commerce—there was no economic thought in the modern sense. There were certainly no economists. This began to change in the 17th and 18th centuries. Although Adam Smith is regularly and reasonably accorded the title of the first modern economist, there are reasons to look before his time to find the beginning of a modern notion of economics. One of the first to address the meaning and ramifications of the new importance of commerce—whose principal work appeared more than a quarter-century before Adam Smith's *Wealth of Nations*—is the French philosopher and historian Montesquieu.

Montesquieu said that modern commerce differs from ancient commerce in that it operates far more widely and broadly. And it has a certain positive effect:

> Commerce is a cure for the most destructive prejudices; for it is almost a general rule, that where we find agreeable manners, there commerce flourishes; and that wherever there is commerce, there we meet with agreeable manners. Let us not be astonished, then, if our manners are now less savage than formerly.[2]

There is, as he says elsewhere, a kind of sweetness (douceur) to a commercial society.

This theme was taken up again and again in the 18th century. Voltaire, for example, spoke of the way commercial societies break down distinctions of race, religion and other sources of potential conflict. There was no group, however, which more assiduously promoted this view than the authors of what is often called the Scottish Enlightenment. The Scot William Robertson said that "Commerce... *softens and polishes* the manners of men."[3] Francis Hutcheson, Adam Smith's teacher, spoke of "the calm desire of wealth."[4] These sentiments were echoed by Adam Smith, by Smith's friend David Hume, by Samuel Johnson and many others, becoming a kind of conventional wisdom among intellectuals in the latter half of the eighteenth century.

How can such a view be plausible? We in the post-Marxist world are more accustomed to hearing about the grasping nature of men who profit by engaging in commerce. We hear frequently that the commercial spirit of a nation may be necessary for the abundant production of goods and services, but it is an ugly necessity often grudgingly acknowledged. Perhaps, it might be argued, the advocates of commerce in the eighteenth century did not live to see the rise of large corporations and monopolistic practices.

But there is another and stronger reason. The advocates of commercial society were comparing it with societies which operated on very different principles.

These societies witnessed continual eruptions of human passions—not simply avarice but the desire for power, ambition, religious domination, glory, honor, vanity and sex. These passions against which theologians inveighed resulted not only in personal venality but calamitous social chaos and injustice as well. It is over and against these passions, which can be both wild and unpredictable, that the spirit of commerce brings a welcome degree of order and predictability. This has been documented in what is still today one of the finest essays in intellectual history ever written.[5] The never very successful theological preaching to "repress the passions" was replaced by a far more successful moderating force, the interest in making money.

Lest this still seem unpersuasive to modern readers, we might think for a moment about recent historical events where passions triumphed over the desire for gain. As of this writing, we are in the twentieth-fifth month of the savagery, depraved morals and wanton destruction caused by the Russian invasion of Ukraine. Here is an event based not at all on the hope of financial gain, but on one man's personal sense of grievance about the borders of his nation. We could think too about the slaughter and butchery which occurred in Rwanda in 1994. Or the actions of Islamic extremists around the world over the past quarter-century. Or mobs lynching Blacks during the Jim Crow era or mobs burning and destroying property in the wake of George Floyd's murder. None of these events was caused by economic motives or tempered by the hope of financial gain; all were driven by other, non-economic passions. In this context it does not seem at all strange to believe that the spirit of commerce channels and softens men's manners. Nor that it softens the relations between nations, which today we generally take for granted until non-economic passions erupt once again.

The advocates of commercial society were not, however, blind to its faults or limitations. Montesquieu observed the leveling force of commerce and its attendant diminution of sublime moral principles:

> The spirit of commerce produces in the mind of a man a certain
> sense of exact justice, opposite on the one hand, to robbery, and

on the other to those moral virtues which forbid our always adhering rigidly to the rule of private interest, and suffer us to neglect this for the advantage of others.[6]

One or another variant of this judgment can be traced through the work of each of the early apostles of the benefits of commercial society. Each understood that human beings are richer and fuller beings—for better *and* for worse—than traders and money-makers. Each investigated the importance of morals for the purpose of living a good life and also as necessary supports for a decent society. Each saw an important role for government to control some of the very tendencies which they prized about commercial society.

One can see the importance of morals especially in the authors of the Scottish Enlightenment. Hutcheson, Smith and Hume all wrote extensively on morals. They sought the basis for moral sentiments which were necessary to lead a good life and also to provide support for a decent society. Though they considered financial gain as the principal preoccupation of most men in a commercial society, they understood that other human passions had not disappeared entirely.

We see this especially in Adam Smith who is, if anything, less sanguine about the benefits of commerce than Montesquieu. Smith argues that "an augmentation of fortune is the means by which the greater part of men propose and wish to better their condition."[7] But he laments the virtues and good qualities of men which are damped down in a commercial society. His description of the baleful effects of the division of labor on the fullness of human life is worthy of Marx. He laments the loss of the courage of mind and the martial sentiments which characterized men before the rise of commercial society. In sum, he says:

These are the disadvantages of a commercial spirit. The minds of men are contracted and rendered incapable of elevation. Education is despised, or at least neglected, and the heroic spirit is almost utterly extinguished.[8]

One might say that the authors of this new view of commercial society were more aware than many of their successors of the limitations of commercial society. They understood far better, as founders often do, what they were rebelling against than did later observers of commercial society who took for granted the primacy of economic motives. We will consider this further when we address the rise of progressivism in America in the early 20th century.

This view of the interrelation of politics, morals and economics was adopted by the framers of the American Constitution. None presumed that a decent political order could survive without the presence of necessary virtues.[9] In the *Federalist Papers* it is Hamilton who speaks most often about economic matters, especially in numbers 11-13. There he asserts the importance of a sound economy to the health of a nation:

> The prosperity of commerce is now perceived and acknowledged by all enlightened statesmen to be the most useful as well as the most productive source of national wealth, and has accordingly become a primary object of their political cares.[10]

He states this on behalf of his argument for the necessity of political union. But he also observes that there are other sources of political conflict including the desire for power and personal ambition. Indeed, he suggests that unless well-regulated, commerce itself can be the source of violent conflict, especially between states.[11]

This theme is taken up by Madison in his famous *Federalist Paper* number 10. There Madison says there are many sources of conflict among men, including the desire for power or pre-eminence, religious beliefs and other passions. He says the greatest source of conflict among men is economic, that is, the unequal distribution of property. Each of these sources of conflict is best addressed, he says, neither by relying on a commercial spirit alone nor by legislating equality, but by a large representative republic which can prevent these passions from animating majorities to tyrannize over minorities.

A properly designed republic cannot eliminate all possible sources of conflict; Madison concludes that "the latent causes of faction are thus sown in the nature of man."[12] This is a far cry from the Rousseau/Marx notion that these causes of conflict can be eliminated altogether by creating a proper form of society.

There was in the 18th and early 19th centuries a nuanced understanding of both the virtues and limitations of commercial society. Enlightenment authors understood that a commercial society was not by itself a panacea for all human problems, but that it needed assistance from a thoughtfully designed, limited government and a solid moral foundation among its citizens. They understood that not only are many destructive passions restrained by commerce but that human virtues are as well. Alexis de Tocqueville sums up the dangers of an over-reliance on the materialism implicit in commercial society: "In all nations materialism is a dangerous malady of the human spirit, but one must be positively on guard against it among a democratic people." This is because, in his view equality "lays the soul open to an inordinate love of material pleasure."[13]

Deirdre McCloskey correctly notes that during this period economics took a large step toward becoming independent of its political and moral context.[14] But it did not become entirely independent and directive as would later occur in both Marxism and in its paler cousin, progressivism. *Homo economicus* did not appear in the full-fledged garb it would later assume. Men were still understood in a broader context which authors of the time referred to as "political economy." This was a phrase which spoke to the continuing connections between politics and economics, and more specifically to the way in which economics is—whatever pretensions it would later assume—rooted in a broader political context. Criticism of commercial society, which has never taken any talent to advance, was particularly unfair concerning this period of nuanced thinking. After all, as Hirschman notes, *"capitalism was supposed to accomplish exactly what was soon to be denounced as its worst feature."*[15]

THE ECONOMIC
INTERPRETATION OF HISTORY

For reasons discussed by various authors, including Werner Sombart's 1906 essay *Why Is There No Socialism in America*, socialism has not found very fertile ground in America. This is especially true of Karl Marx's revolutionary brand of socialism. But this is not to say that the economic interpretation of history advanced by Marx and Engels did not come to America. To the contrary. The late 19th century saw the importation of German thought in the study of history and society. The Wharton School's Simon Patten spoke to this directly in saying that he aimed "to help in the transformation of American civilization from an English to a German basis."[16] In saying this he spoke for many newly minted American Ph.Ds. who had studied at German universities. His book *The Development of English Thought: A Study in the Economic Interpretation of History* was a lengthy criticism of classical English economic authors.

The tendency to reject classical English economists brought with it a complementary belief in a larger economic role for the state, something which had occurred in Germany under Bismarck's social policies. Both views were part and parcel of the development of progressivism in America in the late 19th and early 20th centuries. The major role played by the economic interpretation of history is perhaps best exemplified by Edwin Seligman, who became the President of the American Economic Association in 1903. In his 1902 book entitled *The Economic Interpretation of History*, Seligman argued that what is valuable in Marx and Engels is their economic interpretation of history. Seligman asserts that there can be differing kinds of historical interpretation—political, religious and so forth—but the most important is economic. Morality, he says, is a social product and among the social factors which produce it economic factors are of "chief significance."[17]

Thus far Seligman follows Marx and Engels. But in a manner consistent with the American tradition of individualism, Seligman says that one can be an economic materialist and an individualist at the same time. There is no necessary connection between socialism and the economic interpretation of history. There is nothing in common between the economic interpretation of history and the doctrines of socialism except for what Seligman calls the "accidental fact that the originator of both theories happened to be Karl Marx."[18] Socialism is "teleological," Marx's guess about what will come to be; the economic interpretation of history is a descriptive method for observing what has and continues to occur.[19] In fact, Seligman goes further. He says, contra Marx, that "economic changes transform society in slow and gradual steps."[20] Here we find a full-blown statement of economic causation fitted to the American psyche—a method consistent with many differing conclusions and incremental in nature.

Many progressive authors of the period relied on economic factors as the prime explanation for historical change. Seligman mentions Simon Patten of the Wharton School, George Gunton, an advisor to Teddy Roosevelt, and Brooks Adams. To these names we might add many others, including Charles Beard's 1913 *Economic Interpretation of the Constitution*, Beard's *Economic Origins of Jeffersonian Democracy*, Carl Becker's 1909 *History of Political Parties in the Province of New York, 1760-1776*, and the works of Thorstein Veblen. The essayist Edmund Wilson later summarized this orientation in saying that there is something important to be learned from Marxism, namely, "a technique which we can still use with profit: the technique of analyzing political phenomena in social-economic terms."[21]

None of these authors was a Marxist, if by that is meant a believer in the dialectical inevitability of socialism or the revolutionary role of the proletariat. But they did import into American thought a progressive view that is still resonant today, the primacy of economic factors in explaining human social life. It is for this reason that contemporary religious authors, of which Augusto Del Noce is a good example, conclude that while the specific theories of Marx were largely wrong and have been rejected, Marx still won the "war of ideas" in the West. This he did "by establishing the economic dimension of man as humanity's defining reality."[22]

Part and parcel of the progressive view was the treatment of scarcity and abundance. Progressives followed Marx and Engels in seeing scarcity as the principal flaw in human existence. Scarcity of goods was the engine which drove injustice throughout human history. Economist Robert Nelson says "the state of material deprivation is the original sin of economic theology."[23] They follow Marx, too, in admiring the capitalist mode of production for its extraordinary power to produce abundance. For the first time in human history since Adam was banished from the garden of Eden and condemned to work, capitalism has produced enough goods to satisfy everyone's essential material needs. The abundance produced by capitalism makes possible a completely new chapter in human history.[24] This view was expressed by both neo-classical economists and critics of neo-classical economics.

Thorstein Veblen, who was perhaps the most widely read social commentator of the time, serves as a good example. Veblen argued that modern industrialization allows humanity to produce for the first time enough goods to satisfy all basic human needs. In fact, he said, humanity can now produce so much with the help of machines that many people do not need to work at all. This notion led Veblen, with his stern Scandinavian roots, to express special displeasure over the existence of "waste." Waste of the goods which modern industrialization produces jeopardizes the abundance which can transform human life. Waste arises through inefficiency, through the production of goods designed only to display conspicuous consumption, and in Veblen's case, through the production of armaments for war. Not only the process of production can result in waste, but more importantly the ends to which production is put can also result in waste.[25]

John Maynard Keynes, the most influential economist of the 20th century, held similar views about the possibilities inherent in modern productivity. His 1930 essay "Possibilities for Our Grandchildren" (which was the final chapter in his *Essays in Persuasion*) states that a gradual, incremental process was already leading to a post-capitalist society. These views were carried to America by his acolytes in the mainstream economic community. They are found today in the writings of most liberal economists, at least those who show any interest in history at all. Most mainstream American economists are not socialists, because they understand the power of markets and the private sector to produce innovations and abundance. They wish, however, to regulate these markets to maximize production and perhaps also to achieve what they regard as a more equitable sharing of the abundance which these markets make possible.

Upon what premise do those who aim to regulate the market economy proceed? They act on the progressive premise that this can be done in a rational way, that is, that the economy can be adjusted in ways that ensure both maximum production and a just distribution of what is produced. Two assumptions lie behind this view. First, there must be genuine knowledge of how to achieve these ends. This is generally called "science," a method which provides genuine and unambiguous knowledge as to how to maximize human well-being. We hear echoes of this today in the call to "follow the science," as if there were such a thing as "the science" which provides clear-cut guidance about how to make public policy decisions. More honest thinkers will acknowledge that while the science of economics can provide information about the trade-offs of different policy options, it cannot replace a broader kind of thinking concerning ultimate human choices and ends. This broader kind of thinking we properly understand as political thought.

In addition to the possibility of scientific knowledge concerning human well-being, there must be a class of individuals who possess this knowledge and, equally importantly, act upon this knowledge in an impartial, unbiased way. Who might this class of individuals be? Veblen thought of them as "engineers." Others have called them "technologists." Most often, we refer to them today simply as "experts." These are individuals who are able to rise above self-interest and to act in a genuinely impartial way for the good of the whole, based upon the knowledge which they possess.

This is an idea as old as Hegel, the original progressive from whom American progressives indirectly derived their views. He saw in the bureaucracy of the Prussian state just such a class of men. These individuals—a universal class, as Hegel called them—would be guided by the broadest interests of the state. They would not act on the basis of limited, self-interested knowledge but on a broader conception of the good of the whole. Never before had "science" been given such directive power.

Decisions made scientifically would replace the heretofore sloppy and self-interested decisions of men of business and even men of politics. In short, politics itself would be superseded by administration. There was no clearer exponent of this view than Woodrow Wilson. Wilson thought that deference to experts could overcome the factionalism that had marred American political life since its inception, and create "a single community, cooperative as in a perfected, coordinated beehive."[26] This is the very idea we have seen in both Engels' and Lenin's notion that the governance of men would be replaced under socialism by the administration of things, whatever that might mean.

Today's progressives find this class of disinterested men in the federal bureaucracy. The federal bureaucracy is supposed to act on the basis of knowledge, of science, not on the basis of self-interest as expressed by either the private sector or elected officials. They are experts, but not just experts—they are experts who act in a genuinely impartial way on the knowledge which they possess. Just as Marx and Engels had supposed that the dictatorship of the proletariat would not be driven solely by the interests of one class, but by the interests of the whole, so today's bureaucracy expresses the true interests of modern American society. As the most "scientific" of all social scientists, economists play a central role in this new universal class. As the economist Bryan Caplan correctly observes, "Economic policy is the primary activity of the modern state."[27]

The benefits of trusting enlightened, impartial scientists, including and especially economists, are said to be very great. They can set us on a path to maximize economic well-being and thus to achieve the good life which modern capitalist production makes possible. They take us on a path of day-to-day policy choices which incrementally move the polity forward. In this way, it is possible to "bend the arc of history."[28] This is little more than a faint echo of Hegel's view of historical progress, subsequently taken over by Marx and Engels and then by practicing Marxists.

Government bureaucrats are not merely making day-to-day decisions, but helping to bend the arc of world history. Such a view offers the psychological benefit of knowing one is on the "right side of history." Such self-assurance bleeds very easily into making predictions about the future. Making predictions about the future has often, and correctly been regarded as especially difficult and wisely undertaken with caution. But making predictions when one knows where the arc of history is headed obviates the need for reticence about making predictions. How is this done? Deirdre McCloskey says it is quite easy for economists: "It involves the fitting of a few straight lines to scatters of points, guided in the specification by blackboard economics, and then misinterpreting the result by using statistical significance."[29]

At its worst, the hubris of experts leads beyond merely predicting the future. There is no particular reason to wait around for the future. If one knows where the future is headed, why not help it along? This we know today as social engineering, a practice which McCloskey has identified as today's civil religion.[30] In its more modest form it is known as "nudging" the future forward. It reflects the same impatience which Lenin and Mao demonstrated when they aimed to move Marx's revolutionary goals forward by political action. For many reasons, not least of which is the poor track record of social engineering, it would be wise to temper progressives' enthusiasm to plan the future. As many observers have noted, it is simply not possible to predict the next major technological innovation. The limits of our knowledge of the future are suggested in an old joke about Einstein going to heaven.[31] And another old saw is also correct: both the former Soviet Union and the United States had five-year budget plans; the virtue of America is that we generally ignored ours.

ECONOMICS ASCENDANT

As we might expect in a commercial republic, especially one dominated by progressive views, economics becomes the dominant way to understand society as well as how to bring about social change. We begin to see this in the separation between politics and economics which occurred in the years 1910-1920. It is at this time that the study of classical political economy recedes in favor of the study of economics as a discrete field of investigation. Economics departments spring up at major universities, reflecting the independence and even the pre-eminence of this kind of inquiry.

Though economics becomes the principal way in which human society is to be understood, we should be clear that this is not Marxist economics. Two tenets of Marxism were specifically rejected. One is the historical dialectic which moves society forward; antitheses (going over to opposites and then to a synthesis) are supplanted in modern economics by gradual, incremental changes which move society forward.[32] Movement is still "forward," that is, achieving progress, but progress does not occur by means of revolutionary upheavals as Marx had supposed. Second, modern economics eliminates the importance of social classes as determinants of people's desires. People's demand curves, so to say, are not shaped by their position as a member of a class but as individuals.

Individualism thus lies at the heart of economics practiced in a modern liberal commercial republic. The tastes or preferences of individuals are the basis of modern economics. This of course is a variant of the philosophy of utilitarianism. Most economists as good utilitarians accept people's tastes or preferences as they find them. They do not attempt to argue individuals out of any particular set of preferences which they may have. The ancient doctrine *de gustibus non disputandum* applies fully. This is precisely the sentiment of the father of utilitarianism, Jeremy Bentham, who said the game of pushpin is as good as poetry. All this fits nicely into a tolerant liberal society marked by economic exchanges freely entered into.

There is another assumption which is required for a science of economics. Not only must individuals' preferences be accepted as they are, but individuals must be assumed to try to maximize the satisfaction of their preferences. This is the assumption of self-interested behavior. As Gordon Tullock has said:

> Most economists having observed the functioning of the market
> and government for some time tend to think that most people,
> most of the time, have a demand curve, the overwhelmingly larg-
> est component of which is their own selfish desires.[33]

Economists for this reason tend to look at what we conventionally call altruistic behavior in a very curious way. Many economists have treated altruistic behavior as a form of what is essentially selfish behavior, which of course renders the customary meaning of such behavior more or less meaningless. Here is a case of the world being made to fit economic assumptions in order to preserve the utility of its method. It has been well said that self-interest for economics is equivalent to the idea of gravitation in physics. Adam Smith's teacher Francis Hutcheson said just this: "self-love" for economics was as central to "the regular State of the Whole as gravitation" was to the operation of the physical universe.[34]

These assumptions are of course just that: assumptions upon which to construct an edifice of theoretical propositions. Questions concerning changes in individuals' demand curves—learning, for example—complicate the theoretical basis of economics, which is why they are often ignored. And the question of comparing and measuring demand curves between individuals becomes a very knotty problem. Are we to assume in a small-d democratic fashion that each individual's demand curve is of equal importance with all other individuals' demand curves? Upon what basis would this assumption be made, save for a belief in natural rights which most contemporary economists do not hold? Presumably it is on the assumption that if pushpin is as good as poetry for an individual, there is no way to value one individual's preference for pushpin differently from another's preference for poetry.

This latter question of course is very significant for social policymaking. So too is the related question of whether an equal absolute improvement in one individual's preferences is the same for an individual in very different material circumstances. We tend conventionally to think, for example, that a $100 gain for a wealthy individual is somehow less valuable than a $100 gain for a poor individual. But is this true, and if so upon what assumption?

We have thus far spoken abstractly about the assumptions of individualism and self-interested demand curves. With these assumptions alone, economics would not have attained the significance it did in the modern world. To be given real force and usefulness, these assumptions must be combined with another: material gain is the main way in which self-interest expresses itself. This has been part and parcel of economics since Adam Smith. That economics concerns itself only with material gain has been vigorously disputed by some economists themselves, and we will consider their claims shortly. But in the meantime, it seems safe to say that whatever generality may be granted to economic methods, economics has largely concerned itself with issues of material gain, either for individuals or for nations. Steven Rhoads has summarized this in saying "In their research, economists usually assume that more income means more goods and services, and thus more satisfaction/happiness."[35]

This is true of both microeconomics and macroeconomics. The end of human desire may be called "happiness," but happiness is brought about and secured by greater income or wealth for individuals and a larger economy or increased per capita income for nations.[36]

As to the former, Paul Samuelson said in 1948 "if one can know but one fact about a man, knowledge of his income will prove to be most revealing."[37] As to national gain, it is both the spoken and unspoken goal of economics to aim to maximize national product and/or per capita income. This is the goal both for America as well for foreign nations which America aims to assist.

It may not be possible to aggregate differing individual demand curves into a collectively rational outcome—as per Kenneth Arrow's impossibility theorem—but an increased gross national product and/or per capita income serves for economists (and politicians) as a pretty good and acceptable outcome.[38] In the same manner, it may thus be impossible to define precisely the "national interest" or the "common good," but economists are quite prepared to accept these economic measures as useful substitutes.

There is more. Economic growth and/or redistribution is good not only in and of itself in order to alleviate poverty; alleviation of poverty will in turn help to solve many other social ills including crime, depression, substance abuse and suicide. Despite Arrow's theorem, it seems to be pretty much of a Pareto-optimal outcome to achieve economic growth and/or per capita income growth and thus to alleviate poverty. All of this is of course to say that social causation is at bottom materialistic. Achieving more wealth for individuals and nations is the path to solve the most vexing non-economic social problems.

As we will discuss in the next chapter, economic programs have become the key to the expansion of human happiness. The equation that wealth leads to more goods and services which lead to greater happiness is surely debatable, and indeed has been vigorously questioned by many observers including some economists. How to achieve happiness is a notoriously difficult question. Non-economic costs and benefits are difficult to measure, but that is no reason to exclude them from a judgment about human happiness. Economists tend to ignore these non-economic or psychic costs and benefits. To rule out by assumption these non-economic, psychic factors, and then to rest content with economists' conclusions is to invite continuing surprise about why happiness has not been achieved.

All of this was well understood nearly a century ago by the great Chicago economist Frank Knight. Though himself a first-rate economist, he also knew the limits of economic science. Knight wrote in 1939:

> The idea that the social problem is essentially or primarily economic, in the sense that social action may be concentrated on the economic aspect and other aspects be left to take care of themselves, is a fallacy … Examination will show that while many conflicts which seem to have a non-economic character are 'really' economic, it is just as true that what is called 'economic' conflict is 'really' rooted in other interests and other forms of rivalry, and that these would remain unabated after any conceivable change in the sphere of economics alone.[39]

Knight thought a desire for power was a more basic human motivation than the desire for gain. This again would point to the priority of politics over economics.

Not many economists, or for that matter progressives generally, followed Knight down this path. To the contrary, economics held fast to the view of the importance of material causation. Indeed, the imperial pretensions of economics took a new turn. The definition of economic thought was broadened far beyond its conventionally understood field of production, consumption and the transfer of wealth, that is, material well-being. The earliest and most aggressively forthright statement of this view was offered by Lionel Robbins in 1932. In his *Essay on the Nature and Significance of Economic Science*, Robbins argued that economics was not constrained to look only at issues of material prosperity, but was capable of studying any area of human behavior in which there are ends and scarce means which have alternative uses. As long as any human end is dependent on scarce means, it is a proper subject for economics. Robbins does not quarrel with the assumption of taking individuals' ends as given, but he broadens the ends beyond those of material gain. Economics cannot judge what people want, it can only evaluate the least costly way to get it.

In short, Robbins attempts to transform economics from an area specialty into a general method. That there are more things under the sun than material gain is fair enough. But what Robbins is doing is equating economic thought with human reason itself. Human reason is made equivalent to the instrumental satisfaction of human ends, no more and no less. Robbins' work did not deter modern economics from its long-held orientation toward the study of material causation. But what it did was broaden the applicability of economic methods to the study of all human life.

This broader conception of economics lies at the heart of rational choice theory, which became a new field from the 1950s-1960s onward. Human rationality has been assumed as far back in human life as records take us. But rational choice theory aimed to focus on the ways in which human rationality could be elaborated in logical ways in different situations and with differing rules. This field was considered close to economics given its instrumental understanding of reason, but became very abstract when it lost its grounding in material life. Rational choice theory is applicable to rule-based games of any type. One might say that as a field its methods and findings are often interesting, but it operates at a level of generality such that it does not produce much of value in understanding the actual world. It is akin to a form of pure mathematics which, while internally consistent, struggles to describe in a relevant way actions in the social world.

Rational choice theory, however, did lead to a new set of questions which had never been addressed directly by economics, namely, the role of information in decision-making. Economists from Adam Smith onward tended to assume that individual decision-makers possessed the information they needed, or at least a sufficient amount of it, to make intelligent decisions. Upon what other basis could it be assumed that individuals were making sensible decisions to implement their demand curves? But what if this were not so? Economics would still be predicated on individuals and on individual demand curves, but in the absence of sufficient knowledge their decisions would not achieve their interests. Indeed, perhaps the absence of sufficient information could lead to individuals making decisions very much against their own interests. Further developments in rational choice theory have considered whether there are persistent, or at least recurring biases which mislead individuals as to their true interests. Again, this area of research has produced interesting results at a considerable level of abstraction, but has not undercut the prevailing progressive notion of economic causation.

Nor did the Chicago School of Economics. This school developed as a critique of the liberal/progressive orientation of economics. Central to the progressive view, as we have discussed, is a positive role for government and especially for the administrative state. Government officials are thought to express a view of the whole as opposed to partial, self-oriented individuals. The Chicago School aimed at precisely this assumption. They claimed to look at government—and in this they were largely correct—in a more honest fashion than their progressive colleagues. They found that government officials were also motivated by self-interested behavior. The core premise of their work was well summarized in the Nobel Prize ceremony for James Buchanan in 1986:

> It is hard to believe that these individuals [government officials]
> drop their self-interest and turn into economic eunuchs devoting

themselves completely to social engineering in the service of the general interest.[40]

The work of the Chicago School addressed two separate aspects of government. First, Chicago School economists supposed that government officials were motivated by self-interest just like everyone else. Second, they looked carefully at the incentive structures for government officials to understand how this self-interest would be expressed. They found that incentive structures in government differed from those of the private sector. The desire for re-election among elected officials and the expansion of government programs for bureaucrats better described their goals than the accumulation of wealth (though that is not unknown either). They found too that government decision-makers rarely experienced any immediate consequences for poor decisions. The incentives for making correct decisions seemed closer at hand for private sector decision-makers. Thus the Chicago School argued for reducing the role of government and returning some of its functions to the private sector. This thinking had a significant impact on federal policies, resulting in the deregulation of numerous areas of the economy in the last decades of the twentieth century.

There is no doubt that these were significant political decisions. But the differing political, even partisan orientation of the Chicago School has obscured a deeper area of agreement with liberal, progressive economists. Both see humans as selfishly motivated. Indeed, the Chicago School generalizes self-interest more widely, capturing governmental as well as private sector actors. Some Chicago School economists like Gary Becker look at all human relationships to uncover self-interested behavior as the motivating force of human life, including crime, marriage and other human institutions.

In this way, the Chicago School does not differ from liberal/progressive economists in seeing the goal of economics as creating human well-being, usually understood in material terms. Where it differs is in the means, preferring the private sector because it is more efficient in many cases than the government.

Chicago School economists like Becker say they do not necessarily believe all human action is necessarily economic, that is, that it concerns material gain. They argue that theirs is only a method, a heuristic to discover what can be learned with this assumption in hand. This argument is really too clever by half, however, as the method is fully intended to display self-interested material gain as the basic human motivation. Put simply, Milton Friedman and Paul Samuelson both believe in rational, self-interested behavior and both believe the goal of economics is to assist in the creation of ever more personal and national prosperity. Where they differ is in the second order question, that is, the better means to achieve this.

It is for this reason that the Chicago School does not offer a full-throated critique of liberal/progressive views. It is for this reason, too, that the economic goal of material progress remains at the heart of today's commercial republic. The key to progress is to be found in the proper arrangement of economic incentives. At bottom, economics still determines what is most true about human beings. And more importantly, the way to achieve betterment is through changes in the economic life of men.

Perhaps two anecdotal comments will confirm that the progressive view of economic man is at the heart of today's American government. We have today an economic council made up of Ph.D. economists to offer guidance to the executive branch. Could we imagine a similar political entity comprised of political science Ph.Ds? Or a sociological council comprised of Ph.D. sociology professors? Or an anthropology council? Or a psychology council? In like manner, how did Ronald Reagan—largely sympathetic to Chicago School ideas—aim to prove the superiority of America to the communism of the Soviet Union? He flew Chairman Gorbachev over southern California, with its many private homes and swimming pools. America produced more and better goods, and thus presumably more happiness.

Several other comments are in order. In generalizing the use of economic methods, the Chicago School opened several new fields of inquiry. One was to study political decision-making which progressives assumed to be beneficial correctives to private sector excess. Economics here is no longer embedded in a political context in the manner of political economy; politics is now analyzed as one expression of behavior which is to be studied by economic methods.

This type of research addresses two separate political targets: political officials and voters. Both projects are associated closely with the work of James Buchanan and Gordon Tullock. They argue, consistent with mainstream economics, that there is no organic "general will" which can be discovered by a process other than considering the wills of individuals.[41] Buchanan especially addressed the question of the incentives which elected officials face. He demonstrated, for example, that elected officials have strong incentives to spend more government money than they raise in taxes. This, he argued, was the source of recurring deficit spending.[42]

Much of his work brought him close to the work of political scientists who had already begun to study the role of interest groups as entities which distort the incentive structure for government officials, especially those who must stand for re-election. Buchanan looked at politics as an "exchange relationship," a voluntary and mutually beneficial arrangement between parties—even if one that often skews decisions against what might be more beneficial decisions for the broader polity. This he saw as having more explanatory power than either a zero-sum contest for power or an imaginary high-minded universal class dedicated to the interests of the whole. Of this "economizing of politics" it might be fair to say that it is more relevant in a democratic society than a tyranny in which there is little that could reasonably be considered as an exchange relationship.

The second target was voters themselves. Again, this work has little or no relevance to dictatorships or tyrannies in which voting—if it occurs at all—is a sham procedure. Are voters rational? That is, do they vote according to their self-interest? It has always been the mainstream assumption that individuals do vote according to their self-interest, usually defined in economic, material terms. In order to maintain this assumption economists have gone to great lengths to discover voter self-interest in a world where it often seems empirically absent.

In his ground-breaking book *An Economic Theory of Democracy* Anthony Downs provided a novel and striking way to preserve the twin assumptions of self-interest and rationality. He argued for a theory of "rational ignorance," namely, that it is not worth voters' time and energy to learn about political choices when there is so little chance that a voter will affect an electoral outcome. Perhaps it is wiser for people to focus on their private interests. Better perhaps to focus on one's career or family than to invest time in learning how one's self-interest might be affected by one's political choices. One vote is unlikely to decide the outcome in any event. It may well be perfectly rational—and self-interested—not to bother to vote at all. Downs' view preserves both rationality and self-interest and also, by the way, explains why so many people do not vote at all. Voters often display very imperfect information, but their decision to do so is freely—and rationally—chosen.

The theory of rational ignorance has itself been challenged, most notably in Bryan Caplan's interesting book *The Myth of the Rational Voter*. Caplan argues that we should reject the notion of the rational voter altogether. He argues instead for "rational irrationality" meaning that voters tend to be systematically irrational in some of their beliefs. Voters demonstrate an irrational anti-market bias, an anti-foreign bias, a make-work bias and a pessimistic bias. Why do voters demonstrate these irrational biases? It is because there is a great difference between private costs and public costs. Markets punish individuals who make irrational choices; the cost of voting irrationally, however, is approximately zero.[43] Individuals tailor their rationality to the costs and benefits of error. As one would expect from mainstream economic theory, the less something costs—in this case an irrational vote—the more we will get of it. This is a neat explanation for a nagging question about human behavior: why do individuals who are extremely careful with their personal budgets often vote for politicians who care little or nothing about balancing a government budget?

Two additional points will round out this discussion. First, Caplan suggests that voters often do have strong psychological reasons to vote in an economically irrational way, for example, against free trade. Voters may achieve strong psychological satisfaction from casting an anti-foreign vote, for example, which may make no sense from a purely material, economic standpoint. We should observe, then, that voters in such a case still *are* acting rationally; it is just that the definition of rationality must include more than material, economic matters. This is more than most economists would like to grant. Psychic costs and benefits are difficult to measure, especially in a manner that fits neatly into a mathematical formula. This is why these costs and benefits are often ignored and why Caplan, too, ultimately defines rationality in material, economic terms.

Second, what Caplan's analysis suggests is that politics is very different than economics, not simply an endeavor which can be understood by the usual economic methods. Politics extends to the full range of human interests and passions and while economic analysis can clarify some of its complexity, politics will always run out beyond economic analysis.

Current work in economics which is not simply abstract mathematical modeling is beginning to look at wider patterns of human behavior than a simple rational actor model might suggest, no matter how well nuanced. Complex behavioral patterns demonstrate ways in which human beings actually live and work. They should be studied for their own sake, not simply to see how little or how much they deviate from an arbitrary definition of what is rational behavior. We might then see more studies of what is actually the case and fewer economic models which bear little or no relation to reality, much less aim for empirical confirmation. This is all to the good. So too is the use of "natural experiments" in which economists derive conclusions from roughly comparable social situations. Such experiments come as close as economics can to the controlled experiments of natural science or medicine. One might naively think this would always have been a core interest of economics, but at least its belated Nobel Prize recognition is a step in the right direction. Such studies can offer useful, reality-based information for political decision-making—but of course they cannot substitute for political decisions themselves.

CONCLUSION

What can we conclude from this admittedly brief and incomplete account of economics in the American commercial republic? First, it is no surprise that economics should loom so large in a commercial republic like the United States. It would be surprising if it did not. As Hamilton said, material prosperity is inevitably an important goal in a nation in which commerce defines the heart of its activities.

Second, while economics has played a large role in America since its founding, its importance has been magnified by the progressive movement over the past century. Progressivism has replaced a more balanced understanding that was held by the American framers, by an understanding that sets economic motivation at the heart of human action and social causation. The economic interpretation of history which arrived with progressivism has become nearly universal in American intellectual life. Some modern economists do not subscribe to an economic interpretation of history—but only because they do not consider history at all, preferring economic models that aim to emulate the explanations of physics. The public intellectual Robert Kagan has correctly summarized mainstream progressive sentiment in saying that "the American liberal worldview tends to search for material and economic causes for everything."[44] And as we have seen, conservative economic thought favors the efficiency of the market vis-à-vis the government, but in no way challenges the liberal/progressive belief in the fundamentally economic description of human life. There is simply no doubt that, whatever conservatives may hope and liberals may fear, liberal/progressive beliefs continue to shape the dominant American culture today just as they have since the 1930s.

Third, we might say that the classic definition of political economy has been stood on its head. When early economists in the tradition of Adam Smith spoke of political economy, they referred to an economy embedded in a political and moral system. Politics was the broader human activity, which set the parameters for economic activity. This is a far cry from the economic interpretation of history. Today politics and issues of governance are the subjects of economic analysis, not vice-versa. Economists who equate rational choice theory and public policy with political economy are obscuring this essential difference.

Evidence of this is found in an unmistakably clear fashion in our contemporary discourse. For every mention of the word "citizen" in public policy—and that is usually found only in the context of immigration policy—there are hundreds of mentions of American "consumers." In short, American citizens have become consumers.[45] Politicians today treat citizens as consumers, not as full citizens who have desires for what government can provide but also responsibilities as members of the polity. If they ever existed, the days of "ask not what your country can do for you, but what you can do for your country" are long gone. The principal political question today is the economic question: what can government provide to its consumers?

There is surely nothing wrong in principle with a government which responds to the wishes of its people. Political campaigns which aim to appeal to the desires of citizens do so in ever more crass economic language. But it is a partial and truncated understanding to assume that providing ever greater economic benefits to Americans is the basic, or only task of government or that this constitutes the entirety of what citizens in a republic require.

Fourth, and finally, a number of social scientists are coming to the conclusion that economics does not explain the fullness of political or cultural realities. Robert Putnam's famous study of Italian regions argued that civic traditions are an excellent predictor of socio-economic development rather than the other way around. James Buchanan concluded that most economic work has had very few noticeable public policy accomplishments. And Bryan Caplan has said that because economists tend to focus on the assumptions of economic rationality and self-interest at all costs, they miss the kinds of systematic biases that are familiar to political scientists. He says pointedly "Political scientists' findings are frankly embarrassing to economists who study politics."[46]

None of this is to say that economics is unimportant or that economic thinking does not capture much that is important in understanding human behavior. To the contrary, it remains true as Hamilton said, that "prosperity ... is a primary object of [statesmen's] political cares." Economists can usefully clarify many of the costs and benefits of policy choices which political officials are called upon to make.

But it *is* to say that economics cannot explain the whole of political life. Economics has a positive role to play but it also has its limits. During times of relative stability, when political and economic life is relatively static, it is difficult to see those limits clearly. For example, economics offered a largely useful description of life during the twenty years preceding the economic collapse of 2008. It certainly did not when the collapse occurred. Economics was—and is—far less useful in times of rapid and transformational change.

Like everything, it turns out that economic thinking is useful in moderation. The founders of modern economics understood this. Marx, however, took economics and the economic determination of human life to an extreme, making it the chief underlying agent of all social causation. This disposition (with a deeply modified Hegelian view of progress and minus the role of the proletariat) has been taken over by liberal/progressives who tend to find in economic, material life the source of all human problems and their solution as well. When this occurs, policies adopted on this basis will miss important human motivations and will not succeed in achieving their objectives. We will demonstrate how this plays out in the next three chapters.

PRACTICE

FOUR

DOMESTIC POLICYMAKING

L et us now consider how America's prevailing economic, that is, material orientation—and especially the notion of economic causality—plays out in American federal government policymaking.

SOCIAL ATOMISM

In considering federal government policymaking today, there is only one sensible place to begin. One massive reality overshadows every other consideration: direct transfer payments to and federal programs for individuals. These payments, both absolutely and as a share of total federal spending, are the most salient feature of today's federal government policymaking.

These payments and programs now comprise nearly 70% of all federal government spending and reflect the singular importance which is placed upon them. Moreover, these payments comprise an ever-growing share of the federal budget. John Cogan has observed that from the end of World War II until the present, "all of the increase in noninterest federal spending relative to the gross domestic product is attributable to the growth in entitlement spending."[1] Federal transfer programs include both entitlement programs— which are provided to all qualifying individuals without annual Congressional appropriations—and discretionary programs which are appropriated annually. The largest of these transfer programs are entitlement programs, especially Social Security and Medicare. But other programs like Medicaid, the Supplemental Nutritional Assistance Program (food stamps), Temporary Assistance for Needy Families, Head Start, housing programs, K-12 education programs, Pell grants, job training, the Earned Income Tax Credit, the Women Infant and Children program and roughly 60 more programs expend hundreds of billions of dollars each year.

The concept of an entitlement program is not new; the United States has a long history of such programs. Revolutionary War disability payments for injured members of the Continental Army and Navy, and payments to spouses of those killed in battle were the first such programs.[2] An even larger program was created to make payments to injured Civil War veterans and spouses of those killed in battle. At one time Civil War entitlement programs accounted for roughly 40% of all federal spending.

These programs were entitlements—anyone who met the criteria was eligible to receive these payments. They differed, however, from today's entitlement programs in two significant ways. First, payments went to individuals who actively sacrificed in the nation's service (or spouses who suffered losses as a result of that service). Today's programs—other than Veterans' benefits—require no such service or sacrifice. For most programs it is sufficient only to exist. It is true that today's Social Security and Medicare payments are correlated in a complex way with contributions to these programs. But there is no absolute connection between payments to these programs and benefits derived from them. The average Social Security beneficiary receives back all of his or her contributions in roughly two and one-third years and contributes far less than the benefits he or she receives. The connection between contributions to and payments from the Social Security and Medicare systems could be fairly regarded as an accounting fiction. Second, federal spending during the early years of the republic was a tiny fraction of the gross domestic product, whereas today it regularly exceeds 20%. Today's programs are vastly more expensive in both absolute and relative terms, and far broader in scope.

The nature and scope of federal transfer programs changed dramatically with the advent of the Roosevelt administration in the 1930's. The Roosevelt administration implemented many of the ideas of the progressive social reformers we discussed in the previous chapter. Progressive rhetoric became public policy. And it has remained so to this day. About this there should be no illusion: progressive thinking dominates American politics and culture today. It is indeed, as some have remarked, a "cultural hegemon." Both major political parties accept this reality; In fact, "the growth of entitlement spending over the past century has been greater under Republican administrations than Democratic ones."[3]

As Joseph Epstein has pointed out, the dominance of the progressive agenda throughout government often makes it difficult for Republicans to offer more than a pale policy echo of progressive programs:

> With their specific programs, the Democrats seem always on the political offensive; with their general principles the Republicans on the defensive, seeing it as their chief task to block costly Democratic bills...[4]

Where is the political passion in always playing defense, and never quite succeeding at that? Once it is accepted that the government's role is to cure economic necessity, is it not always more attractive to do more rather than less?

Though it is today somewhat obscured by the passage of time, the original progressive motivation to provide (ever-greater) transfers of money to individuals was two-fold. First of course it was to provide economic assistance to those in need. As Roosevelt said, necessitous men cannot be free men. This goal itself had two aspects. First, in providing economic, material assistance to qualifying individuals, these individuals would be able to escape poverty. As George Will says:

> Thus was the "well-being" of the citizen defined exclusively with reference to material conditions, without reference to how the citizenry's character might be affected...[5]

But the progressive vision actually went much further than this. It was, and still is, based on the premise that federal transfer payments will lead not only to economic gain, but economic gain will in turn cause individuals to make better life choices.[6] It has been fairly said that economic gains are thus equated with happiness, but it would be more accurate to say that economic gains will cause individuals to make better all-round life choices and thus achieve a greater level of happiness. Economic gain will thus bring about many other social goods, including declines in alcohol and drug addiction, smoking, suicide, compulsive gambling, depression, violence and crime. Once again we see the notion of economic causation.

The evidence for this is not very compelling. There are numerous studies that address the thorny issue of what brings about human happiness, but few suggest there is more than a partial role for economic or material gain. It is not our purpose here to review the extensive literature which demonstrates this.[7] At the risk of over-simplifying a broad category of research with many dimensions, perhaps it is fair to say there seems to be a correlation between increased income and happiness among the very poorest individuals, but this correlation disappears above that level. Indeed, some studies suggest that certain social diseases are more likely to arise among wealthier individuals. For example, Liah Greenfield notes that "[the evidence] suggests that functional mental illness is a characteristic disease of prosperous and secure liberal democracies."[8]

What certainly *is* fair to conclude is that improvement in economic circumstances is not a panacea which can solve non-economic problems. Some bases of human happiness and human action are quite independent of economics. One thoughtful observer asks "Does the possession of money exempt one from human vanity, acquisitiveness, arrogance and pride?[9] This of course has been the hope of social thinkers from Marx to modern progressives: a more equitable society will reduce social ills which result from economic insecurity and poverty. If further evidence were needed of the limits of this view, we might consider the behavior of some wealthy individuals. Why do wealthy businessmen engage in fraud and financial manipulation? Why do extravagantly paid professional athletes risk their careers by getting into gunfights outside nightclubs? Why do politicians risk their careers with sexual affairs? Why do politicians risk their popularity by circumventing their own rules at the French Laundry?

We might discuss in a bit more detail one aspect of the relation of income and happiness: the question of work or labor. Roosevelt said that necessitous men cannot be free men. In this he followed a long train of left-leaning thought. Engels, for example, said "the urge towards happiness thrives only to a trivial extent on ideal rights. To the greatest extent of all it thrives on material means."[10] For Marx and Engels, however, this did not mean that the provision of material means would mean the end of labor. To the contrary, for them work or labor was critical for human flourishing. They believed the social system was poorly organized under capitalism; their goal was not to eliminate human labor but to eliminate its alienated form and make it self-directed. Roosevelt's policies followed this notion in creating many jobs programs in the 1930's.

Modern progressives seem to have lost sight of the importance of work. One after another progressive author asserts that the aim of their project is to achieve leisure. It seems that unlike Marx and Engels, who thought that alienated labor was the problem, modern progressives—fully in the mode of modern economists—seem to think that labor itself is the problem. Wherever possible, progressives aim to disconnect transfer payments from work requirements, which has led to a lower percentage of people in the work force. A clear expression of this view can be found in Speaker of the House Nancy Pelosi's comment that a high unemployment rate during the pandemic was positive, in that it freed Americans for leisure activities.

What is at stake here is this: whether human happiness is a simple function of greater income, or whether it matters how that income is realized. There is no doubt that "earned happiness" provides deep satisfaction. This is a feeling which most of us have experienced, and it carries with it a sense of accomplishment which is absent in the case of government-provided transfer payments. One sees this same phenomenon among lottery winners, who are no doubt pleased with their winnings but who often display a sense of disorientation and doubt about why they deserve such an outcome.[11] Perhaps too this same feeling characterizes those who have inherited great wealth compared with self-made men. Senator Susan Collins of Maine spoke to this on the Senate floor:

> We will not build a more prosperous, just, and equitable society characterized by opportunity, dignity, and meaning just by issuing government checks. The time-tested way to achieve those goals for American families is by supporting and rewarding work. It is by recognizing the dignity of work.[12]

In investing so much in the provision of ever-greater transfer payments, progressives often seem surprised that this does not accomplish other social goals. These payments are at an all-time high today, yet drug use is up, suicide is up, crime is up and educational test scores have cratered. This should be surprising only to those who see the provision of economic assistance as the source of human flourishing. About this Robert Nelson notes "the conviction that material causes explain lying, stealing, and bad behavior has been characteristic of [Paul] Samuelson's whole generation of liberals."[13]

Why do progressives invest so much confidence in greater income—economic determinism—as the cure for so many social ills, especially in light of its rather poor track record in addressing non-economic problems? The notion rests on poor social science and even worse psychology. When progressives observe that Americans with greater income and wealth commit fewer violent crimes, for example, their default assumption of economic causation suggests that greater income is the cause of this. They fail to consider that perhaps the non-economic traits that lead some Americans to enjoy greater income are the source of both the income and the social behavior. Reducing all problems to economics results in a misapprehension of the complexities of human beings and in domestic policies that promise too much and deliver too little.

There was also a second goal of the progressive project: to achieve greater social cohesion. High taxes on the rich and extensive transfer payments to the poor would express a new sense that Americans are "all in it together." No longer would individuals be understood as independent actors but as parts of an organic social whole. The destructive individualism of the natural rights tradition would be replaced by a society in which each was interconnected with others as part of an organic society. The progressive reformer Mary Follett said:

> We see that to obey the group which we have helped to make and of which we are an integral part is to be free because we are then obeying ourself... The state must be no external authority which restrains and regulates me, but it must be myself acting as the state in every smallest detail of life.[14]

Pure Hegel, pure Rousseau and pure nonsense, a formulation which assumes away every genuine political question.

The progressive goal was to create a smoothly functioning society in which transfer payments would moderate the selfishness of individuals and achieve social harmony. William Schambra says that progressivism envisioned:

> a genuine national community which could evoke from the American people a self-denying devotion to the public good, a community in which citizens would be linked tightly by bonds of compassion and neighborliness.[15]

Though he defined the outcome more in terms of security than compassion, this was the goal of the very first progressive ruler, Otto von Bismarck, who spoke of the broad social benefits his newly emergent welfare state would bring.

This goal came to fruition in America during the Roosevelt administration and it has remained here ever since. The Roosevelt administration's principal and most lasting legacy was called "Social Security." The name is interesting, especially in light of how this program has unfolded. Its intent was to provide social cohesion by addressing the economic needs of retired Americans. How has this worked out? Transfer payments go to individuals under the Social Security program, just as with all other entitlement and discretionary transfer programs. These payments are understood as "rights," which is the meaning of an entitlement. As such, they constitute a modern version of "property."[16] Progressives have not succeeded in abolishing or even reducing the importance of property; they have succeeded only in changing its form.

We might ask, as Proudhon did, what is property? And the answer is not theft, which is a clever but mistaken slogan. It is that which one has a right to manage and to dispose of as one sees fit. American individuals have property in their transfer payments, to which they are entitled. A recent radio commercial by a financial planning firm asked, "what is your most important asset?" The firm's answer was not one's house or automobile but one's right to a guaranteed stream of government payments until death.

There is nothing really social about Social Security. It is a program which might better be labeled "individual security." No connection with another person is involved. Since the advent of direct deposit, there isn't even a chance to see a neighbor on the way to the mailbox. Despite what progressives may think, the Social Security program—and its many relatives—have created a clientele of fully atomized individuals. Much else today shares this contractual, individual character, including marriage and no-fault divorce, the all-volunteer army and many other social institutions. Where once Americans had property in themselves—that is, liberty—this property has been supplemented and now dominated by a new kind of property in entitlement programs. These programs are "rights" which are owned by individuals. These programs are defended every bit as vigorously as other rights. These programs reinforce an individualist ethos, and the result is a pervasive social atomization.

This suggests an answer to what is on the surface a somewhat puzzling question: why do we have the maximum amount of transfer payments ever provided by government and at the same time a nation of citizens who are unhappier with government than ever before? There are surely many reasons

Americans may be unhappy with government including policy reasons, incompetence, corruption, the role of the media and other broad cultural factors.[17] That there has been a decline in confidence in government, however, is indisputable.[18] What seems odd is that this has occurred almost in direct proportion to the growth of entitlement and discretionary transfer payments. Transfer payments may be providing economic assistance to many American individuals, but it is obvious they are not providing a greater sense of community.

What transfer payments provide is not gratitude or community but a sense of self-entitlement. Recipients see these payments as simple justice, defined as economic justice at that. Transfer payments result in about as much gratitude and sense of community as an ATM machine, which also provides money which is the property of the recipient. It is difficult to imagine much loyalty to an ATM machine; it is there to facilitate the payment of what is owed to the recipient.

Authors as far back as Walter Bagehot have argued that dignity is the most important attribute of a successful government. What is the inherent dignity of an ATM machine? There are good reasons to think that when government reduces itself to a provider of money to American consumers, that Americans quite naturally become disenchanted with government.[19] It is a widely observable phenomenon that people become quietly resentful of those who provide for their economic well-being. Perhaps a feeling of self-entitlement, as we use the term disparagingly, is a defense against this. At any event, there is in fact more social connection in a typical market exchange that in receiving a government transfer payment.

It is the heart of the progressive project that more is better; larger Social Security COLAs, more inclusive and extensive Medicare and Medicaid benefits, more reliance on food stamps, and the expansion of social welfare programs generally. These programs, as their advocates are fond to say, reflect a deeply moral and compassionate society. They also seem to reflect the personal incentives of government officials who aim always to expand the scope of programs they manage. Whatever good these programs do for individuals, they do not produce a sense of community, leave aside a sense of pride in being an American. The occasions which do—a successful moon landing, an Olympic team victory or the horror of 9/11—are all clearly non-economic in character. They testify to a different origin for a sense of community or national pride than economic transfer payments. Economic, that is to say, material gains do not satisfy such needs. *Homo economicus* is not a very grateful being. It would be folly to think that increasing transfer payments to individuals— expanding the welfare state—will foster more social or political harmony. The record points to the opposite, the increasing social atomization of America.

Perhaps we should conclude with a word about the fashionable idea of a guaranteed income, also called by Milton Friedman a negative income tax. This notion received considerable publicity during Andrew Yang's brief presidential campaign and has been adopted on an experimental basis by several localities.

It is easy enough to see why economists would like this idea. If it were adopted in lieu of the confusing and overlapping welter of current welfare programs—this being by the way an unlikely political outcome—it seems it would offer far greater efficiency, always a positive outcome for economists. It would simplify the welfare state, leading perhaps to the elimination of numerous government officials who administer the current welfare state. These government officials are often among the major beneficiaries of these programs.

But efficiency is not the main reason for economists to favor a guaranteed income. Unlike transfer programs dedicated to specific ends like food or housing or education, a guaranteed income would allow recipients themselves to decide on the uses to which their guaranteed income would be put. This would, in other words, rely on a rational choice model in which beneficiaries' preferences would be king.[20] It would replace government micromanagement and allow recipients the freedom to make their own choices.

This of course assumes that recipients of a guaranteed income would know their own true interests, but this is merely the same assumption that underlies economic theory generally. Steven Rhoads has said that the Earned Income Tax Credit (EITC) is the favorite current transfer program of economists.[21] Like a guaranteed income, this program allows recipients of the tax credit to choose where they wish to spend the money. There is, however, a major difference between the EITC and a guaranteed income; the EITC pays only individuals who are employed and it supplements their earned wages.

If a guaranteed income were to replace completely the current panoply of transfer programs it is possible it could actually provide more benefits to recipients at a lower net cost to the government. This is even more likely if a guaranteed income were means-tested and provided only to recipients below a certain income level. All this has its attractions from a purely economic standpoint.

Over the past four or five decades the American government has moved very far from its initial orientation, which was to provide *common goods* such as defense, roads, the post office, and so forth. The vast bulk of today's government expenditures goes to individual recipients rather than to what is used in common. This has often been observed to make more Americans economically dependent on the government for the satisfaction of their needs. This much is clear. But it seems not to have resulted in any positive benefit for the common good or to citizens' connections to one another. It seems instead to have resulted in a widespread sense of self-entitlement and social atomization. A guaranteed income is likely to accelerate that process, further loosening social bonds and further deepening a sense of personal entitlement. It is also likely that over time upward pressures on a guaranteed income would be similar to those of today's transfer programs. Annual COLAs and politicians' promises to raise and expand a guaranteed income are fully predictable.

Simplification of today's many transfer programs makes good economic sense. A guaranteed income, however, is predicated on a very poor psychology. If the goal is to create a citizenry which thinks of itself ever more fully as a consumer and not as a citizen, a guaranteed income is likely to achieve it. The outcome is likely to be a vast agglomeration of atomistic, entitled consumers with little sense of social cohesion or attachment to the nation. Citizens will be ever more fully shrunken to the status of consumers, whose interests are far narrower than those of citizens. As Thomas Paine said in *The American Crisis*, "What we obtain too cheap, we esteem too lightly."

THE FEDERAL BUDGET

Let us turn in more detail to the non-entitlement programs and activities of the federal budget. Congress does pass non-economic legislation, including occasionally major legislation like the Civil Rights Act. For the most part, however, non-economic legislation which Congress passes in any given session is largely insignificant. Legislative proposals often name federal buildings, honor various causes or industries, or express the non-binding "sense of the Congress" on various matters. The annual appropriation bills are where the real action is, and this is truer than ever today. If a member of Congress has any hope of passing a provision into law, the best and sometimes only way to do this is to attach it to a "must pass" spending bill. Spending bills are the principal legislative activity of the Congress.

The very same notions of economic determinism we encountered with entitlement spending are found here too. Even when there are policy provisions embedded in spending bills, they are often conditions or limitations on spending, which is the true purpose of legislation. It is federal spending which drives federal policy debates and not vice-versa.

This is well illustrated in the recent Build Back Better legislation promoted by President Biden and the Democratic House and Senate leadership. This legislation was not a part of the annual appropriations process, but a freestanding bill meant to supplement regular appropriations. Almost the entire debate about this legislation concerned one thing: what was to be the "top line" spending of the legislation?[22] After the initial fantasies of Senator Bernie Sanders were set aside, the Biden administration and Democratic Congressional leadership settled on the number $3.5 trillion. There was certainly nothing sacrosanct about this number, its essence being the most that its advocates thought was politically feasible. Nor was it derived from a careful adding up of programs thought to be necessary and in what precise amounts. Rather, the process worked as it usually does—by filling in programs to add up to reach just this pre-determined total. This was simply where the administration and the leadership drew the line. More was better than less and if the $3.5 trillion number could not be reached, the closer to it the better. Why is more better? Because more dollars would solve more problems, and it seems there is an infinite number of programs waiting in the wings to solve both economic and non-economic problems. So it is with every proposed spending bill, where money is the federal solution to any and all problems whether they are economic problems or not. Virtually all federal issues resolve themselves sooner or later into budgetary issues. The average American citizen would be appalled at the way in which budgets are put together.

One can see this same dynamic across virtually every federal government program. It can be described as a kind of "signaling." By seeking to spend more on any specific program, members of Congress or the executive branch can signal their heartfelt devotion to the beneficiaries of a government program. It does not matter so much that a well-researched investigation has determined the precise amount that is required for a given program; what is important is that more, not less, is spent. Upon what premise could this possibly make sense? It is only on the premise that providing more money is the real way to benefit people, that is, once again the notion of economic causation—and the resolution—of social problems.

There is neither time nor space available here to demonstrate this with all federal domestic programs, though it could be done. Perhaps several examples will serve to illustrate the general point. Let us briefly consider federal programs concerning education and criminality. These are especially instructive because unlike, say, SNAP, the federal government is only a small contributor to overall national spending on both education and crime. Here one can see clearly what is supposed to be the added value of federal policy contributions.

The United States spends more than $775 billion annually on primary and secondary education. Of this only 7.7% is provided by the federal government, the vast preponderance of spending coming from states and localities. The national average per elementary and secondary pupil spending is approximately $13,000. This number has risen faster than inflation in recent years; it has increased more than 12% in real (not nominal) dollars. Why is this spending increasing? It increases on the premise that per pupil spending is the key to better education. But what has been the actual result of this increased spending? Test scores today are lower and by any reasonable measure elementary and secondary students today are less well-educated than the previous generation. This is true even leaving aside whatever negative impact the Covid pandemic contributed. There seems to be no observable correlation between spending more education dollars and better results.

Consider too education spending by individual states. According to the U. S. Census Bureau, New York State is at the top with annual per pupil expenditures of $25,500 for elementary and secondary students. At the bottom Idaho spends $8,272 per pupil, roughly 1/3 of New York's annual spending. Are Idaho students 1/3 as well educated as New York students? It would be fair to say that New York pays its teachers more because of its generally higher cost of living, and teacher's salaries are the largest share of education spending. But for all of this are New York students three times better educated than Idaho students? There is no evidence to suggest this.

We might look too at Chicago, which in this as in all things is perhaps too easy a target. Per pupil spending in Chicago is among the highest among American states and localities. Yet only 24% of middle school students test at or above proficiency in reading and only 21% in math.[23] There is simply no demonstrable correlation between greater spending and student success. That this should be at all surprising is due only to the implicit assumption that more money is the cause of educational improvement.

What is the federal contribution to education? It is to provide money in the form of grants to states and localities to improve student success. If one looked at declining test scores alone, matters have gone entirely backward since the creation of the Department of Education in 1979. This is not an enviable record for a federal cabinet department. All this might suggest to a reasonably thoughtful person that factors other than money are involved in achieving quality education. What are essentially federal bribes to entice state and local jurisdictions to adopt new programs based on the same economic assumptions have not been helpful.

A significant source of federal spending for education is the school lunch and breakfast program. This program has expanded rapidly in recent years. It is premised on the reasonable idea that a hungry student cannot learn well. This is perhaps fair enough. But test scores have declined in the face of this additional federal spending. Are we to suppose that they would be worse yet without this program? Here again the model of economic causation militates against asking deeper questions about the reasons for student success and failure. Perhaps the family milieu at a time when parents packed their children's lunches had something to do with better test scores. And perhaps too the disappearance of this family environment has something to do with their decline.

The federal government is more deeply involved in post-secondary education. What has been its contribution? Here too it has been the provider of economic resources, often in the form of loans and loan guarantees for students. The premise: more money leads to better and more widely inclusive education. The actual result: inflated college costs, larger administrative staffs, greater student debt, a general decline in educational quality, and recently the notion that students need not fully pay back their loans. The federal government—prompted again by the default assumption of economic determinism—is complicit in an overall approach to education which former Purdue President Mitch Daniels has called "a venture flawed in concept, botched in execution, and draped with duplicity."[24]

In the same vein, let's consider federal spending to address crime. Here too the federal government plays a minor financial role compared with states and localities. The federal role consists largely of providing grants to states and localities. On May 20, 2021 the Biden administration announced a new "Comprehensive Strategy for Reducing Violent Crime." As to this, we might ask a la Walter Mondale "where's the beef" in this new strategy? The answer is simple: on December 2, 2021 the Biden administration announced $1.6 billion in grant money for states and localities to implement this program. This is in addition to the Justice Department's $20.6 billion in discretionary grant funding for law enforcement programs. And this in turn was a small pittance of the $350 billion in state and local pandemic funding, much of which states awash in cash struggled to figure out how to spend.

Grants from the federal government support a number of different programs, some of which are well-established and some of which are recently invented. The premise behind all of them, when all the bells and whistles are stripped away, is the general notion that poverty is a "root cause" of crime and must be addressed with a variety of economic programs.[25] The premise behind this notion is that people with more money commit fewer violent crimes. This is true as a general matter, though there is no precise correlation between rising incomes and declining violent crime. Once again we encounter the economic causal notion that more money and less poverty is therefore the solution. But again, if we can set aside the thoroughly ingrained notion of economic causation for just a moment, it might be possible to ask deeper questions. Perhaps life choices which have caused some people to have more money may be the cause of both their economic fortune and their lower violent crime rate.

As with education, the lion's share of money directed to combat criminality is provided by states and localities. There is also a vast difference between how much states spend to address crime, ranging from $1,296 per capita in Nevada to $387 per capita in Kentucky. Is there any correlation between dollars spent and the level of criminality? Overall, states which tend to be governed by Democrats spend roughly 38% more per capita than Republican-governed states. But there is absolutely no correlation between greater spending and less crime. Given that correlations between poverty, spending and crime are poorly related across both time and geographical locations, a degree of humility if not outright skepticism about economic causation would be in order. It would improve our policies to be more honest.

Much the same could be shown across every federal spending program. About this one additional point is in order. The premise of economic causation has one very unfortunate side effect: it justifies federal spending wholly in terms of economic inputs. It justifies programs by measurable, dollar-denominated inputs, with little or no attention paid to outputs, that is, the quality or success of federal spending programs. It is enough that more is spent, not that it is spent wisely. But of course this is a poor way to justify government programs. My friend Stanley Weiss used to say "more is not better, better is better." Perhaps the best summary of this unfortunate tendency appeared in a column by David von Drehle several years ago. He spoke of the enormous gusher of federal spending during the pandemic saying "It seems the federal checkbook is the only tool Washington knows how to use."[26]

Former Office of Management and Budget Director Charles Schultze has observed that the relation of inputs and outputs has become increasingly complex in the modern era.[27] This may be true, but considering inputs alone results in a massive gap between what is promised and what is actually delivered.[28] Von Drehle says "Overpromising and underdelivering feeds the cancerous collapse of confidence in America."[29] And he adds:

> Democrats in power would help themselves—and the nation—by focusing less on spending and more on capacity ... The most important question for Washington should be 'how'—not 'how much.'[30]

This is excellent advice for Democrats and Republicans alike. This is especially true since the long historical default position of balancing budgets has completely collapsed. For the greater part of American history a balanced budget seemed like an obvious goal. Keynesianism replaced this with the notion that budgets need not be balanced each year but should be balanced over a business cycle. Today Keynesianism is long gone; the federal government runs deficits, and massive deficits at that, in good years and bad. The result has been a massive increase in debt repayments as a share of the federal budget. Though Republicans as a rule still favor less spending than Democrats, they seem to have decided to stop playing the Grinch at every party. Old-fashioned deficit hawk Republicans wish this were not so. Honest Democrats probably wish this were not so either. It is no mistake that the one type of legislation which Senate rules permit to be passed by less than a filibuster-proof majority concerns spending and taxing.

The principal argument for spending on economic programs today is that such spending is an "investment." The innovator of the notion of social capital, Chicago economist Gary Becker, has lightheartedly—but truly—said this field was ultimately widely accepted because it was a useful tool to secure government money.[31] That there is such a thing as social capital is surely true, and the concept is essential to understand the comparative success of different national economies. But it is hardly a justification to call any and all social spending an investment. It is the nature of a true investment to be able to measure its actual return. As we have discussed, this is exactly what input-dominated federal government spending fails to do. "Investing in people" has become an all-purpose rationale for spending money on social programs without any reasonable clue about their return, that is, their success or failure. Chris DeMuth has rightly said that the government has gone from investing in the future—by means of expenses for the common good—to borrowing from the future—for payments to individuals to fund current consumption.[32]

SOME FURTHER CONSEQUENCES

There are additional consequences to the reliance on economic solutions to resolve all social problems. One is the progressive confusion about why working-class Americans—and increasingly working-class minorities—vote for Republicans. Don't working-class Americans understand that progressives offer more economic programs and payments? How can these groups fail to understand their own "self-interest?" Jonathan Haidt calls this one of the "great puzzles in recent years: why do rural and working-class Americans generally vote Republican when it is the Democratic Party that wants to redistribute money more evenly?"[33]

This may sound like a straightforward neutral question, but it is not. Buried within it we find again the same deeply mistaken premise: self-interest is to be understood in purely economic, material terms. Progressives, who simply cannot seem to abandon economic determinism, have proposed a variety of answers. One is that working-class white Americans hate minorities. Another is that they fear the end of a patriarchal system (which by the way already seems pretty much to have disappeared). Another is that they are simply ignorant, clinging to their guns and their Bibles. In other words, hatred, fear and ignorance have blinded working-class Americans to their true (economic) interests. These are all low, base motivations which risk alienating entire swathes of Americans in order to preserve the sanctity of economic determinism. Perhaps working-class Americans have been fooled by clever disinformation? But why would Americans fall victim to this unless it is because of hatred, fear or ignorance?

This political phenomenon was noted and discussed in Thomas Frank's interesting 2004 book *What's the Matter with Kansas: How Conservatives Won the Heart of America*. Frank puzzles over why Kansans have responded to their very genuine (economic) problems by charging off "in exactly the wrong direction."[34] Theirs is:

> A crusade in which one's material interests are suspended in favor of vague cultural grievances that are all-important and yet incapable of ever being assuaged.[35]

Working-class Kansans do not vote for their "interests" because for Frank all genuine interests simply must be economic interests. All else is delusion.

The same sentiment lies at the basis of modern economic theory. Many empirical studies have noted that people do not necessarily vote their pocketbooks, that is, their economic interests.[36] How can this be reconciled with the assumption of economic rationality? Authors from Anthony Downs forward have sought ways to preserve the notion of economic rationality at all costs, including developing theories of rational ignorance and rational irrationality. All this is in the service of maintaining the notion that rational interests are economic interests. The progressive failure to move beyond the twin assumptions that people know their own economic interests and will vote accordingly is no mere corollary of progressivism but lies at its very heart.

It is thus the reflexive progressive view that so-called cultural issues are merely distractions from the most important issues, that is, economic issues.

That is why progressives invariably explain any political failure as a communication failure rather than the quality of the message itself. Fareed Zakaria says:

> To me, one of the most striking things about the rise of populism in our times is that it is driven by cultural issues. It is strange at some level, but in uncertain times—even in economically uncertain times—instead of moving left on economics, people tend to move right on culture.[37]

That this should seem "strange" is entirely a result of assuming economic self-interest as the bedrock human motivation. Give us the old-fashioned economic populism of William Jennings Bryan.

Two of the Democratic Party's most thoughtful figures have broken the code. They argue that several comforting "myths" held by the Democratic Party have jeopardized its hold on working-class voters. One is what they call "*economic determinism*:"

> Too many [Democrats] believe that economic issues are the "real" issues and cultural ones are mostly diversions invented by their adversaries for political purposes. But for Americans across the political spectrum, social, cultural and religious issues are real and frequently more important than economic ones. These issues shape their identity and reflect their deepest convictions … The myth of economic determinism goes a long way toward explaining why Democrats have had such a hard time winning back the votes of the white working class—and why they seem to be losing support among Hispanic working-class voters as well.[38]

None of this is of course to say that economic issues are unimportant. Economic issues are invariably ranked as the most important political issues in poll after poll. But it *is* to say that they are not the only important issues. This seems increasingly true as most Americans now have secured the basic economic necessities of life.

It would really be quite easy—in principle at least—for economists to preserve their assumptions and their models of human rationality. It would require that rationality be defined more widely than economic rationality. This has of course been acknowledged rhetorically by many economic theorists, going back at least to Lionel Robbins. But actually doing this would make it far more difficult to develop complex economic theories and models because non-economic, psychological desires (demand schedules) are not so easily measured as are desires that can be expressed in monetary, economic terms. Politically, however, this would require less difficult and fruitless searching for why a candidate like Donald Trump could be elected. Why don't people always vote for their (economic) interests? Because people are deeper and more complex than the cramped portrait of economic man who seeks nothing but ever more federal largesse.

A second consequence of over-reliance on economic causation is a false view of the role of money in politics. As a general matter Americans believe that too much money is spent in election campaigns. The question is, compared with what? I have never seen a persuasive answer to that question. A brief conversation with an average American citizen will reveal there is no independent ground for this opinion, but that it simply reflects more or less what is heard from the media.

It is true that lots of money is spent in American election campaigns, and the trend is clearly upward. In each federal election cycle more money is spent than in the previous cycle; in 2020 more than twice the amount was spent than in 2000.[39] 2022 broke all records for mid-term election spending. It is interesting to note, however, that election contributions as a share of the GPD have remained relatively flat, trending only from about .05% in 2012 to about .06% today.

The more significant argument, usually pressed by progressives, does not concern total spending but the claim that money buys elections. This is especially true since the advent of so-called dark money. Here is where we encounter once again the premise of economic causation. What is the evidence for this claim? In its simplest form the evidence is that the better funded federal candidate has won 80-88% of federal elections in recent years. There are of course many highly visible exceptions including the presidential election of 2016, where Hillary Clinton vastly outspent Donald Trump yet lost the election. The textbook case is Congressman Eric Cantor's loss to Dave Brat in Virginia. Cantor spent more on steakhouse campaign dinners than Brat spent on his entire campaign.

Anecdotal examples are interesting but hardly dispositive. What is more important is that once again when progressives see a correlation between campaign money and victory, they take this as ground truth and fail to see there are many other factors which contribute to a high correlation—but not causation—between spending and victory. Chief among them is incumbency, which itself correlates with high spending. Other factors such as "earned media," personalities, name recognition, media bias and late-breaking issues are examples. Indeed, after adjusting for these other factors the role of money seems to be quite small. Perhaps the fairest conclusion is that other things equal—which they never are—there is a slight advantage for candidates who spend more money than their opponents.

One variant of this claim is that large campaign contributions lead to corruption in the American political system or even that they "undermine American democracy." It is true that about ¼ of one per cent of Americans, or roughly 800,000 people, contributed approximately 68% of all political campaign funds over $200 in 2020.[40] The share of national income held by the upper one per cent of Americans was roughly 20% and their share of wealth was roughly 40%. The income of the top 20% of American comprised about 50% of total income and the top 20% held close to 90% of national wealth. These statistics track the share of income taxes paid by wealthy Americans. The top one per cent of earners paid 38% of all income taxes and the top 25% paid roughly 86%. If money is buying favors for the wealthy, the wealthy are not doing a very good job of it.

Wealthy Americans contribute to candidates for many reasons. Though they contribute more and vote more often than the poor, they do not necessarily vote their pocketbooks. Their motivations for voting and providing funding include very abstract ideological preferences which do not necessarily benefit them economically either directly or indirectly. It should be no harder to accept this view about wealthy Americans than that the working-class does not always vote its pocketbook either.

The fact is that money is far less significant in political races than is often assumed. Bryan Caplan summarizes this in concluding that "most empirical work finds weak effects of money in politics. The typical study reports little to no effect on how politicians vote."[41] Political commentator Robert Samuelson echoes this conclusion: "In short, campaign contributions matter a lot less than most people assume."[42] He says that "The crusade for campaign finance 'reform' captures a defining delusion of our time."[43]

Why then do Americans, and especially progressives, over-estimate the role of money in politics? Political consultants are surely one source of the notion that raising more and more money is imperative for electoral success; after all they are the principal beneficiaries of these funds. This is true of both Democratic and Republican political consultants, so does not explain why the progressive left believes so strongly that money buys elections.[44] Progressive support for limiting or ending private sector funding for political campaigns rests at bottom on the belief in the power of economic, material causation. Neither the working-class nor the wealthy regularly vote their narrow economic interests. It seems it is difficult for empirical evidence to dislodge the fundamental underlying progressive belief in economic determinism.

A third consequence of the dominance of economic causation is what might be called incrementalism. From time to time one hears the concept of zero-base budgeting. Zero-base budgeting is budgeting which is not based on last year's budget; it is a budget constructed from the ground up, based on a clear-eyed assessment of what is needed for the coming fiscal year. In short, zero-base budgeting aims to create budgets which are rational. This is precisely *not* how federal budgeting works. Almost every federal budgeting decision is based not on a ground up construction but on the previous year's budget.

Programs should not be funded simply because they were funded in prior years. This is fair enough. This results in programs like the legendary mohair program, which was funded for decades beyond the time when it made the slightest bit of sense. But this is illustrative of the inertia of the federal budgeting process. This is very different from the administrative rationality which progressive theorists thought would characterize modern government. Budgets are not drawn up scientifically—whatever that might mean—but from a clash between advocates with differing priorities. And the battle lines will inevitably be drawn in one very clear place: how much did we spend last year, and should we spend more or less this year?

Why should this be so? Former Budget Director Charles Schultze has offered one of the most thoughtful accounts of this and other budget-related questions. Schultze acknowledges that there are from time to time brand new programs and significant departures from past spending practices. We have seen a clear example of this in new funding to address the Covid-19 pandemic. Covid-19 spending had no precedent in previous budgets. But Schultze says "the number of radical decisions that any political leadership can effect at one time is strictly limited."[45] He concludes that "most of the individual budget decisions made each year are incremental in nature."[46] He observes that whatever program currently exists is one that has already made it through the political process. It is far easier to adjust spending up or down (usually up) than it is to create a new program. This is true enough, as anyone who has ever observed an executive department budget request drawn up, its treatment by the Office of Management and Budget, or a Congressional committee mark-up can testify. This is also true, by the way, of appointees who require Senate confirmation. Nominees who have been previously confirmed, no matter how successful or unsuccessful in their previous assignments, are generally easier to confirm than new appointees.

There is another reason as well. Non-economic legislation is often all or nothing. Legislation regarding abortion or voting rights will be enacted or not. It is true that compromises on the scope of legislation are possible, but programs that are subject to economic, monetary tweaking are far easier to achieve in principle. This fosters a kind of policy incrementalism which characterizes most federal programs.

This is entirely consistent with the nature of economic theory. Deirdre McCloskey says "Economic science of an orthodox character is good at explaining routine."[47] When the economy is operating in a more or less routine way, and federal government programs are growing incrementally, economics can offer good descriptions of what is occurring. It is when there is a shock to the system and there are radical departures in the economy that economics offers poor explanations of what is occurring and poor prognostications about what will occur. We will consider this outcome further in our discussion of intelligence failures.

There are, to be sure, advantages to budgetary incrementalism. This was confirmed in an experiment I ran in several classes at the University of Virginia. I asked students to assign percentages of their tax contributions to different federal budget functions. The results were interesting. The blended results of each class were wildly different than current federal budget priorities. This of course could easily be explained by the sample—generally middle-class young adults. No doubt a sample of the entire American populace would come somewhat closer to current federal spending priorities.

But results also varied wildly in the face of real-world events during the previous year. If a foreign policy crisis arose, far more was allocated to that budget function than was allocated by federal budgeteers. The same was true if issues related to poverty or education took center stage among the public. It would be difficult to run a government on wildly fluctuating inputs each year, the likely result of direct citizen participation in budget decisions. It was of course the intention of the framers of the American Constitution to mediate direct citizen participation by electing representatives who would "refine and enlarge" the sentiments of citizens. Whether members of Congress actually refine and enlarge public opinion is open to question. What is not open to question is that their decisions reflect a decided tendency toward incrementalism.

While incrementalism has its practical virtues, it also has one very negative result: it reinforces the failure to review and judge the success or failure of programs after they are initially adopted and funded. If programs are adjusted incrementally year by year, there is little incentive to review these programs and determine whether they are successful or whether they merit changes or elimination altogether. Charles Schultze says:

> Unfortunately … too few programs are routinely subjected to an evaluation of results. Indeed, it is not uncommon for programs of an avowedly experimental nature to be inaugurated with no provision for a systematic evaluation of performance.[48]

This unfortunate tendency is true of both the legislative branch which authorizes programs and the executive branch which administers them. Schultze calls this one of the weakest links of the current budgetary system. The entire annual spending process is fought out over whether to increase, maintain or decrease spending from the prior year's budget. This process is driven from beginning to end by the notion of economic causation, that is, that money is the solution to all social problems.

A NOTE ON REPARATIONS

Here we might consider briefly the notion of economic reparations as a recompense for the institution of human slavery. One might naively think that the salience of this notion would have receded over the course of time. The United States is now 160 years from the Emancipation Proclamation and only a few years less from the adoption of the XIII Amendment which formally abolished slavery. Depending on how generations are measured, we are today at least six generations beyond the end of slavery in America.

Though the demand for reparations is often couched in terms of slavery, this is not what it is really about. It is about the fact that median incomes and wealth of black Americans trail that of whites and other racial minorities. Given that some minorities have arrived more recently in America, and that some did not speak English when they arrived, what could be the source of this discrepancy? For progressives it only could be the lingering effect of slavery. Given that other minorities often faced some degree of discrimination, it cannot be discrimination alone that would justify reparations. It must somehow be traced back to slavery, at least rhetorically.

There are numerous practical difficulties facing proponents of reparations. These have been widely observed, so only a few need be mentioned here. To whom precisely are reparations to be paid? To descendants of slaves or to all black Americans? Should reparations be paid to highly successful blacks whose income and wealth exceed national norms? From whom should reparations be required? From all Americans, including those who themselves or their families came to America one or more generations after slavery had been abolished? From descendants of union soldiers who lost their lives in the civil war to end slavery? How large should reparations payments be, and in what form? What amount of reparations would be "just?" Should reparations be paid to individuals or somehow to institutions or programs which largely serve black communities?

These and a host of other practical questions make the idea of reparations very difficult to imagine in practice. But they do not touch the idea of reparations at a deeper level. There are more difficult questions. What, for example, would be the likely effect of reparations? Would recipients of a one-time reparation payment be likely to achieve continuing parity with other ethnic groups? Many would, especially those who have made wise life choices on their own. Extra money would no doubt be welcome and have its uses. Those who have made unwise life choices on their own, however, would be unlikely to benefit in any lasting way. No doubt extra money would come in handy, but for how long? When the money runs out, these recipients would be likely to be in the same economic position they are today. In short, those who most need financial assistance would be least likely to benefit from it in any lasting way.

Another effect is easily predictable: deepened resentment on the part of non-black Americans who are below the median income and wealth levels of the American population. One sees this resentment today, where federal transfer payments—as has been shown by Phil Gramm—often level up

the income of people who do not work with those who do. This is one reason that working-class-Americans—of all ethnic groups—have been trending toward the Republican Party in recent years. Reparations would deepen
this resentment and also give it an unfortunate racial tinge. Why should a
black working-class citizen receive reparations when non-black Americans
who are in the very same economic position do not? This is not a formula
for racial harmony.

What lies behind the idea of reparations is the same economic/material
point of view we have already encountered over and over again. The good of
reparations may be framed as "justice," but it is a purely economic understanding of justice at that. For proponents of reparations there can be no genuine
redress other than economic redress. Economic causation lies behind both
the description of the problem and its proposed solution. The root problem
is economic—now fashionably called equity—and its solution must therefore be economic as well. Legal and other forms of redress for the sin of slavery simply cannot be sufficient; economic redress is required.

A purely economic program like reparations will fail because economic
determinism is not an adequate understanding of human motivation. This
has been addressed at least since the time of Plato. In his *Republic* Plato speaks
of a cave in which men are chained and see only the images of things on
the cave wall. One man breaks free of his chains and steps into the sunlight
where he can see clearly. But it turns out that breaking free of one's chains is
not the same as genuine liberation. Breaking one's chains is a purely external event; his circumstances have changed but he is not yet fully liberated.
Full liberation cannot be provided by one's external circumstances; it must
come from inside.

For this reason Plato's character returns to the cave, where he finds life
unchanged. Those still living in the shadows mock him because he does not
see as they do. Are we really to suppose that reparations for the enslavement
of one's ancestors more than 160 years ago will liberate anyone? Genuine liberation is taking responsibility for one's own life, not a change in external
(economic) circumstances. It is a cramped notion of justice to seek salvation

from a one-time change in economic circumstances. Reparations are likely to perpetuate the illusion of an economic solution to human problems.

FIVE

FOREIGN ASSISTANCE AND INTERVENTION ABROAD

L et's turn to the role of economic or material causation in the conduct of American foreign policy. We should be clear from the outset what we do and do not mean by this. American foreign policy has long and widely been understood to pursue both economic interests and idealistic goals which run out far beyond these interests. Bob Kagan has demonstrated this brilliantly in his book *Dangerous Nation.* In calling America a "dangerous nation" Kagan points to the way in which a nation founded on universal ideals and not on geography or ethnicity quite naturally aims to bring these same principles into practice around the world. He shows too how these ideals implicitly (or even explicitly) threaten other nations which are not governed by them.

Countries like Russia and China, to name several of many, do not much care about the nature of the foreign regimes with which they deal. Their foreign policy goals are self-interested and their policies are thoroughly transactional. For America, on the other hand, there is often an unstated but not so subtle view that nations which are not founded on the consent of the governed—even those run by friendly governments—are not fully legitimate.

It is often difficult to separate American interests from its ideals. In many cases, such as opposition to Russia's invasion of Ukraine, interests and ideals overlap. In other cases, such as American policy toward Saudi Arabia, they do not. Marxist theorists occasionally attempt to simplify this difficulty by arguing that American ideals are a façade and that American foreign policy can be accounted for entirely by American interests, and economic ones at that. This usually results in extraordinarily weak, even ridiculous arguments. For example, Marxist theorists argued that the American invasion of Iraq was undertaken to secure Iraqi oil. It somehow escaped these hard-headed, unsentimental analysts that Saddam Hussein was eager to sell Iraqi on the world market. It was America, through its leadership on United Nations sanctions resolutions and its military forces, which prevented this. Simple American acquiescence to Saddam's desire would have been far easier—and far less costly in terms of lives and treasure—than removing Saddam from power, extinguishing the massive fires he set in Iraqi oil fields and helping to rebuild the Iraqi oil industry from scratch. This is all the truer as America did not take any ownership of Iraqi oil, which was used to help rebuild the country.

THE STATE DEPARTMENT BUDGET

The argument we make here is very different. It is not a neo-Marxist view that American policies are invariably driven by economic interests, but rather that the *means* by which America's interests and ideals are pursued rest very heavily on the notion of economic or material causation. The programs and policies of American foreign policy rest largely on the premise that the principal driver of world problems is economic and the way to bring about social change is by means of economic change. Chief among the economic drivers is poverty. This we can see in the State Department budget, the foreign assistance program, trade policy and economic sanctions.

To begin, we see this reflected in a concern over the "top line" of the State Department and Agency for International Development (AID) budgets. How can an administration or the Congress demonstrate their concern about foreign policy challenges? By providing a higher top line of overall spending. To spend more is to care more. The Biden administration is pleased to note that it is requesting a 15% increase over FY 2022's top line appropriation. This equation of increased spending with improved outcomes is the way in which global challenges are addressed.

This approach is not unique to the State Department. In addition to the domestic programs we discussed in the previous chapter, it is also true of the Defense Department and other national security institutions. Defense Department budgets—and the Defense Department plays an increasingly large role in what were once thought of as State Department issues—are also often evaluated by the level of top line spending. This is reflected in abstract calls for a certain percentage increase in the Defense Department budget or by calls for defense spending to achieve a certain percentage of the GDP. To be sure, it is not possible to construct national security budgets entirely from the ground up, based on documented threats and needs. The international environment changes too rapidly for this. And other things equal, when it comes to defense there is a good case for erring on the side of too much rather than too little. But it would be a welcome development to see national security budgets more closely tailored to a persuasive argument of what is needed rather than what is politically possible to squeeze out of Congress in a given year.

In recent years the State Department has undertaken several steps to try to justify its funding requests in terms of a larger strategic framework. This began with the Quadrennial Diplomacy and Development Review (QDDR), modeled after a similar Defense Department exercise. The first QDDR was begun in 2009 and completed in 2010. The second and last QDDR was begun in 2014 and completed in 2015. In the place of the discontinued QDDRs, the State Department and AID produced a four-year Joint Strategic Plan in 2018 and another in 2022. These exercises have as their goal, which is a worthy one, to provide strategic guidance for State and AID activities and programs. Would that this were so in reality. These exercises do not produce documents around which anything could be—or actually is—planned. A brief look at them will reveal that they are largely reverse-engineered justifications for whatever programmatic spending is already underway. At best, if this is even the correct word for it, they re-describe existing programs in the language of newly minted political goals such as inclusion, equity or global warming.

National security expert Kori Schake has argued along these lines in saying that "mission focus" is one of the State Department's major deficiencies.[1] The planning documents, such as they are, are rife with vague and non-measurable aspirations such as "to identify solutions," "to sustain and enhance," to "seek to" and "to ensure." When State Department officials are asked what they need to do their job better, they say simply that they need more money, without explaining how additional money would transform anything about how the State Department actually works.[2] A quick look at the word salad which comprises the Department's so-called planning documents would quickly convince the reader of one thing: nothing concrete, meaningful or measurable could possibly be planned on the basis of these documents.

The reality is that the State Department and AID build their annual budget requests not from any strategic viewpoint, but from the budget request and/or Congressional appropriation of the previous year. To sit around the table as this exercise takes place at State is to remove all doubt about that. Is country X more or less deserving than last year? How will a cut from the previous year be taken by recipient country Y? Here we find the same "signaling" that characterizes domestic discretionary programs. This is true of both the administration's budget request and Congressional deliberations over annual appropriations.

Herewith a case from many possible examples. When I was serving at State the Egyptian ambassador called me in a panic. It appeared the House Appropriations Committee intended to cut Egypt's military assistance from the previous year's level as a signal of its displeasure with Egypt's human rights record. This, the ambassador said, would be disastrous. I might have been more moved if this had not been the sixth such call I had received that week from ambassadors worried about their country's foreign assistance levels. I assured the ambassador the State Department opposed this action, though he was scarcely mollified.

It is interesting to note that in my several conversations with the ambassador, the question of precisely how much money the Egyptian military needed to accomplish its missions never arose. Not once. Not once were the actual merits of the military assistance program ever discussed. The conversations were never about the substance of the matter but about its optics. How would a cut in military assistance be taken by the Egyptian government?

This question never arose on the American side either. The threatened cut by the appropriators was not based on a careful analysis of the requirements of the Egyptian military; it was intended to send a message. It too was all about optics. A cut in U. S. aid was meant to signal displeasure with the recipient government. This process works the other way as well; an increase in foreign assistance is meant to convey American satisfaction with, or support for, a recipient government. The signal is far more important than whatever the additional aid is actually supposed to accomplish.

There is another angle as well. How much military aid Egypt receives also reflects on the Egyptian ambassador. The ambassador would not like to have to report to Cairo that Egypt's aid is being cut on his watch. How much aid a country receives is a clear marker of how well an ambassador is doing his job.

Not every expenditure of U. S. tax dollars is determined in this way. But it would surely surprise the average American taxpayer how many funding decisions are based on this practice of signaling. Just as with domestic programs, the equation of more money with better results attaches excessive importance to inputs as opposed to results.

To its credit, in recent years the State Department has made additional efforts to evaluate its programs. This is especially true of AID. AID observes that its work is "evidence based," with more than one hundred evaluations of its programs conducted each year. These can be accessed at the State Department's website "Foreign Assistance Evaluations," and the State Department estimates it expends roughly $500 million annually to conduct these evaluations. In theory this is all to the good. In practice it is nearly worthless. A survey of the evaluations reveals a somewhat standard format. First, programs are described in positive terms in some detail. Then evaluations proceed to recommendations for the future. There is virtually no meaningful measure of success or failure. The typical evaluation suggests a program is "on target." But on target to accomplish what? Or that it demonstrates "substantial progress." But substantial progress toward what end? Or that it is "productive." But productive of what? Kori Schake summarizes the problem: "the Department of State contents itself with exhortation rather than establishing metrics [of success]."[3]

This outcome is only to be expected; the people who review and evaluate AID programs are largely the same people who carry them out. In many cases the individuals are not government employees but private contractors who have an obvious financial self-interest in promoting the success of their programs. The result is often a recommendation that more money should be provided to continue and to expand these programs. One evaluation (chosen from many possible candidates), for example, suggests that its program would be more successful if its foreign participants were expanded from 383 to 500. Why 500, and to exactly what end? The answer is baked into the process: more is always better.

The Government Accountability Office (GAO) undertook an independent study in 2017 of State and AID programs. Predictably its results were less sanguine. It concluded that 4% of State programs and 26% of AID programs were "successful," 48% of State programs and 48% of AID programs were "acceptable," and 48% of State and 26% of AID programs were ranked "low" in terms of success.

Congress has also intervened on the question of program evaluations. It passed the "Foreign Aid Transparency and Accountability Act of 2016." This act required that within 18 months the president must set forth guidelines for "measurable goals, performance metrics and monitoring and evaluation plans," which should be applied across time with reasonable consistency. This too is an admirable goal, but two facts about it should be noted. First, Congress once again makes the executive department the judge of its own programs. Predictably little has changed as a result of this initiative. Second, Congress has managed in its typical fashion to offload all responsibility for program evaluations from itself. In a better world Congress might take some responsibility for evaluating programs which after all it has authorized and funded. This would require the work of holding genuine oversight hearings. What passes for Congressional oversight these days is the occasional "gotcha" hearing to score partisan points on an all too obvious programmatic failure.

As it stands, once a program is funded there is a strong, built-in constituency to continue it. The private contractors, executive branch officials and Congressional authorizers and appropriators are all responsible for the monies expended on programs, and they are all loath to acknowledge shortcomings or failures. The Defense Department's military after-action reviews are a far better example of genuine program reviews. The surest sign that honest evaluations were occurring at State and AID would be an occasional conclusion that a program had failed to accomplish its intended goals, or even that its goals made little or no sense in the first place. There is nothing like this on the horizon today. Far simpler, it seems, is to fall back on the economic causal view that money solves all problems. If and when programs fail, then, the inescapable conclusion is that they were not sufficiently funded. The answer must always be more.

FOREIGN ASSISTANCE AND THE STAGES OF ECONOMIC GROWTH

These questions are significant because of the high percentage of the State Department budget that goes to fund foreign assistance programs. In recent years the State Department budget—the 150 account in budget terms—has been roughly $60 billion. Of this roughly 2/3, or $40 billion annually is spent on foreign assistance. The remaining $20 billion goes for salaries, buildings, security, travel and other expenses associated with the conduct of diplomacy. The provision of foreign assistance is clearly a major State Department activity and the core mission of AID.

This was not always the case. Although there were occasional instances of foreign assistance delivered in the late nineteenth century, foreign assistance did not become a major tool of U. S. policy until the years just prior to America's direct involvement in World War II. Though it was characterized differently, the Lend Lease program for Britain was essentially a large-scale foreign assistance program. In all, 38 nations received assistance with an estimated value of $48 billion under the Lend Lease program. This program reflected the fact that in the years after World War I America had become the world's dominant economy. It was not until after World War II, however, that American foreign assistance began to assume the shape it has today. In those years American assistance was provided to an array of foreign governments in a variety of forms, including especially security assistance. Chief among them, of course, was the Marshall Plan (officially the European Recovery Program) provided to 16 European nations between 1948 and 1952. This program provided a total of $17 billion, roughly equivalent to $137 billion in today's dollars. The purpose of the program was to assist European nations in rebuilding their devastated economies and to reduce trade barriers between European nations.

Scholars today debate the significance of this aid. Some suggest that the European recovery was already underway by 1948, and in any event the program provided only 2.5-3 percent of total European GDP at the time. Nevertheless, the Marshall Plan was deeply appreciated by European nations and retains a very positive reputation to this day. The reason is not hard to see: European economies bounced back quickly and within a decade all were operating at or above pre-war levels.

The favorable reputation of the Marshall Plan was an important predicate for the expansion of American foreign assistance programs. European nations not only became economically self-sufficient but were weaned away from the temptation to align themselves with the Soviet Union. It is hard to imagine today, when European nations are part of a NATO alliance solidly opposed to Putin's Russia, but in the late 1940's and early 1950's it was by no means beyond imagining that one or more western European nations might fall under the sway of Eurocommunism.

Favorable results in Europe gave the Marshall Plan a positive cachet that it retains to this day. There are from time to time calls for a new Marshall

Plan to address pandemics, global warming and a host of other issues. Most recently there has been a call for a new Marshall Plan to assist Ukraine in recovering from the devastation Russian forces have inflicted on Ukraine's economy. These calls are not based on an assessment that there is any similarity with post-war European recovery; a new Marshall Plan simply means large dollar expenditures.

Indeed, it is easy to over-generalize from the success of the Marshall Plan. Spending more money, even lots more money, does not guarantee success in situations unlike those of post-war Europe. It is important to recall that post-war Europe was building on an already developed social and economic base. As Dambisa Moyo correctly notes, the Marshall Plan was "a matter of reconstruction, and not economic development."[4] The economic development of poor nations with no history of modern political, social or economic institutions is an entirely different matter.

Afghanistan makes this point in spades. According to the U. S. Inspector General for Afghan Reconstruction (SIGAR), the U. S. provided Afghanistan with $137 billion in economic assistance over 20 years. This was in addition to $837 billion in military assistance and many billions of additional economic and military assistance provided by American allies. This is a staggering amount provided to one country of approximately 41 million people, a fair test of whether Marshall Plan-like spending guarantees success. This is what economists might refer to as a "natural experiment." What little Afghanistan has to show for this is rapidly disappearing. Robert Nelson makes the same point about assistance to post-communist eastern Europe. Where nations had decent pre-communist norms, they have done well; where they did not, they have not.[5] This distinction has been largely lost in America's foreign assistance program.

In 1961 the American foreign assistance program we know today came of age. In 1961 President Kennedy asked, and the Congress agreed, to create a new organization committed to the idea of "development assistance." The provision of security aid and emergency economic aid continued, just as they have right up to today. What was new, however, was a new type of aid which was to operate independently from day-to-day American diplomatic goals. The newly created Agency for International Development assumed a quasi-independence from short-term State Department goals. It should be noted in fairness that a national security goal was still implicit in development aid. President Kennedy said that many newly independent nations were "without exception … under communist pressure" and that these nations required assistance to achieve "sufficient economic, social and political strength to stand permanently on their own feet."[6]

There was a long policy syllogism at work here, namely, that economic growth would lead to freer, friendlier governments which in turn would be bulwarks against the temptation of communism. Nevertheless, development aid could run on its own track independent of short-term American policy preferences; its payoff would come in the longer term. As we shall discuss, this implied a development process which would bring nations to the happy result of mature, free and anti-communist developed nations. The key to this was the stages of growth through which nations were assumed to travel on the path to development.

The concept of "development" spoke volumes about its authors' premises. The word is taken from biology, which understands the growth of organisms as a natural, uni-directional process. Organisms begin small, they mature, and unless attacked from the outside, naturally become mature and self-sustaining. In applying this metaphor to poor nations there is an implication that social changes are not arbitrary or random but have an implicit directionality. This is of course an altogether debatable notion, to put it politely; nations seem to be able to become richer or poorer, more or less developed, depending on the policies chosen by their governments. Venezuela, for example, was once a relatively prosperous nation which has descended into desperate poverty and chaos. The notion of development suggests a natural course through which nations travel on their way to maturity. As Robert Nisbet says, actual history is not the same as "the language of developmentalism, with its hoary concepts and premises of imminence, continuity, directionality, necessity and uniformitarianism."[7] Belief in the natural economic development of nations is another version of the belief that the arc of history bends toward justice.

How then does economic development occur and what role does foreign assistance play? Virtually every development model advances a clear path for development. But none was more persuasive than the notion of "stages of growth" and no stages-of-growth model was more persuasive than Walt Rostow's. Rostow's *The Stages of Economic Growth,* which was published in 1960, played a deep and influential role in the theory and practice of development assistance. Rostow's book was subtitled *A Non-Communist Manifesto,* and Rostow challenged the Marxist view of economics as the ultimate cause of all social change. He stated upfront that while economic changes cause social changes, economic change itself can be based on non-economic factors.[8] Fair enough, though Rostow proceeds to ignore this dictum throughout his book, which treats economic growth as a purely economic phenomenon. He sets out five stages of economic growth: traditional society, society with the pre-conditions for economic takeoff, economic takeoff, the drive to maturity, and the end stage of high mass consumption. Rostow's stages are all economic, and the impetus for progressing from one stage to another is economic as well.

Rostow proposed that the underdeveloped world was largely at the pre-condition for takeoff stage.[9] What is required for takeoff is to get a nation's investment rate up from 5% to 10% of GDP; more savings for investment is required. Rostow suggests that developing nations' governments could do this, though it is very difficult for a poor nation which tends to consume most of what it produces. This is the role for foreign assistance; grants or loans from developed nations can play this key catalyzing role. In short, money is required to produce more money which in turn is required to produce more money yet. In fairness, Rostow says "it is necessary to avoid linear projections."[10] But Rostow's book is essentially one long linear projection, and it is founded on the notion that economic change is the motor to produce economic, social and political development.

Foreign assistance is to be the catalyst to set into motion the process of economic development which will proceed through an orderly pre-defined sequence of stages. And the more economic assistance, the greater the like-lihood of worldwide development. In his book Rostow calls for substantial increases in foreign assistance, a call which he and M. F. Millikan had already proposed several years earlier.[11] Here we have both the gist and the rationale for the American development assistance program. It is founded on the premise that economic assistance (often coupled with technical assistance) is the key to the development of poor nations. America is historically far and away the world's largest provider of development assistance, though many other devel-oped nations also contribute. Some contribute at a far higher per capita basis than America, and in certain circles it is a point of pride as to which nation contributes the highest per capita amount of official development assistance (ODA).[12] Needless to say, this friendly competition is all about inputs with no mention of actual results.

Given the trillions of dollars that have been expended in the past six decades, one might wonder why foreign assistance is still necessary. This is not an unfair question. Indeed, the United Nations recently announced that donor nations would have to provide a total of $2.5 trillion beyond their cur-rent programs to achieve sustainable development among poor nations by 2030. More is always the answer. Is economic causation—providing more money—really the key to broad social and political development, or for that matter even of economic growth itself?

This question lay behind a new American initiative which was undertaken in 2004. In 2004 Congress authorized and the executive branch stood up the Millenium Challenge Corporation (MCC). This initiative did not replace traditional development assistance but was added alongside it. The think-ing behind this new entity was solid—though its execution has often been sketchy—and reflected well-founded doubt about the premise that provid-ing development assistance was sufficient to bring about economic growth. In this way it was a half-step away from the pure economic causation model that lay behind traditional development aid programs.

The goal of the MCC was the same as that of traditional development aid programs: "to reduce global poverty through economic growth." Economic growth remained the goal, which in turn would bring with it other kinds of social progress. But the means to create economic growth were understood differently. The idea was to bring about political and legal changes which would provide the proper context for economic growth. In other words, the capital accumulation model of the stages of growth and traditional development aid was insufficient by itself to achieve significant economic growth. What was required was a political context in which predictable laws, contracts, property rights and a sphere of citizen independence were necessary conditions to achieve sustainable economic growth.

The core of this new view has been expressed by Daron Acemoglu and James A. Robinson in their book *Why Nations Fail*. They argue that "economic institutions shape economic incentives ... It is the political process that determines what economic institutions people live under."[13] They say further that "while economic institutions are critical for determining whether a country is poor or prosperous, it is politics and political institutions that determine what economic institutions a country has."[14] This thinking is clearly a step in the right direction, less because of its institutional orientation than because of the priority it assigns to politics. This in turn points to a difficult set of questions. Why do some nations have political institutions which permit economic growth and others do not? And how can nations which lack these political institutions be led to create them?

It might seem as if the answer to the latter question is education. By educating rulers, whom we might assume wish to do the right thing for their nations, we can create a political process which permits, or even encourages, good economic institutions. This is another version of the process of writing new constitutions for nations which has been in vogue since the second half of the eighteenth century. But as constitution writers have found out, the problem is not so simple. In many cases, rulers are financially benefiting from their current political processes. This is especially the case in those nations whose political and economic systems are heavily based on extractive industries. In these cases rulers often have strong financial incentives to maintain current arrangements because they are so profitable—for the rulers. Not every ruler sets aside his or her economic interests when making policy.

In many nations this harmful system—with perverse incentives for economic growth—grew quite naturally out of colonialism. Colonial powers generally used their colonies to extract wealth from them. To do so they often relied on local rulers to assist in this process. In some cases they even strengthened the power of local rulers. When colonialism came to an end in the decades after World War II local rulers kept in place the extractive policies of their former colonial rulers, now for their own financial advantage. In short, many post-colonial rulers have a significant financial stake in maintaining political and economic institutions adverse to broad economic growth. Albert Hirschman recognized this as early as 1958. In his book *The Strategy of Economic Development,* Hirschman noted a deep tension: "universal desire for economic improvement oddly combined with many resistances to change."[15]

The MCC approaches the issue of political institutions through a process of "conditionality." It negotiates what it calls "compacts" or partnerships with recipient governments. For their part recipient governments must agree to put in place conditions such as "ruling justly" or "economic freedom" or "investing in people." In exchange for this the MCC provides multi-year economic assistance. Economic assistance is still the presumed solution for economic growth, but at least there is an awareness that for assistance to work it must do so in the context of better political institutions.

The MCC has its critics. Proponents of traditional development assistance have always been wary of the MCC, fearing that it might supplant the development assistance model. On the other hand, Dombisa Moyo argues that any type of assistance which flows through governments—even if conditioned—provides the basis for corruption and dependence. Still others criticize the MCC on narrower grounds, namely, that in recent years the MCC has added new kinds of conditionality to reflect current priorities of the American government. These include global warming and gender issues which seem at best to have a tenuous correlation with economic growth.

We might conclude this discussion of the MCC by agreeing that while it takes a step in the right direction, it is still tied to what is essentially a capital accumulation model of economic growth. It is indeed necessary to have decent political and legal institutions to create economic growth. But how does the MCC propose to help create such institutions? Ironically, it does so by providing economic assistance. Economic causation is still at work here, this time in the form of a kind of "bribe" to create better political institutions. We have already considered the assumption that providing money to individuals will lead them to make better life choices. Here at the macro-level, the assumption is that providing money to governments will lead them to make better political choices. It seems it is difficult, if not impossible, for American government policymakers to escape the fundamental belief in economic causation.

In fairness, we might ask the following hard question: if we do not rely on economic causation, how can we help to achieve significant change in poor nations? Economic growth depends less on capital accumulation than on a social-political context which allows for freedom and which encourages innovation. What is the lever by which to create such conditions? Surely, as many observers have noted—Moyo and McCloskey, for example—government-to-government aid is unlikely to be the lever. Perhaps to the contrary.

We might use the case of Afghanistan to address this question. For more than 20 years the United States aimed to help Afghanistan create new and better institutions. It did not just hand out money—though it surely did that—but it aimed to create democratic institutions including regular elections and a national parliament. It aimed to create new agricultural, health care, education, police and military institutions as well. Yet all this disappeared in an instant. Why? The institutions were formally correct, in many cases following American institutions, but they simply did not take deep root in Afghan society. If they had, the Afghan proponents and beneficiaries of these institutions would not have allowed them to collapse so quickly in the face of Taliban pressure.

Formal political institutions may be admirable on the surface, no doubt about it. But how to ensure they take root? This suggests the limitations of a purely institutional approach to creating sustained economic growth and complementary political processes. The institutions themselves must rest on something deeper to be successful. The philosopher Immanuel Kant was fond to say that human reason was so powerful it could balance and shape institutions in such a way that they could produce good government even for a nation of devils. It seems this is simply not true, being a long and unfounded deduction in a period when practical reason seemed able to rule the entire world. If they are effective, institutions may be able to shape some human behavior and outcomes; but they in turn must rest upon a pre-existing set of widely accepted social norms, including a moderated form of self-interest and a general level of trust in one's fellow citizens. This was the understanding of the American framers, who referred again and again to what they called the necessary "virtues" of the citizenry.

The importance of this foundation has been noted by many wise observers. Daniel Moynihan called it "culture," Albert Hirschman called it "attitudes," Deirdre McCloskey calls it "sentiments," and Robert Nelson calls it "trust." A kind of social, non-economic capital seems necessary to buttress institutions so that they are not mere formalities but have genuine force. It has often been noted that many tyrannies have constitutions with a long menu of political rights comparable to those in the American Constitution. All are mere words resting on no social/cultural base.

FOREIGN TRADE AND SANCTIONS

Fortunately, there is another way for the United States to influence positively the economic prospects of other nations, including and especially poor nations. This way is through foreign trade and investment. As we will discuss, the utility of foreign trade and investment is also limited in its ability to influence non-economic practices of foreign nations; the limits of economic causation exist here too. But foreign trade and investment are far more useful tools to bring about economic growth than foreign assistance. This is acknowledged by almost everyone who studies international economics. The economist N.

Gregory Mankiw says of the often-fractious science of economics that "few propositions command as much consensus as that open world trade increases economic growth and raises living standards."[16]

The process of worldwide trade expansion was led by the United States after World War II. This was a strong reaction against the trade-restrictive policies which were adopted by the United States and other nations in the years between the two world wars. As we have already noted, an important aspect of the Marshall Plan was to remove trade barriers between European nations. This goal was expanded with the adoption by 23 countries of the General Agreement on Tariffs and Trade (GATT) in 1947. This agreement was further broadened and deepened considerably by subsequent rounds of trade negotiations over the following decades. In recent years worldwide trade totals have exceeded $20 trillion annually.

This is of course not to say that more open world trade has no downsides. Individual workers and entire industries have experienced financial harm from expanded foreign competition. But overall it is impossible to deny the astonishing positive effects of international trade on both developed and developing nations. The Word Bank has concluded that worldwide poverty has been reduced from 38% in 1990 to 8.4% in 2019. Walter Russell Mead summed this up in saying foreign trade "has done more than all of the world's foreign aid bureaucracies to raise living standards and increase opportunities for people in emerging economies."[17]

There is especially strong evidence for this proposition in East Asia. Nations like Japan, South Korea and Taiwan which opened their economies to the world and which focused on export promotion, have experienced astonishing economic growth and increases in their per capita GDP. This was a far more successful approach than one taken by nations which have failed to integrate their economies into the global trading system and have instead relied on foreign assistance provided by developed nations.

There has been no greater example of the benefits of trade and openness than China. When Deng Xiaoping and then Jiang Zemin opened the Chinese economy, they produced results which have often been described as a supremely successful anti-poverty program. Tim Groser, for example, says this was "the largest poverty-reduction program in human history. Hundreds of millions of Chinese were lifted out of destitution, and huge opportunities opened up for China's trading partners."[18]

There is no doubt about the importance of maintaining a broad commitment to an open world trading system. Lifting another billion people on the world's bottom economic rung depends upon it, as does the economic health of the world's developed nations. Adjustments along the way will certainly be needed to protect individuals, industries and nations which are harmed by foreign competition, especially by competition which emerges rapidly and in some cases unexpectedly. Adjustments will also be needed to provide the political will of developed nations' leaders to maintain a broadly free and open world trading system. But the importance of openness cannot be doubted; there is simply no way for foreign assistance to achieve the positive results of expanded foreign trade.

What we must note here, however, is the excessive faith placed in international trade to achieve more than economic growth. Once again we see the notion of economic causation, namely, that economic growth will bring about non-economic benefits. And once again China serves as the best example. The United States led the world in bringing China into the world trading system. The United States provided Permanent Normal Trade Relations to China, bringing tariffs into line with those levied against other nations. It also supported Chinese entry into the World Trade Organization. In and of themselves, there was nothing wrong with these steps. But accompanying them were untested and, as it turns out mistaken hopes about the consequences of these steps. Chinese entry into the world trading system was seen as a pathway toward moderating China's dictatorial rule and self-centered mercantile policies. The hope was to make China a "responsible stakeholder" in the world trading system, that is, a nation which would play by the rules of liberal democracies and gradually become more politically akin to them. President Clinton said, for example, that this process would bring about "reform" in China, that it would offer "new hope for change in China," and that it would help to "bring about peace" in the world.

These were not fringe notions but were deeply and widely held by the political center of the American polity. In the spirit of full disclosure, this author entertained a modest degree of such hope as well. But the notion turned out to be a misplaced hope rather than a reality. What we have learned once again is the futility of expecting economic change to bring about non-economic benefits. It may well be true that expanded trade gives nations an incentive toward international stability. The Germans especially, who had several motivations to believe in the politically liberating effect of trade (including their reluctance to meet their defense spending commitments to NATO) saw trade as a powerful diplomatic as well as economic tool. This was enshrined in their saying *Wandel durch Handel*—change through trade.

In its simplest form, the overweening faith in economic causation was expressed in Thomas Friedman's "golden arches" theory of peace. "No two countries," he argued, "that both have a McDonald's have ever fought a war against each other." Since Russia's invasion of Ukraine this is obviously no longer true. While commerce undoubtedly softens the sentiments of people, as we have discussed in an earlier chapter, it does not necessarily soften the sentiments of their rulers, especially if they are autocrats. As Clifford May has written, what Friedman "failed to appreciate is that if those countries are unfree, undemocratic and ruled by tyrants, most of their people don't matter."[19] The golden arches theory essentially recycled a popular pre-World War I notion that economic interdependence would lead to the end of war. It took only a handful of years before World War I in 1914 disproved that theory, an outcome which should have tempered any enthusiasm for it in our own time.

As to war, we might note that the connection between economics and the state of war is very weak. Neo-Marxists who seek the basis of war in economic conditions must torture their interpretation of reality beyond all recognition. Think for a moment of the several wars in which the United States has been engaged in the past half century. Vietnam, Iraq I, Iraq II, Bosnia,

Kosovo, Panama, Lebanon, Grenada, Libya and (indirectly) Ukraine—none had anything to do with economic causation. Nor does the bellicosity of Russia, China, Iran or North Korea today. Autocrats offer the starkest proof of the limits of economic causation.

It seems all too easy for economists to observe a simple economic fact and to over-generalize from it. It is hard to believe today—and it certainly does these authors no credit—to look back at mainstream economic thinking about the former Soviet Union. From observing a few years of economic growth in the Soviet Union, economists came to precisely the wrong conclusion. Both Paul Samuelson and Robert Heilbroner said the Soviet economy would surpass that of the United States in a generation.[20] Once again, these authors failed to recognize that politics is prior to economics and can and does shape economies. This became evident within a decade or two after their pronouncements. Perhaps there is a lesson here about contemporary China as well. Chairman Xi seems determined to rein in the Chinese economy and to reassert political control over it. If he does not handle this carefully and in a limited way, he has it within his power to derail the very economy which has elevated both him and China.

In an interesting article Gerald Seib has proposed a different view. He says "Economic globalization was supposed to make wars harder to start. What if the experience with Russia right now is demonstrating that globalization actually makes them harder to prevent?"[21] Perhaps, he suggests, Putin is willing to pay the economic price for invading Ukraine, calculating that the West is not prepared to pay the price to defend Ukraine. Perhaps so too with Chinese calculations over whether to invade Taiwan. Whatever the truth of this, it is certain that decisions about war are political and not economic decisions. It is often said, and not without some reason, that Japan's decision to go to war with America was based on economic factors, namely, Japan's declining ability to obtain natural resources. But Japan had many possible choices to deal with this problem, including foregoing its imperial expansion. Economics may set the table, but economic causation does not determine whether nations go to war or not.

Let's switch gears and observe the way in which an over-dependence on economic causation works exactly the other way around. Although international trade remains a core priority of the United States, there are many occasions when America aims to restrict trade. The tool to do so is economic sanctions, which can be levied against nations, sub-national entities or individuals. Economic sanctions differ from measures like tariffs which are implemented to address purely economic competition from foreign nations. Tariffs are designed to protect American economic interests from foreign competition, some of which is fair and some of which is not.

Economic sanctions are an entirely different matter. They are not an economic tool designed to address primarily economic problems. They have non-economic purposes ranging from expressions of disapproval of other nations' policies, to forcing change in other nations' policies, to regime change. Economic sanctions are an economic tool designed to address non-economic problems.

Sanctions have become America's most frequently employed foreign policy tool. The Treasury Department whose Office of Foreign Assets Control (OFAC) enforces U. S. sanctions currently lists 38 active sanctions programs aimed at foreign nations or sub-national entities. Some of these programs are made up of numerous partial sanctions which have been adopted at different times. In addition, OFAC lists 6,300 sanctions against individuals who fall under the Specially Designated National and Blocked Persons list. Other organizations which track U. S. sanctions estimate the total number of sanctions at almost 12,000. Castellum ai's Global Sanctions Index, for example, lists 11,652 separate U. S. sanctions, including sanctions on nations, entities, individuals, vessels and aircraft. Fletcher School professor Daniel Drezner summarizes current American foreign policy in saying "it has become obvious that the United States relies on one tool above all: economic sanctions."[22]

How did we come to this place? The United States first imposed economic sanctions with the Embargo Act of 1807. This legislation sanctioned both England and France because of their maritime policies, including in the case of England impressing American seamen. The Act, which cut heavily against

Federalist New England as well as England and France, has been generally regarded as a failure. It was repealed only two short years later in 1809. For the next century the United States used economic tools like embargoes only to address economic challenges.

This changed entirely after World War I. The notion of economic interdependence having obviously failed to deter war, the victors were in search of another weapon that might prove more effective. In creating the League of Nations, Woodrow Wilson and other leaders turned to economic sanctions as a way to deter nations from using violence or going to war. Article 16 of the League of Nations charter states that such aggression will be met with:

> The severance of all trade or financial relations, the prohibition of all intercourse between their nationals and the nationals of the covenant-breaking State, and the prevention of all financial, commercial or personal intercourse between the nationals of the covenant-breaking State and the nationals of any other State.

Several points should be noted about this initiative. First, as Nicholas Mulder observes in his comprehensive book *The Economic Weapon,* this approach relied on economic sanctions not only during war, as had traditionally been the case, but during peacetime.[23] Sanctions were to be imposed not only as a tool of war, but as a deterrent to aggression in the first place. This was a new departure, and a much higher bar for sanctions to meet.

Second, in light of what has been discussed in previous chapters of this book, it should come as no surprise that this new approach should be adopted by Woodrow Wilson and other progressives who were firm believers in the power of economic actions to shape non-economic behavior. Wilson believed there was great power in economic sanctions, which he said in 1919 were something "more tremendous than war" itself. Here again we see the notion of economic causation expand beyond the economic sphere to the political sphere.

How effective is this economic tool in bringing about non-economic change? Though Wilson was not alive to see it, the League of Nations was completely ineffective when it used the full measure of this tool against Italy in 1935. It failed to deter Mussolini from invading Ethiopia, nor did it have any effect on Mussolini's war once it had begun. This was an inauspicious start, pointing clearly to the limits of economic causation.

Despite this initial failure, the use of economic sanctions has exploded in recent times. How effective have economic sanctions been in the past decades during their growing use as a foreign policy tool? The answer to this question depends entirely on the goal when sanctions are enacted. As a tool to signal displeasure they can be said to be very effective, more so than a simple diplomatic or Congressional statement of displeasure. As a way to change behavior, however, their record is very poor. Their best chance of success is when they are directed against smaller, less powerful nations which do not have the economic strength or flexibility to respond to them. Chances of success are also far better if the sanctioned nations care what sanctioning countries think and which have few allies inclined to help them. And chances are better yet when imposed multilaterally in a comprehensive way. Economic sanctions against South Africa were a rare success because they combined all three of these conditions. South Africa was isolated politically, sanctions were comprehensive and multilateral, and the South African government thought of itself as a western nation which cared what western sanctioning nations thought.

In most every other case, sanctions can succeed in causing economic pain to sanctioned nations, but this economic pain is rarely sufficient to bring about significant policy changes, much less to bring about regime change. We might consider several high-profile examples. The United States has imposed significant economic sanctions against Cuba for more than 60 years. This has not been sufficient to change Cuban policy in any significant way, nor has it threatened the Castro regime or its successor's hold on power.

This is also the case with regard to North Korea, Iran and Venezuela, three of the most heavily sanctioned states in the world today. The case of Venezuela is instructive. If economic sanctions cannot effect political change there—in a poor country in this hemisphere with a long tradition of democratic rule— the role of sanctions does not auger much hope for success against stronger nations. Iran is a good case in point. The "maximum pressure" sanctions against the clerical regime there have not succeeded in deterring either Iran's nuclear weapons program or its role as a leading state sponsor of terrorism. Rueul Marc Gerecht and Ray Takyeh describe the limits of economic sanctions precisely:

> American politicians, mesmerized by economics, often think of foreign policy as a corporate transaction. Mr. Khamenei is neither impressed by sanctions nor enticed by financial rewards. He recently said, "In the economic area indicators are not good … but the economy is not the only criterion for power, progress and success."[24]

We might consider too the role of sanctions in regard to Russia's invasion of Ukraine. The threat of extensive sanctions clearly did not deter Putin from invading. That much is clear. Nor are economic sanctions forcing a negotiated end to the war. Sanctions are doubtless having a negative effect on the Russian economy, an effect that will likely grow if maintained into the future. But they have not changed Putin's policy or actions in any way, and there is no reason to think they will succeed going forward. As Janis Kluge of the German Institute for International and Security Affairs says, "The Kremlin is convinced it can withstand a few years with a bad economy and wait for better days. Russia is emboldened by its own success in fending off the West's sanctions."[25] One might ask rhetorically which tool has been more effective against Russia: economic sanctions or the provision of modern, highly capable weapons to Ukraine?

The Peterson Institute estimates that economic sanctions have succeeded roughly 20% of the time they have been utilized. This estimate depends fully on the goals of the sanctions when utilized. Sanctions have failed nearly 100% of the times they have aimed to bring about regime change. And their record has not been much better in leading to significant policy changes by sanctioned regimes. They are unable to achieve these goals because the autocratic regimes against which they have usually been directed:

think differently. They are educated in the much harder school of autocratic politics, and they are aware of a range of human ambitions that modern liberal states, from their earliest foundations, have sought to suppress in the name of peace and comfort.[26]

The limitations of economic sanctions have been eloquently summarized by Nicholas Mulder. He writes:

> While history shows the power of material calculations, it illustrates equally important countervailing motives ... The same aspect of economic sanctions that makes them philosophically appealing to liberal internationalism—their reliance on a *homo economicus* rationale—also limits their salience ... Sanctions would no doubt work better in a world of perfectly rational, consistently self-interested subjects, but this is not the world we inhabit. Most people in most places at most times make collective choices on the basis of a wider set of considerations.[27]

Amen. To which we might also add that when sanctions are applied against autocratic regimes—which is most of the time—there is not really a genuine collective choice being made, but one in which autocratic rulers can avoid most of the pain which is inflicted on their nations. The hardest consequences of sanctions do not fall on autocratic rulers but on their populations, and especially the poor.

Economic sanctions also have a negative economic effect on the sanctioning nations themselves, either directly or as a result of reciprocal sanctions put in place by sanctioned nations. This accounted for the unpopularity of the Embargo Act of 1807 in New England and New York, whose trade was jeopardized by American sanctions. There is no need to discuss this in detail here, but perhaps one example will serve to make the point.

A New Jersey firm processed a product called gum arabic, which has uses in the food and beverage, printing and pharmaceutical industries. Acacia trees grow across a belt in central Africa, including and especially in Sudan. Because of massive human rights violations by the Sudanese government, the U. S. placed economic sanctions against Sudanese exports. This policy was understandable, but unfortunately the French put no such sanctions in place. French businesses continued to process the material they bought from Sudan, and they sold it directly to American food and beverage, printing and pharmaceutical companies—of course at a higher price. The New Jersey firm was soon to go out of business, not because it did not make a good and competitive product, but because of a legal action taken by the United States government.

Though no one had an interest in being complicit in serious Sudanese human rights violations, the well-intentioned U. S. government policy had the following result: American end users were getting all the gum arabic they wanted; French processors were making more money than ever; American processors were going out of business; and worst of all, Sudan was selling as much gum arabic as ever. Here was an obvious self-contradictory result.

This is not an argument for never imposing economic sanctions. But what we find with economic sanctions is similar to every other instance of economic policymaking, that is, its ability to shape non-economic outcomes is very limited. Both the Congress and the executive branch favor sanctions because they are rather easy to put in place, far more so than the use of violence. They signal good intentions, but as in all other such cases the entire emphasis is on the economic policy input, not on the effectiveness or result of the input. There is no more compelling proof of this than a Government Accountability Office report in 2017. This report looked at the role of the Treasury, State and Commerce Departments and found that each of them "stated they do not conduct agency assessments of the effectiveness of sanctions in achieving broader U. S. policy goals." Nor, we might add, does the Congress. As with Congressional spending to achieve non-economic ends, there is simply no concern whether these economic inputs are successful or not, or whether they are even measured. The reliance upon the notion of economic causation to bring about non-economic results runs very deep. It is no wonder that policies based entirely on faith in economic input often fail.

TERRORISM AND POVERTY

In addition to the policies we have already discussed, the U S. government has confronted a relatively new problem over the past three or four decades: the problem of terrorism. Though nations like Iran actively support terrorism, acts of terror are more frequently engaged in by sub-national groups or individuals. Although acts of terrorism, including domestic terrorism, have occurred occasionally throughout American history, terrorism has only occurred frequently enough in the past several decades to require a policy response. After 9/11, the 9/11 Commission proposed new initiatives including the creation of the office of the Director of National Intelligence and the creation of a counter-terrorism center.

What can explain the newly emergent rise of terrorism? John Kerry spoke to this question following his meeting at the Vatican in 2014. There Kerry said:

> We talked about the common interest of Pope Francis and President Obama in addressing poverty on a global basis ... This issue of poverty, which in many cases is the root cause of terrorism or even the root cause of the disenfranchisement of millions of people on the planet.[28]

In remarks made the previous year at the Global Counter-Terrorism Forum, Kerry made a similar point about the need to address terrorism by "providing more economic opportunities for marginal youth." In fairness, on another occasion Kerry also called corruption a root cause of terrorism. Kerry is not alone in this view of terrorism. President Obama also made similar statements associating terrorism with poverty and marginalization. And:

> In the aftermath of the tragic events of 9/11, several prominent observers—ranging from former Vice President Al Gore to

President George W. Bush, as well as academics, including Joseph
Nye, Dean of the Kennedy School of Government, Laura Tyson,
Dean of the London Business School, and Richard Sokolsky and
Joseph McMillan of the National Defense University—have called
for increased aid and educational assistance to end terrorism.[29]

In short, it is the prevailing governmental view that terrorism is at bottom an economic problem.

What exactly is a "root cause" as opposed to, say, a simple cause? It is certainly a rhetorical flourish meant to provide emphasis to the point being made.
But it also suggests that whatever specific motivations a terrorist may have
in any given case, poverty lies behind that motivation as a somehow deeper,
more general cause, likely unknown even to the terrorist himself. Terrorists
may have their own justifications for terrorist acts, but these can somehow
all be subsumed under their common origin in poverty.

What shall we make of these claims, especially in light of most scholarly
studies which show no such connection between poverty and terrorism? For
example, a comprehensive study considering 65 possible correlates of terrorism concludes that "economic development as measured by GDP per capita
does not matter for the amount of terrorism ... The preponderance of evidence suggests that the level of economic development is of minor importance
at best."[30] What seems to matter more than the absolute measure of poverty
is the degree to which political regimes provide an open economic system.

This study confirms the work of Alan Krueger, whose 2007 book *What
Makes a Terrorist: Economics and the Roots of Terrorism* is a classic in the field.
His views are summarized in an article addressing the subject of poverty, education and terrorism. There he and his co-author say "there is little reason for
optimism that a reduction of poverty or increase in educational attainment
will lead to a meaningful reduction in the amount of international terrorism,
absent other changes."[31]

Indeed, one study found an inverse relationship between poverty and terror. It concludes:

> The threat of terrorism systematically rises as low income polities become richer, peaking at an income level of about $12,800 per capita ... but then falls consistently above that level ... Thus, alleviating poverty may first exacerbate terrorism, contrary to much of the proposed recipes advocated since 9/11.[32]

There are many additional studies which arrive at similar conclusions, and no serious study that suggests the contrary. The science, we might say, seems to firmly contradict the conventional views of political leaders.

To this science we might add several further considerations. The most obvious of course is that during recent decades nations have generally become richer than before, as we have mentioned in citing World Bank figures. This hardly squares with the rise of terrorism during this same time period.

Second, there are nations (such as Nigeria, for example) which contain differing religious groups with roughly the same economic characteristics. Yet systematic acts of terror arise entirely from within one religious group and not the other. This offers a decent case of what economists call a natural experiment regarding the economic causes of terrorism. It would be difficult, in fact impossible to lay the cause of Boko Haram terror at the feet of economic conditions.

Third, suicide bombings are a frequent tool of terrorists. Blowing oneself up seems to have no conceivable connection with lashing out at poverty or any other economic cause. One could perhaps make a case that the grotesque bounties paid to families of suicides has an economic end, but this is a pretty far-fetched argument.

Finally, there is no known case of a terrorist ever mentioning poverty as his motivation, or the elimination of poverty as his goal. Other motives, both religious and political, are invariably mentioned. Political leaders must ignore the words and self-understandings of terrorists and go behind them, as it were, to find a truer economic form of causation of which terrorists are themselves unaware.

Why the split between science and common sense on the one hand and the prevailing views of political leaders on the other? A cynic might suspect that blaming terrorism on economic rather than political or religious causes is a more politically correct way to proceed. But at a deeper level, any problem which is described as an economic problem must also have an economic solution. If poverty is the so-called root cause of terrorism, then alleviating or eliminating poverty is the solution. Happily, we have in hand programs designed to address just this problem. Foreign assistance programs which aim to address poverty have the added advantage that they can also be justified by addressing the problem of terrorism.

Alan Krueger says there is a "surface appeal" to blaming economic circumstances for terrorism. This could not be truer. But why? The answer is to be found in the material philosophy of economic causation which runs straight through the progressive liberal democracy of the United States. As a significant social problem, the roots of terrorism simply *must* be found in economic causation, in this case poverty. When economics is the root cause of a problem the solution must be economic as well.

As we have just discussed, terrorism is simply not an economic problem, root problem or not. Terrorism is a political problem, not an economic problem. Krueger and Maleckova speak to this directly. They argue that terrorism is best understood as a violent form of political engagement. More educated and more economically privileged people are more likely to participate in politics of any kind, violent or not. They are able to concern themselves with more than the daily problem of economic subsistence. For this reason, Krueger and Maleckova conclude that "terrorism is a political, not economic, problem."[33]

The political urgency to prevent and respond to acts of terrorism does not permit the usual indulgence in airy theories of economic causation. We are fortunate that presidents are impelled, whatever their views of the so-called root causes of terrorism, to choose political and military responses to acts of terrorism. Waiting for the eventual elimination of world poverty to address terrorism is not a winning political hand. Joshua Muravchik praises George W. Bush for recognizing that combating terrorism must rest on a political and not an economic strategy.[34] This is all to the good. But it is unlikely to put a serious dent in the widely mistaken and abiding progressive view that this problem, like all other social problems, is at bottom an economic problem.

SIX

INTELLIGENCE FAILURES

In this chapter we will consider the way in which an economic determin-ist orientation leads to intelligence assessment failures. This should not be taken as an across-the-board indictment of the work of the intelligence com-munity. The intelligence community has a record of many successes, not all of which by any means have been made public.

In general, the intelligence community is able to provide policymakers an astonishing amount of information—facts—about what is occurring around the world. How many missiles China has deployed along its coast facing Tai-wan, how many tanks Russia moved to the border with Ukraine, what a given world leader said to one of his associates—all these kinds of information, and more, are provided to policymakers in a very useful way.

As well, the Central Intelligence Agency's (CIA) operations side of the house undertakes a variety of activities, some of which require great personal courage to implement. This chapter does not address either the provision of facts or covert operations. It addresses intelligence community assessments, especially regarding significant transformative events around the world.

Despite its successes, the American intelligence community has had its share of major intelligence failures. Its mission, after all, is not only to discover "what is"—the facts—but also "to warn of potential threats." Here the record is far less positive. Various commentators, including former directors of the CIA, have acknowledged numerous significant intelligence failures. Among these failures critics have included Pearl Harbor, the Chinese entry into the Korean War, Pakistan's nuclear explosion, the Bay of Pigs, the fall of the Shah, the Yom Kippur War, the Soviet invasion of Czechoslovakia, the rapid success of the Solidarity movement, the Soviet invasion of Afghanistan, 9/11, Iraqi weapons of mass destruction, construction of the Syrian nuclear reactor, the Arab Spring, the post-Iraq War insurrection, the rise of ISIS, post-Qaddafi anarchy in Libya, and the origin of Covid and the depth of consequences flowing from its initial outbreak in China. One critic has wryly concluded that "The U. S. has been surprised by every major world event since 1960."[1]

In many of these instances, defenders of the intelligence community have disputed these claims, often laying blame for failure on policymakers rather than the intelligence community. We will discuss some of these claims and counterclaims later in this chapter. But there is no doubt, as intelligence agency leaders themselves have acknowledged, there have been numerous intelligence community failures. Why should this be so? Reasons have been widely discussed by both outside critics and those within the intelligence community itself. Critics have focused on the need for better coordination between intelligence agencies, insufficient human resources abroad, the need for partnerships with non-intelligence community sources, better language training, politicization of intelligence reporting, and problems inherent in the lowest common denominator conclusions of the sort that "we judge" or "we assess."

In fairness to the intelligence community, it has often been willing to study the reasons for its failures in a way in which, for example, neither Congress nor domestic executive departments and agencies ever do. At times reforms have taken place in the intelligence community after external or internal reviews. Perhaps the most extensive review was conducted by the 9/11 Commission, which led to the creation of the position of Director of National Intelligence (DNI) and the national counter-terrorism center. After-action studies and responses to what can be learned from failures surely have their merits. However, they invariably share one feature: they tend to be "internal" criticisms which address bureaucratic, institutional issues. The purpose of this chapter is quite different. It aims not at institutional or organizational issues, but at a deeper problem: our intelligence community shares the same economic determinist assumptions that characterize our domestic and foreign policymaking communities. Indeed, it would be surprising if it did not.

THINGS WE CAN COUNT AND LINEARITY

Predicting transformative events is difficult and will always be prone to a degree of error. If these errors were random, correcting them would be difficult or impossible. But intelligence failures to predict, or even to warn of possible transformative events, rest on common and repeated mistaken assumptions. Major intelligence failures always fail in exactly the same way. For example, intelligence failures surrounding the fall of the Shah in 1979 or Ukraine's resistance to the Russian invasion share the very same mistaken assumptions.

An internal intelligence review of how better to measure the will of militaries to fight—as is underway currently after the Russian invasion of Ukraine—is fine as far as it goes. But it is only one manifestation of a deeper problem. The failure to predict transformational changes rests on two very deep and mistaken premises which go deeper than the specific form they take in any given case. The first is the progressive assumption of economic determinism and the second is its corollary of incremental, linear thinking.

The intelligence community tends to focus on tangible, material factors and assumes these are the basis of what is real, as well as the causal basis for significant social, political and military change. This material, economic orientation captures much that is important about reality, but it also misses much. It leads to a pattern of looking primarily at things which can be counted and drawing inferences from them. One thoughtful critic has said, "whatever... cannot be counted is then treated as nonexistent for practical purposes."[2]

One such non-tangible factor—but not the only one—which has been slighted is the importance of religious belief, especially in the contemporary Middle East. In America, where CIA analysts grow up and form their impressions of reality, religion is scarcely ever thought of as a significant human motivation that intrudes into political life. When it is thought about at all, it is often thought of disparagingly as the province of "deplorables" who misunderstand their own best (economic) interests. The social class from which CIA analysts is drawn is not about to make that "mistake." In America religion and politics are separated and religion rears its head in politics only in unhappy, marginal ways. The powerful role of religion in people's lives is thus entirely missed. As Deirdre McCloskey says, religion is understood as a kind of social club with costs and benefits, much like other voluntary associations, not as a potentially powerful source of human motivation.[3]

Religion is only one non-economic factor that tends to be overlooked in favor of tangible, countable factors. As former Senate Intelligence Committee staff member Angelo Codevilla says, analysts tend also to miss "love, hate, devotion to God, lust for vengeance, the cruel joy of conquest, or political ideology."[4] In short, they tend to miss the importance of ideas and their ability to move and inspire people. Putin's decision to invade Ukraine, for example, had nothing whatever to do with economic or material considerations, but with an idea in his head about greater Russia. Nor was Ukraine's choice to fight a decision motivated by tangible, economic factors.

An economic/material orientation to the world is a clear expression of the rational actor model we have described in earlier chapters of this book. Rational men are prudential men, that is, somehow always concerned with their (economic) well-being and who always act upon the tangible realities they observe. But even economic men are driven in significant part by non-economic goals. There is no surer way to fail to understand human motivations than to ignore this reality.

This will emerge quite clearly in the case studies we will analyze. We can also observe this in the "Global Trends" report which is issued by the CIA. A look at the current "Global Trends 2040" is instructive. It begins with a discussion of so-called "structural forces," as if these were somehow fated from above and not dependent on human choices or human innovation. These structural forces include economics and technology which are said to "shape the contours of our future world."[5] Only then are human responses to these (apparently set in stone) realities considered. Global Trends concludes with five scenarios for the year 2040. It is at least positive that five different scenarios are offered, but it turns out that all five are variations of one another based on these mysterious structural forces. Genuinely diverse outcomes—such as that China might not be a world force in 2040—are never hinted at. Nor is there any reason to suspect that any one of the five scenarios will come to pass. Moreover, each is described so abstractly as to offer no guidance to policymakers in any event.[6]

Critics have accused intelligence analysts of "mirror imaging." American analysts tend naturally to see foreign leaders and their motivations as quite like themselves and their own motivations. What we aim to do here is to give mirror imaging a more well-defined form. What we suggest is that mirror imaging tends to mirror the progressive economic determinism which dominates the American intellectual landscape. Foreign leaders, groups or individuals who act on non-economic motives are thought to be making mistakes or acting wrongly. Putin, for example, is said to have misjudged the true needs of Russian citizens in invading Ukraine. Such leaders are judged like the Kansans in *What's the Matter With Kansas?* who do not understand their real (economic) interests. The real interests of people and the real forces impelling change must somehow always be understood in terms of American economic determinism.

And thus the actual interests of foreign leaders who operate on different principles are not well understood, if not ignored altogether. Analysts tacitly assume that because they would not do what a foreign leader is considering, the foreign leader is unlikely to do it either. Such an action is simply not rational or prudential, and if a foreign leader undertakes such an action anyway, it is understood as a mistake by a leader who does not know his true interests. It is easy enough to see why simple mirror imaging comes across abroad as complete and utter arrogance.

An implicit corollary of an economic determinist orientation is linear thinking. Just as Global Trends illustrates, what is at issue in understanding the world is trends, that is, projections of the recent past into the future. But what is the warrant to assume the future will be a projection of current trends? Investment advisors regularly warn that past performance is no guarantee of future results. That would be excellent counsel for the American intelligence community. As a matter of fact, the least likely outcome is a straight line which reaches out forever into the future, or even to 2040. I recall sitting in a Senate hearing with senior intelligence and other administration witnesses in the late 1970's. Based on a few years of recent experience they predicted a straight-line increase in the price of oil, which suggested that soon enough Saudi Arabia would possess all the money in the world, rather like a late stage in the game of Monopoly.

Linear thinking commits two kinds of mistakes. First, it assumes that change will continue in one direction. This is part and parcel of an economic determinist orientation. More investment, or more growth, leads to further investment or growth, which in turn leads to further investment or growth. Trends are definitive.

The second, and equally significant mistake is incrementalism. What is it that trends reveal but a steady movement in one direction? If the Chinese economy is growing at a certain percent each year, a radical change from this baseline seems outside the bounds of possibility. Modest fluctuations, yes. But a radical change? Global Trends 2040 makes an incremental assumption in all five of its future scenarios. Is there no possibility of a radically different future for China? Upon what grounds can this be ruled out?

What incrementalism misses, of course, is the possibility of radical, transformative change. As we will demonstrate in the following case studies, this is precisely what is missed in each and every case. As Deirdre McCloskey says, a materialist routine cannot in its nature explain surprises.[7] But why should we be at all surprised by sudden breaks in what is moving in a predictable, incremental way? It is not as if steady, incremental change—without radical breaks—is a natural, inevitable process. Malcolm Gladwell's book *Tipping Point* makes just this point. He points to moments where what has been steady, incremental growth—or decline—suddenly undergoes rapid transformational change. Examples in nature abound. At a certain point, lowering the temperature of water suddenly turns it to ice. At a certain temperature rain turns to snow. At a certain point a gradually warming object suddenly bursts into flames. At a certain point sperm and ova unite to form brand new beings. At a certain point a gradually weakening bridge suddenly collapses. And at a certain point an incipient epidemic begins to grow geometrically.

If these things occur in nature, they are that much more likely to occur in the human world. Gladwell's book would make excellent reading for the intelligence community, to impress upon it the ever-present possibility of radical change. It would be a strong antidote to the somewhat lazy tendency to see the future as just like the past, until transformational changes are fully on top of us. Ernest Hemingway speaks to this in *The Sun Also Rises*. There his character Mike Campbell is asked how he went bankrupt. He says "Two ways. Gradually. Then suddenly."

CASE STUDIES

The Fall of the Shah

On January 16, 1979 the Shah of Iran abdicated his throne and fled into exile. The Shah had been one of America's principal allies in the Middle East. Iran and Saudi Arabia were referred to as the "twin pillars" of American Middle East policy. Under the Shah Iran was called the "guardian" of the Persian Gulf. The Shah's regime served as an insurance policy against hostile forces threatening the flow of oil to the world economy.

How did the Shah's abdication come about and, more to our purpose here, what was the intelligence community's role in warning of this possibility? What was the intelligence community's role in alerting American policymakers in a timely way, such that policymakers could have had more options than simply observing from the outside the fall of the Shah? We will find here many specific intelligence failures, each of which, however, is rooted in the same underlying mistake.

How do we know the intelligence community failed in this instance? Apart from the evidence we will consider below, the intelligence community publicly acknowledged its failure. The former director of the CIA, Stansfield Turner, later said "In 1979, Islam as a political force was not on our radar scope. The intelligence community was not prepared to understand it."[8] In June of 1979 Robert Bowie, the head of the National Foreign Intelligence Center, asked for a study about why the intelligence community failed in Iran. This report, written by John Devlin and Robert Jervis, was titled "Analysis of NEAC's Performance on Iran's Domestic Crisis, Mid-1977—11/7/1978." Jervis later used the core of this report as the basis for his 2010 book *Why Intelligence Fails: Lessons from the Iranian Revolution and the Iraq Wars.*

Much has been written about the reasons for the intelligence failure in Iran, including the usual criticisms concerning tasking, collection and reporting. A frequent criticism was that the intelligence community had only four full-time Iran experts on staff, which is perhaps a fair enough criticism. What is missed in this criticism, of course, is what good additional analysts would have done if they shared the same perspective as those who were already there. Quantity is not always a good substitute for quality.

At the deepest level, the intelligence community was blinded by its own assumptions. It never took the role of religion seriously, and when it considered the role of religion at all it did so in several mistaken ways. The Shah himself confirmed the intelligence community's bias against taking religion seriously. He demanded that American intelligence agencies limit their outreach to religious opposition figures within Iran. The CIA was only too happy to follow this course, as it did not think the Shah's position was tenuous. It preferred to focus its contacts on the Shah, his immediate circle and western-inclined elite groups. In this way American intelligence missed the power of the Shah's religious opposition as well as the widespread hatred of the Shah these opposition groups were fomenting.

All along, the CIA and its partner agencies were more concerned about communist opposition than religious opposition to the Shah. There was what has been described as a "general belief" that serious political problems always arise from the political left, not from religious opposition groups. The CIA was particularly focused on the security of U. S. sites located in northern Iran which were used to monitor Soviet ICBMs. In short, the CIA had its own assumptions and its own concerns, and the significance of religious belief was not among them.

When the CIA considered religion at all, it misjudged it in several ways. First, it did not understand the axial importance of the Ayatollah Khomeini among Iranian religious leaders. Khomenei after all was far away in Paris and not on the ground in Iran. Khomeini regularly issued tirades against the Shah from his perch in Paris, but their import was not clear. Khomeini was seen as but one of many religious leaders. American intelligence saw religious opposition to the Shah as splintered and assumed it would not act in a concerted way. Even then American intelligence assumed there were religious "moderates," figures who never appeared then or any time since.

A SAVAK (the Shah's secret police) official saw the situation far more clearly, though his views were not credited. He argued that other religious leaders could not act independently of Khomeini, as they feared Khomeini's reaction. Khomeini was not one of many equal religious leaders, but the one who held a virtual veto power over the others. His radical opposition to the Shah effectively cleared the field of other religious leaders. And by the way, when he arrived in Tehran in 1979 he proceeded to do exactly what he said he would do.

The intelligence community treated religious opposition to the Shah in just the way Deirdre McCloskey described, as social clubs with costs and benefits and not as a powerful source of human motivation. From this viewpoint, the intelligence community assumed that religious groups were like other political groups, willing to compromise principles in order to secure a power sharing relationship. Nothing could have been further from the truth.

Yet another mistake was made about religion. So determined to see a communist threat to the Shah, analysts wondered aloud in late 1978 whether the Soviet Union was the motive force behind religious opposition to the Shah. Surely religious leaders on their own, with their only weapon their endless verbal denunciations of the Shah, could not pose a serious threat to the Shah's rule. Somewhere behind religious opposition must be a strong military/

economic power. However implausible this was, it reflected the low estima-
tion by the intelligence community of the power of religious belief to move
people. Finally, when it became apparent to virtually everyone in the last
months of 1978 that the Shah was in deep trouble, American officials were
busy advocating some kind of military-religious government as a successor
to the Shah. Misapprehension of Khomeini and of religious belief generally
seemed difficult for American officials to give up.

These mistaken assumptions were fully reflected in the intelligence community's analysis throughout the second half of the 1970's. The CIA confi-
dently reported that Iran was not in a revolutionary, or even a pre-revolutionary
situation. The Defense Intelligence Agency (DIA) confirmed this view. In
1977 the CIA reported that "the Shah will be an active participant in Iranian
life well into the 1980's" and judged there would be no significant change in
Iran's governance in the near future. This was re-confirmed again in 1978. A
year later the Shah was gone. The State Department's Bureau of Intelligence
and Research (INR)—which is occasionally a dissenting voice from the larger
intelligence agencies—was also on board. In INR's January 28, 1977 report
#704 entitled "The Future of Iran: Implications for the U. S.," INR foresaw
stability in Iran for the coming years. It said there would be "clear sailing" at
least into the mid-1980's."[9]

The CIA began work on a National Intelligence Estimate (NIE) in September of 1978 titled "Iran to 1985," in which it saw no prospect of religious
leaders coming to power. This draft was subsequently shelved and was soon
enough overtaken by events on the ground. Even in November of 1978—less
than two months before the Shah's fall—the CIA judged in one of its weekly
summaries that there was "no serious domestic threat" to the Shah.

The American intelligence community made a second major mistake. It
supposed that the Shah would respond to any domestic insurrection with the
use of force. This view was widely held in the intelligence community, as was
the further inference that if the Shah did not use force, he did not believe his
regime was in danger. There had been hints, however, that the Shah would
not use force if and when a crunch came. He had used force in September of

1978 to put down protests in what came to be known as "Black Friday." This use of force had two predictable consequences. First, it both enlarged and deepened the opposition to the Shah's rule, which made the Shah wary of using force as a tool to crush dissent. Second, the Shah received predictable warnings from American officials against the excessive use of force. Although the Shah's rule could be brutal, he was also influenced by notions of western liberalism, and his first instinct was not always the use of force.

American intelligence and diplomatic officials assumed that if and when the Shah's regime was seriously threatened, he would deploy his force called "the Immortals" to shoot protesters and restore order. At the same time, however, the Shah was receiving mixed signals from the Americans, some of whom believed almost until the end there was a middle way, a more inclusive government that might include Khomeini and either the Shah or a hand-picked successor. Why this was ever thought to be possible is hard to say. The Shah was in a difficult place, to be sure.

Despite this dismal record of intelligence predictions, there are some who defend the intelligence community's work. How is this possible? It is possible because only in the last two months before the Shah's abdication, it became apparent to even the most casual observer that the Shah was in trouble and might not retain power. This possibility finally began at this late date to be reported to policymakers along with the rosy predictions cited above. In short, the intelligence community began to hedge its bets. Defenders of the intelligence community thus argued that after November of 1978 the fall of the Shah was a policy failure, not an intelligence failure. This is a rather standard defense of intelligence community shortcomings, which we will see in each of the other case studies we will examine. It takes no talent to make accurate predictions when outcomes are so clear that anyone can see them.

In November of 1978—again, just two months before the fall of the Shah—U. S. Ambassador to Iran William Sullivan began to see the writing on the wall. On November 9th he wrote a memo titled "Thinking the Unthinkable." In it he reflected on the possibility of a new government in Iran. He suggested at that late date the possibility of some kind of moderate successor government to that of the Shah and argued that the United States might be able to live with such an arrangement. To say that this memo, not to mention slowly emerging negative intelligence assessments, was too little too late would be an understatement.

It is of course difficult to say how far in advance of events a correct intelligence assessment must be in order to allow policymakers a decent range of actions to respond. This was perhaps especially true for the Carter administration. Despite Zbigniew Brzezinski's hawkishness there was not much sentiment in the Carter administration to intervene in Iran, or anywhere else for that matter. Only under the pressure of a presidential primary challenge from Senator Ted Kennedy in April 1980 did President Carter use force to attempt to rescue American hostages there. The unhappy outcome of that effort is well known.

Behind the several intelligence mistakes of the intelligence community in Iran there is one deep, underlying failure. The intelligence community's preoccupation with the military and economic power of the Soviet Union blinded it to the very real power of religion. All other mistakes trace back to this failure. The physical, material power of the Shah—his troops, his weapons, his secret police—seemed to suggest there could be no real threat from religious opponents. Whatever the religious protests, the Shah would enjoy smooth sailing as far out as the analytical eye could see. All this was nicely summed up afterward by a State Department official who asked, "whoever took religion seriously?"

The Implosion of the Soviet Union

If being short-handed is any defense of the intelligence community's failure in Iran—and I have already suggested that more of the same would not have helped—there is certainly no such defense regarding the collapse of the Soviet Union. The Soviet Union was for nearly half a century the principal preoccupation of American policymakers and the intelligence community alike. There was no remotely close target of intelligence interest. Over many years thousands of analysts were deployed and billions of dollars expended to gather information about every aspect of the Soviet Union. These included both human and technological assets, and no stone was left unturned to provide intelligence about the Soviet Union.

The dissolution of the Soviet Union occurred in two major steps. The first was the fall of the Berlin Wall in 1989 and the second was the departure of Mikhail Gorbachev on Christmas day in 1991. Neither of these events, nor any of the intervening steps was predicted by American intelligence agencies. If there is a reason for these failures, it must lie elsewhere than in insufficient staffing and attention.

In fairness, the fall of the Berlin Wall—when it occurred one evening—was difficult to predict. It rested in the first instance on the hasty, reactive decision of a border guard commander. This action was not predicted by either American or West German intelligence, and it no doubt came as a surprise to the governing authorities in East Germany and the Soviet Union as well. Events on the ground moved quickly and this is not a formula for accurate intelligence predictions which, as we have discussed, tend to see linearity everywhere and never speedy transformations. Conventional wisdom, etched in stone over many decades, exercised a gravitational effect over observers, even careful ones. When asked in June of 1987 about the chances of German reunification, Gerhard Schroeder replied "there are none."

Much the same could be said about the 1991 abdication of Gorbachev. By 1989 Gorbachev had already largely lost control of events. His announcement of new initiatives like perestroika (restructuring) and glasnost (opening) were not in fact far-reaching visions but efforts to remain relevant. Gorbachev was looking for a basis on which to create a stable government. Nevertheless, the CIA continued to act as if Gorbachev was the beginning and end of all wisdom regarding the future of the Soviet Union. This was a continuation of a long pattern of looking to the center to determine the course of Soviet developments. CIA analysts devoted far less attention to other forces which were arising in the Soviet Union, including both forces looking for firmer direction from the center and those looking for a more pluralistic society and empire.

Once again, linear thinking blinded analysts from understanding the rapidly changing groundwork of Soviet society.

Is it true that American intelligence agencies failed to predict the rapid dissolution of the Soviet Union? Many critics have said so. But once again we need not guess, because after 1991 CIA directors themselves have said so. Robert Gates, one of America's most respected and honest public servants, concluded that while the CIA had some successes, its work on the collapse of the Soviet Union had serious shortcomings. And in a 1991 *Foreign Affairs* article Stansfield Turner wrote, "we should not gloss over the enormity of the failure to forecast the magnitude of the Soviet crisis."

Once again, we confront the question of whether the intelligence community failed entirely or only in part. Defenders of the intelligence community can point to the work of individual analysts who warned about Soviet weaknesses, and especially closer in time to the Soviet collapse. Whatever their merits, these views were filtered out in overall intelligence community judgments about the Soviet Union. Stansfield Turner referred to the lowest common denominator assessments of the intelligence community as the "corporate view." The conventional wisdom of the intelligence community pointed clearly to the permanence of the Soviet Union. Conventional wisdom was reinforced at every stage by the process of arriving at a joint intelligence judgment. Conventional wisdom which fosters linear, incremental thinking no doubt permeates all government bureaucracies. If anything, however, these tendencies are magnified in secret organizations whose views are not subject to public scrutiny and debate. As Daniel Patrick Moynihan argued in his book *Secrets*, secret organizations develop a radical disjunction between "insiders" and "outsiders," and the views of outsiders are regularly dismissed as less well-informed. In 1995 Moynihan proposed legislation to remove from the CIA its analytical functions and transfer them to the less secretive State Department.

Intelligence misjudgments about the Soviet Union were not limited to the speed of its collapse. There is a record of frequent and significant failures from World War II forward. In 1943 the War Department advised President Roosevelt that the German army would conquer the Soviet Union within one to three months. This was not a small mistake. The War Department prediction was based entirely on the material assessment of the number of German troops, tanks and aircraft which were massed against the Soviet Union. Non-material factors such as will to fight or winter weather were minimized. This eerily foreshadows the intelligence community's assessment about the Russian invasion of Ukraine, which we will consider shortly.

American intelligence agencies produced a long track record of mistaken judgments about the Soviet Union throughout the Cold War period. Intelligence agencies were able to track reasonably accurately the types and numbers of weapons systems the Soviet Union was producing and deploying. This was a matter of counting, at which intelligence agencies excel. Where its estimates were mistaken—and often far off the mark—was in regard to the overall economy of the Soviet Union.

Entire books have been written about the size of the Soviet economy during the Cold War. Suffice to say here that intelligence judgments were not random errors; they were errors that displayed a systematic bias. Mistaken estimates of the intelligence community always occurred in the same direction: overestimating the size of the Soviet economy. There are of course difficult methodological questions involved in comparing the size of different economies, not the least of which are how to compare market and non-market economies and the proper dollar-ruble ratio to employ. This was the topic of a lengthy GAO report for Senator Moynihan in September of 1991, just prior to the opening of the Berlin Wall.[10] This report, like many outside observations as well as the work of Team B, concluded the CIA had regularly overestimated the size of the Soviet economy. As we have noted, this overestimation was consistent with the views of a number of academics including Paul Samuelson, Robert Heilbroner and John Kenneth Galbraith. As far back as 1957 the Gaither Commission had estimated that the Soviet economy would surpass the American economy by 1993—two years, as it turned out, after the Soviet Union ceased to exist.

Had CIA estimates misjudged the Soviet economy in random ways—sometimes larger and sometimes smaller than we now know it to have been—these errors could perhaps be accounted for by the complexity of comparing market and non-market economies. But they were not; CIA estimates consistently overestimated the size of the Soviet economy. The CIA put the Soviet economy at roughly half the size of the American economy and estimated that it was growing over more than three decades at an average rate of 3.9 percent. These estimates were not off by degrees but by magnitudes. The same is true of CIA estimates of the East German economy. In 1987 the CIA made perhaps its most bizarre estimate ever, concluding that East German GDP per capita was greater than West Germany's.

What can account for these regular and consistent misjudgments? First to say is that the CIA considered economic data and ignored every non-economic fact or impression that was available. As Daniel Moynihan suggested, an East German cab driver could have made a more accurate estimate of these matters. The CIA preferred a scientistic framework—based entirely on numbers—to shape its estimates. No actual real-life impressions were allowed to disturb this fact-based analysis or cause the CIA to reflect on its methodology. Second, this problem was compounded by another: the information the CIA relied on was simply not true. Though analysts occasionally expressed skepticism about Soviet data, they simply could not believe the magnitude of Soviet lying. This of course reflected a mirror imaging problem, in which American analysts and academics could not easily credit a practice they would neither adopt nor condone in America.

Massive Soviet falsifications of statistics occurred in construction, health care, agricultural production, consumer goods and every other non-defense sector of the Soviet economy. Outside estimates, except for American academic economists who also relied on spurious statistics, were generally much closer to the truth than intelligence estimates. For those who are interested, open archives containing more than 14,000 pages of more than 600 CIA estimates of the Soviet economy are available. Only during the 1980's did American intelligence estimates begin to adopt a somewhat more pessimistic view of the Soviet economy, though one nowhere near suggesting the true difficulties which the Soviet Union faced.

The one area where U. S. intelligence agencies presented a different assessment of the Soviet Union was in the area of defense expenditures. As we have said, the intelligence community was able to identify and count quite accurately Soviet military equipment and weapons systems. Here, however, the CIA consistently *underestimated* the military's share of the Soviet economy, for decades putting Soviet military expenditures in the range of six percent of Soviet GDP. If the Soviet economy were (wrongly) pegged at half the American economy, this would put Soviet military expenditures on a par with American military budgets of roughly three to four percent of the U. S. GDP. It would have been miraculous, however, for the Soviet Union to produce its massive quantities of military hardware with a six percent share of its actual GDP. This would—and should have—beggared the imagination.

The answer, of course, as Team B proposed, was that the Soviet Union was spending a far greater share of its economy on the military than six percent of GDP. Faced with the presentation of these views, the CIA began to revise its estimates upward from six percent to 12 percent. And when in retrospect, the Soviet economy was more accurately judged to have been between 30 and 40 percent of America's GDP, the real share of Soviet military spending had to be revised upward in the range of 25-30 percent or higher of its GDP. When combined, these revised assessments of Soviet GDP revealed an economy which was far from healthy, and which could not seriously compete with the United States. Robert Gates said in 1986 that "the Soviet Union is a despotism that works." That was true enough at the moment, but not for much longer than that.

What are we to make of all this? There was surely no shortage of analysis of the Soviet Union. First, there was a misplaced reliance on economic factors at the expense of other human factors which might have produced a more balanced judgment. This mistake was compounded by excessive trust in Soviet economic statistics. Second, the relative permanence of communist governance over half a century led to an overly optimistic assessment of its capabilities, its staying power, and even what benefits it was delivering to its subjects. One intelligence study, for example, referred to the "pride" East

Germans had in their communist regime. This was an obvious, even incredible, mistake. When I traveled to eastern Germany immediately after the fall of the Berlin Wall, I sensed no such pride at all. There was an understandable degree of fearfulness about the uncertainties of a transition to a market economy, especially among older people. But pride? Only an overly rosy picture of Soviet and East European economies could disguise for American analysts peoples' genuine hatred of living under a tyrannical regime.

The hollowness of Soviet and East German social-economic realities was heavily discounted, even missed, by American intelligence agencies throughout most of the Cold War. Such is the over-reliance on economic statistics to the exclusion of non-economic factors. This record of failure has caused more than one critic to wonder aloud whether the CIA's methodology led to its mistaken assessments or whether the methodology was designed to produce these mistaken assessments. However this may be, an over-reliance on the importance of economic, material factors—just as we have seen in other areas of American government policy—will invariably miss important information and perspectives necessary to understand the human world. A beautiful chart containing reams of economic statistics has all the look of a fully objective, scientific product. But there is no true science when vast amounts of relevant non-economic data are omitted. The result of such an approach is to be surprised that rapid transformations can occur.

The Collapse of the Afghan Government

When we look at the rapid collapse of the Afghan government in August of 2021, we will discover the very same reliance on counting and incrementalism on the part of the American intelligence community. The lack of focus on non-economic factors clouded intelligence judgments about the Afghan government's ability to survive without American forces on the ground.

Was there in fact an intelligence failure in Afghanistan? Once again, we do not have to guess about this, as both intelligence and policymaking officials have acknowledged their failure after the fact. Barely six months after the failure to gauge properly the fighting strength of the Afghan military, the intelligence community made precisely the same mistake in under-estimating the will and the capability of the Ukrainian military. Members of the Senate Intelligence Committee sent a letter to the Director of National Intelligence, the DIA and the CIA on May 10, 2022 asking the intelligence community to re-examine its methodology for measuring the fighting ability of foreign militaries.

National Intelligence Director Avril Haines had already set in motion a review of just this question, which is entirely appropriate. To go to the heart of the matter, however, such a review should not restrict itself to what went wrong in the specific cases of Afghanistan and Ukraine. These cases are simply instances of a deeper problem, namely, the inevitable shortcomings of an economic/materialist orientation which rests on what can be counted and its attendant bias toward linear, incremental change.

Some former intelligence officials have argued that the intelligence community did not fail in Afghanistan, but that the debacle in August of 2021 was a policy failure. This argument has been advanced, for example, by both Mike Morrell and Michael Allen. Both blame the Afghan military collapse on the Biden administration's precipitous withdrawal of American forces. Allen says, for example:

> The intelligence community's job is to gather and analyze the secrets of foreign governments, not our own .... As far as the intelligence community knew, Mr. Biden intended to withdraw troops as he said he would ... in full coordination with our allies and partners.[11]

Allen observes this was very different from the "poorly executed" and "stealthy" withdrawal which actually occurred. Allen is certainly correct that there is blame to go around, to include senior policymakers of the Biden administration.

The U. S. Army also issued a report which laid a good deal of the blame for the poorly executed American troop withdrawal on Biden administration policymakers. President Biden rejected the findings of this report. On September 28 and 29, 2021 Defense Secretary Austin and Joint Chiefs Chairman Milley testified to the House and Senate that they had recommended that 2,500 U. S. troops should remain in Afghanistan to support the Afghan military.

Much of this back and forth is a standard blame game in Washington. But however much the Biden-engineered withdrawal contributed to the collapse of the Afghan government, this does not exonerate the role of the intelligence community. It is certainly no warrant for CIA Director William Burns' misplaced pride in the work of the CIA. Burns said he was "very proud of the analysis, with all its imperfections, that we tried to provide to policymakers over the six months leading up to the withdrawal."[12] Imperfections indeed.

Despite all attempts to disclaim responsibility, the fact is that in April of 2021—the very month President Biden announced the timetable for American troop withdrawal from Afghanistan—the CIA assessed that Afghan National Security Forces could hold off the Taliban for "18 months to two years." This was less than four months before the Taliban entered Kabul. Intelligence predictions before and after the April 2021 assessment were all over the map, ranging from shorter to longer assessments of the Afghan military's staying power. None, however, was remotely correct.

What caused intelligence estimates to be so far off the mark? There was certainly no shortage of embassy employees, which numbered roughly 4,000 not too long before the August collapse of the Afghan government. Some critics have argued that due to security concerns, U.S. embassy officials were unable to be in regular contact with Afghans throughout the countryside, and thus unable to form a true sense of Afghan sentiments. Apparently, they were also unable to understand the degree to which the Taliban had penetrated both local Afghan governments and the regime in Kabul itself. This has rightly been called a counter-intelligence failure by Joel Brennan, who was a national counter-intelligence officer from 2006-2009.[13]

Given their inability to move freely about the countryside, both American intelligence officials and diplomats relied heavily on military reporting. Military intelligence provided a generally rosier picture of the situation in Afghanistan than other intelligence agencies. William Burns' pride in the work of the CIA no doubt reflects the fact that the CIA had all along been on the more pessimistic side of reporting in Afghanistan. There is really nothing new about this; despite silly caricatures from the political left about the U. S. military's thirst to engage in war, the U. S. military is generally more hesitant than civilian agencies are to engage its enormous power in conflict. Nevertheless, once engaged, the military tends to produce reports to show it is succeeding in achieving its objectives.[14]

Military reporting reflects a strong tendency to base its reports on what can be counted. This includes the number of enemy forces that have been killed or wounded and, in the case of Afghanistan, the number of Afghan military forces that were trained. As we have said earlier, reliance on what can be counted provides a superficial impression of solid, objective reporting. In fact, undervaluing what cannot be counted paints a picture that is anything but complete.

There is no reasonable way to assess favorably the intelligence community's role during the last months and years of the Afghan government. It is not a persuasive argument to point to increasingly negative reporting ever closer to August 14, 2021. In fact, in May of 2021—a month after President Biden announced his withdrawal timeline—the CIA issued a report claiming the Afghan government could hold out until year's end and possibly as long as two years. In July of 2021—only a month before the Afghan government's collapse—the Defense Department assessed that the Afghan government could hold off the Taliban long enough to achieve a political settlement, should that be necessary. This betrays an obvious inability to understand the forces at work and is eerily similar to late-stage notions of a political settlement between the Shah and his Islamic opponents in late 1978. As late as August of 2021—the actual month of the Afghan collapse—the intelligence community was in the process of preparing a report suggesting the Afghan government could hold out against the Taliban for a moderately long length of time.

It is fair enough to say the intelligence community was correct in terms of the direction of events in Afghanistan. No intelligence agency argued that the

Afghan government was gaining an advantage against the Taliban over time. Nor was the goal of defeating the Taliban a concern of the Biden administration, which mainly hoped for better optics, that is, to put a decent interval between an American withdrawal and a Taliban victory. The problem was the speed with which the collapse occurred. Because of the implicit linear, incremental thinking based on what could be counted, the intelligence community completely missed the speed of the Afghan government's collapse. Not one intelligence agency saw this coming. This too-optimistic view was reflected in statements of policymakers. Ambassador Zalmay Khalilizad saw no prospect of an immediate collapse of the Afghan government and Secretary of State Tony Blinken stated flatly there would not be "another Saigon" in Kabul.

Based on various material indicators including the number of Afghan government troops and the number and quality of its American-made weapons, the intelligence community simply could not adjust its thinking to the possibility of rapid transformational change. There is no better statement of the prevailing American view that material strength will dictate outcomes than President Biden's final phone call with Afghan President Ashraf Ghani on July 23, 2021. In that call President Biden said to Ghani: "You clearly have the best military, you have 300,000 well-armed forces versus 70,000-80,000 and they're clearly capable of fighting well."[15] Admittedly this was a bit of a pep talk from the American president. But what was missing was what was always missing in American intelligence and American policy toward Afghanistan: the proper evaluation and weighting of non-economic, non-countable factors.

Some of these factors were described by a civilian advisor to the U. S. military, Carter Malkasian:

> The Taliban exemplified something that inspired, something that made them powerful in battle, something closely to what it meant to be an Afghan. In simple terms, they fought for Islam and resistance to occupation, values enshrined in Afghan identity. Aligned with foreign occupiers, the government mustered no similar inspiration.[16]

This description of the Taliban is far too charitable for my taste, omitting as it does the Taliban's threats, torture and use of brute force to terrorize the Afghan population. But it correctly points out that non-economic, non-material forces were in this instance decisive. And that the power of these forces cannot always be comprehended by linear, incremental thinking.

These shortcomings were summarized in the August 2021 report of the Special Inspector General for Afghanistan Reconstruction (SIGAR) titled "What We Need to Learn: Lessons from Twenty Years of Afghanistan Reconstruction." In assessing how the U. S. failed in Afghanistan despite military spending of $837 billion, 2,443 American combat deaths and $137 billion in economic aid, the report concluded that "Money spent, not impact achieved, became the primary metric of success." Amen.

The Ukraine War

In considering the role of U. S. intelligence in the Ukraine War, we can begin with positive news. American intelligence was able to observe with great accuracy the Russian build-up along the Ukraine border as well as other signs of Russia's military movements. It was able to track closely the movement of Russian military vehicles and forces. These were of course items that could be seen and counted. In passing this intelligence along to the Ukraine government, both before and throughout the continuing conflict, American intelligence has provided significant assistance to Ukrainian forces.

In addition, the Biden administration made a wise decision to share publicly its knowledge of some of Vladimir Putin's plans. In particular, it was able to get ahead of and undercut Putin's public stance that Russia was simply responding to Ukraine's provocations. It denied Putin the ability to pretend that Ukraine had initiated the conflict. Putin lost the public relations war early and has been unable to regain his footing ever since.

Finally, U. S. intelligence had reasons to think that Putin was not bluffing, but that an invasion was likely. Neither American allies nor the Ukraine government itself were as clear about this and kept open the hopeful presumption that Putin was bluffing about an invasion. This is surely to the credit of American intelligence agencies.

There were, however, two significant intelligence failures. Before discussing these failures, we might note that Russian intelligence was at every step worse than American intelligence, and especially worse in the key dimensions in which American intelligence failed. First, Russian intelligence completely misjudged Ukraine's ability and willingness to fight. The Russian Federal Security Service (FSB) was so confident that Ukraine's government would quickly collapse its officials were picking out apartments in Kyiv in which they would live while standing up a new pro-Russian government in Ukraine. This was a colossal failure which is difficult to explain. Russia had been gathering detailed intelligence on Ukraine for many years and should have been thoroughly familiar with all aspects of Ukrainian politics, economics and military life. There is no good excuse for the FSB's failure to misjudge Ukraine's willingness to resist a Russian invasion. It is hard to imagine the FSB believed its own propaganda that Zelensky was deeply unpopular in Ukraine, and despite his Jewish heritage, was presiding over a quasi-Nazi regime. The only reasonable defense for the FSB's and Putin's mistaken views was the relative ease with which Russia had captured territories in Ukraine's east and Crimea in 2014. But this required wholesale ignorance of changes within Ukraine during recent years, as well as the impact of western training of Ukraine's forces.

Secondly, Putin clearly underestimated the solidarity of western, especially NATO nations, in responding to a Russian invasion. Putin assumed that after loud but brief and ineffective objections to his invasion, the west would soon enough come to terms with Putin's conquest of Ukraine. In fairness, if Russian forces had succeeded in capturing Kyiv in three or four days, western opposition might well have been temporary. Confronting a *fait accompli* in Ukraine, western nations might well have split apart, especially given the importance of European imports of Russian energy. This was the pattern after Putin's earlier invasions of its neighbors. A bloody ongoing conflict, however, was a totally different matter and one which solidified the western response.

American intelligence succeeded in what it could see and count, but not in its intelligence assessments about what this meant. It would be fair to say that the American intelligence community made not one, but two major mistakes in its assessments. The first concerned Russia and the second concerned Ukraine. American intelligence overrated Russian military capabilities and underestimated Ukraine's. Neither mistake necessitated the other.

As to Russia, the American intelligence community and especially the military intelligence agencies, vastly overrated Russia's conventional force capabilities. Former Army Brigadier General Kevin Ryan, a former military attaché in Moscow, said "I, along with many other people, misjudged Russian military capabilities before this war began. I thought that they were much better prepared for a war like this."[17] Ryan was surely correct that he was not alone in this; this was the conventional wisdom of the American intelligence community.

Why were the estimates of Russia's capabilities so wrong? Ryan also correctly observed that the U. S. often overestimates the power of its potential enemies. This may well be true, and it is surely better than underestimating them. But in this instance, as in so many others, the answer has to do with material factors. Russia had a military force of 900,000 men and an enormous stockpile of military vehicles, ammunition and weapons. Quite apart from Russia's nuclear arsenal, which is of no particular value in the Ukraine war, Russia held a massive dominance of troops and weapons, some of which were of Soviet vintage but some of which had been developed in recent years as part of Putin's military modernization program. Hugh Gusterson, a drone warfare expert, summarized the intelligence community's failure in this way:

> They count weapons systems and soldiers under arms, and they respect military judgments about the relative effectiveness of different weapons systems.[18]

This is precisely the same mistake intelligence agencies made in Iran in the late 1970's and in Afghanistan in 2021. Insufficient attention was paid to non-material factors such as training, doctrine, tactics, morale and civilian support. It thus failed to see that the Russian military was an over-rated, corrupt and largely hollow force which is not very well-adapted to modern battlefield conditions. American intelligence estimates were too much about counting size and not enough about quality and other non-tangible factors.

American intelligence estimates about Ukraine were no better. In fairness, the State Department's Bureau of Intelligence and Research (INR) under-stood Ukraine somewhat better than did the larger intelligence agencies. INR had sponsored polling about Ukrainian attitudes toward Russia, and polling data pointedly clearly to the animus of most Ukraine citizens against Rus-sia. Even in eastern provinces where there are large Russian-speaking minor-ities, Ukrainians overwhelmingly opposed the idea of Russian control of Ukraine. Polling pointed to the possibility that Ukraine would vigorously resist an attempted Russian takeover. Other U. S. intelligence agencies, not to say Putin, would have done well to give more weight to this kind of poll-ing information.

As it was, INR's views were subsumed in the broader intelligence com-munity's assessments. Ukraine fielded an army of only 196, 600 and pos-sessed nowhere near the quantities of Russian missiles, artillery, tanks and other weapons of war. The CIA was sufficiently certain of Russia's ability to quickly subdue Ukraine, it began planning for the possibility of a Ukraine insurgency once Russia had seized Kyiv.

Interestingly, the American intelligence community was more or less in agreement with the FSB about the rapid conquest of Ukraine. As is usual in an autocracy, the FSB was eager to tell its leadership what it wanted to hear, so much so that it elaborated on Russian advantages and blurred the line between intelligence and propaganda. The notion that Ukrainian citi-zens would rise up and support Russia's effort to rid Ukraine of its alleged Nazi leanings seems genuinely outlandish. But on the core question of Rus-sian and Ukraine military strength, both intelligence services were singing from the same hymnal.

CONCLUSION

As we have said, the intelligence community is currently involved in a review of its methodology for assessing the military strength of foreign nations. This kind of assessment will be more difficult than counting what can be seen. The Director of the DIA, Lt. General Scott Berrier says, "I think assessing will, morale and a will to fight is a very difficult task."[19] Arkansas Senator Tom Cotton, never one to mince words, agrees. He observes:

> Will to fight is not a discrete area of intelligence you can go out
> and collect on it. It's not like how many working fighters did an
> air force have. There's a lot of subjectivity.[20]

That it is difficult, and far more difficult than counting what one can see, is certain. There is no doubt a legitimate fear of subjectivity intruding into what are presented as objective intelligence reports. But this is a risk worth taking. Material strength is surely important, but there is more to analysis than that. For whoever is willing to look, there are many clear signs of where to look. And the repeated intelligence failures we have experienced by focusing too fully on material, tangible factors demand that we try.

It would help to have a check list of non-tangible factors to consider in assessing the strength of foreign militaries, both those of opponents and those of allies. The collapse of the more numerous and better armed Afghan security forces barely six months prior to Russia's invasion of Ukraine offered an object lesson in the importance of non-tangible factors for anyone willing to look. It still could. Beyond this, there is an even more compelling example. The Revolutionary War—the basis on which this country was founded as an independent nation—proves that the more numerous and better armed force is not always victorious. This is especially true when important ideas are at stake.

As Yogi Berra said, predictions are hard, especially about the future. What offers hope that intelligence estimates can be improved is that their failures are not random. Despite the specific details of each instance, intelligence projections fail *in exactly the same way.* They fail because they rely too much, if not entirely, on material/economic factors as determinants of human outcomes. The cases we have considered above are but four of many possible examples which demonstrate this shortcoming.

It seems that American intelligence agencies cannot get past this orientation any more easily than can other domestic or foreign policy departments and agencies. Economic determinism, along with its attendant incremental, linear thinking, runs deep in the contemporary American psyche. The 9/11 Commission spoke to this in a very general way. The Commission said what is needed in good intelligence work is to "institutionalize imagination." This is a very high bar, as the regular operation of institutions is in some ways the very opposite of imagination. It is the purpose of this book to make actionable the idea of institutionalizing imagination. We are not talking about a flight of fancy into modern-day astrology. What is needed is to be certain that our thinking transcends today's prevailing economic determinism and considers the ways in which non-economic human choices can and regularly do shape our world.

SEVEN

SOME MODEST PROPOSALS

Having now illustrated many of the ways in which the notion of economic or material causation both shapes and constrains our national policies, the reader might reasonably expect a series of suggestions about how to improve these policies. These will appear, but first we must begin in a more difficult, more honest place. Not every proposed reform, however worthy, is possible to implement at any given time.

THE DOMINANCE OF
PROGRESSIVE MATERIALISM

We must begin by acknowledging the depth to which progressive materialism is rooted in today's American psyche. There should be no doubt about this: progressive materialism dominates the entire political and cultural landscape of 21st century America, as it has for nearly 100 years.[1] This dominance is expressed through many channels: today's Democratic Party, the federal executive branch, the so-called mainstream media, the entertainment industry, academia, the K-12 school system, most not-for-profit organizations, the tech industry, and increasingly the leadership of large American corporations across the board. In short, it is expressed by most of America's intellectual class, who earn their living by manipulating words and symbols. No less a thinker than Alexandr Solzhenitsyn has observed:

> The current of materialism which is most to the left always ends up by being stronger, more attractive and victorious, because it is more consistent.[2]

As we have also noted, today's Republican Party does not stand in total opposition to the notions of progressive materialism. Many Republicans seek to temper the advance of progressive materialism and the economic programs which are built upon it, but they do not fundamentally oppose these programs. Girded with the work of conservative economists, they too look at economic man and argue they can achieve greater material satisfaction in a more efficient way. Regulations can be reduced and greater economic output will occur. Taxes can be cut and greater revenue can be achieved, both for individuals and for the government. Even conservative natural rights advocates often advance their views through the lens of economics, that is, elevating to the first rank the right of individuals to keep more of the money they earn.[3]

This suggests that moving outside the realm of progressive materialism will not be easy. There is no obvious institution in America today which could serve as a vehicle to place progressive materialism into a broader socio-political, moral context. This brings us to a conclusion somewhat akin to that of the economist Joseph Schumpeter. Like Marx, Schumpeter thought there were strong forces within capitalism which were leading to socialism. He argued that capitalism was creating an intellectual class which would undermine the foundations of capitalism. Unlike Marx, however, Schumpeter was no advocate of socialism, which he saw as a generally bland, homogeneous form of organization, lacking the important qualities of innovation and reward for merit. As an honest thinker, he went where his thinking, not his preferences, took him.

In similar fashion, it seems that today the major forces in American leadership circles are entirely oriented toward progressive materialism. This is not to say that Americans are trapped in a web of their own making; as human beings, Americans always have options. But it is to say that a major re-orientation which places progressive materialism into a broader human context faces very significant obstacles. We will speak to this deeper question toward the end of this chapter. Meanwhile, for those seeking to improve our current public policies at the margins, there are steps that can be taken.

POLICY REFORMS

Domestic Policy

The essential quality of successful domestic policies would treat Americans as citizens, not as consumers. This means to treat Americans as agents with both demand schedules, as economists might say, but also with obligations. The task of government is not simply to provide ever more economic goods, whether directly as financial aid or indirectly as food aid, housing aid, health care aid, childcare aid or other forms of what are in the end economic assistance.

The debate over whether economic assistance should be direct or indirectly targeted to specific ends is an interesting academic exercise. Economists would no doubt prefer direct financial assistance, as this maximizes the ability of recipients to choose their own ends. It allows a degree of latitude for recipients to choose among competing financial ends. On the other hand, legitimate questions exist as to whether taxpayer money should be used to subsidize certain ends that recipients might choose, such as liquor, drugs, gambling or similar choices. The SNAP program, for example, limits which items at grocery stores can be purchased using food stamps. However interesting this debate, there is a deeper problem which lies behind these considerations, namely, that in either case there currently seems to be no examination of outcomes. The success of government programs cannot be fairly judged simply by the amount of financial assistance provided, whatever form it might take. Financial assistance can be helpful in many cases but will always fall short of success if it is both the beginning and the end of domestic policymaking.

We can illustrate this across many policy areas. For present purposes, we might choose federal programs which address the three main stages of life for most Americans: education, work and retirement. We have already discussed education, suggesting there is no connection between the amount of either federal or state spending and positive educational outcomes. Indeed, given the track record of educational decline, it is unclear if there is a positive role for the federal government at all. But even if there were no federal participation, the same question would exist for the states, which fund the lion's share of K-12 education.

Higher pay for teachers and modernized school facilities do not equate to better educational results. This is not an argument against fairly compensating teachers or providing facilities which are necessary for successful teaching. But it is to say that the formula of measuring outcomes by inputs omits very important factors. The quality of teachers—again, which is not determined solely by higher salaries—the nature of what is being taught, and the role of both students and their parents are important determinants of educational success. None of these is best addressed by purely economic measures.

It is of course easiest to judge success by inputs; spending money, which is the particular forte of the federal government, is a faux sophisticated way by which to gauge educational progress. Addressing non-economic factors in student success is more difficult and would require a sea change in attitude, one which addressed the role of non-monetary factors in genuine education. Much of what would be required in this regard could not be provided by the federal government or, for that matter, by state governments. Thoughtful state and federal guidelines could bring about some necessary changes, but there must be greater involvement by students and parents in students' education. This is likely to entail other changes in federal programs such as those, for example, which have assisted in destroying lower-income families.

An honest study which addresses the role of non-economic factors in student success would be a good place to start. It would be far more meaningful than yet another study which tries to demonstrate, against all evidence, that more money equals better education. There have been several efforts in recent decades, most notably No Child Left Behind, to connect test scores with federal funding. These efforts are well-intentioned, but end up as do so many federal programs, providing funds regardless of outcome. Indeed, the argument is often made that failing programs require more, not less, money. This simply rewards failure. Federal and state programs must be based on the fact that there are non-economic as well as economic reasons for student success and failure.

It is unlikely, for example, to achieve greater student success without clear familial expectations. This is a difficult issue for progressives, because it requires moving beyond an economic mindset. It requires actions on the part of students and parents, rather than the simple provision of more money for schools and teachers. But without changes in parental and student attitudes, there is no chance of real educational success. As it is, many students arrive at school in their early years lacking both motivation and a foundation on which to learn. This puts an impossible burden on teachers, who are then blamed for what is in part a problem beyond their capability to solve.

What is true of K-12 education is also true of higher education, where the federal government plays a larger role. Connecting student buy-in with educational assistance is critical. At the moment, the Biden administration is proposing to move in exactly the wrong direction. Federal loan programs offer at least some nexus, some connection between financial assistance and student motivation. Most programs are structured as loans, which provide at least some student motivation because loans must be repaid. To forgive these loans is to break this nexus and, by the way, also to send a very disheartening message to those students who have repaid their loans.

There is a further consideration. In providing easy credit for students, loan programs have created an enormous incentive for colleges to raise fees well beyond cost-of-living increases. College loan programs should be restructured to require colleges, many of which are quite flush financially, to put some "skin in the game" by sharing responsibility for student loan risks.

As a whole, the intervention of the federal government into education has not been helpful. It may well be impractical at this moment to abolish the

Department of Education. But if it is to be involved in education, it should do so in a way that points to reforms that do not put money at their center. It should always and everywhere promote greater student agency. It should encourage greater parental responsibility. It should not encourage a sense of victimhood among students. It should encourage education which points to the common American good rather than the further balkanization of America. And as an aside, it might discover that that best way to promote a greater sense of the social whole is not to preach about it but to illustrate it with stories about great Americans who can model this behavior.

What is true of education is true of every other domestic social program. Reliance on federal assistance without recipient buy-in is unlikely to produce results beyond dependence on that assistance. One way or another, work is the principal occupation of adult Americans, just as it has been since the beginning of the republic. Work is not simply a means to secure the material necessities of life; it is also one of the principal ways in which people today find, just as they always have, a sense of achievement in life. As the medieval monks said, *laborare est orare*, that is, to work is to pray. To work is to come up against a kind of resistance, which strengthens the moral fiber of human beings.

As we have noted, Marx sought a society in which there was no longer what he called alienated labor, in favor of a society in which people were free to take up many forms of activity. People could choose to do whatever it might please them to do, on the assumption that these choices would be broadly harmonious. But it is not hard to imagine that people might choose less idyllic options than hunting, fishing or criticizing poetry. Progressives today have not thought even that far. Progressive materialists hope for a time in which human work is vastly diminished if not largely eliminated altogether. But what is to take the place of work?

Progressive intellectuals tend to look down on physical labor. People who undertake physical labor, however, report that they are largely satisfied by their work. Until and unless human beings can structure a world where meaningful activities can replace work, the satisfaction which derives from work should not be tossed overboard without thought. Forced idleness due to Covid lock-downs provided a good natural experiment in this regard; many forms of social pathology increased. Reducing or eliminating work on the airy assumption that the purpose of work is solely to secure material ends—economic man once again—would likely produce a world with more, not less unhappiness.

For this reason, government financial assistance should retain a connection between work and federal aid wherever possible. Work requirements should be set in place for federal financial aid programs not as a form of punishment, as progressives today conceive it, or even simply as a way to wean people away from government programs. Work requirements should be put in place to help recipients understand the importance of work for their own sense of agency and accomplishment.

Programs funding retirement—which are the largest of all government funding programs—are a bit different. They necessarily have only an indirect nexus between financial assistance and work. But in creating the Social Security program Franklin Roosevelt believed that it was important for citizens to make dedicated contributions to this program. This, he argued, would preserve the idea that Social Security was not a welfare program but was funded by citizen contributions. The same is true of Medicare which, when it was established, adopted a similar model. The residual effect of this can still be seen today: whenever changes are proposed to the Social Security program citizens react with a special indignation one does not see with proposed changes to the food stamp program or the earned income tax credit, for example.

As we noted in Chapter Four, the connection between inputs to and benefits from the Social Security system is hardly one-to-one. Social Security payments go into the Treasury Department's funds and are paid out from the Treasury's funds. It is only as an accounting matter that these funds are segregated from general Treasury expenditures. Thus we hear that the Social Security system is running low on funds and might need to reduce payments to Americans within the next decade. All proposals to increase the age level for beneficiaries, to alter the formula for benefit increases or to raise the amount of Social Security contributions are rightly made in the spirit of maintaining the nexus between inputs and outflows. This is all to the good, as the alternative is to treat Social Security as a vast welfare program. The same is true of Medicare.

As a general matter, no federal programs should provide benefits without requiring citizen participation in some manner. To do less is to treat citizens as mere consumers. We see this in its most grotesque form during election campaigns in which candidates aim to outdo each other in what new or expanded benefits they promise. There is perhaps no better example than the Biden FY2024 federal budget proposal, which has made such promises into an art form. As we have noted, we have clearly come a long way from the rhetorical flourish of asking not what the country can do for its citizens but what its citizens can do for their country.

There is no connection between providing more financial assistance to Americans and Americans' satisfaction with either their own lives or their government. Hope, much less expectation, that this will change if evermore financial assistance is provided is completely misplaced. What is required is moving away from government programs which are judged entirely by their inputs. How can this happen? However well-intentioned, preaching is unlikely to bring this about. What is required is a way to compel both legislators and executive branch officials to move away from input-dominated policies toward policies which are judged on their outcomes. This is tantamount to saying that genuine program oversight is required. But how can that happen? How is it possible to require legislators to consider not just the intent of their work but its outcome?

There is no easy answer. Perhaps the only practical way to move toward program oversight today is to include in all federal funding legislation a sunset clause. This is by no means a new idea, nor is it a panacea. It has been tried on various occasions by both the federal government and by as many as 36 state governments.[4] The concept is simplicity itself. Requiring federal spending programs to be reauthorized after, say, five or seven or ten years, would compel debate about what a program has and has not accomplished. It is true that Congress might choose to rubber stamp existing programs. But a sunset provision would set the default position in a different and more helpful place;

rather than extending programs by default, this would set the termination of programs as the default position. It would eliminate the implicit assumption that once authorized, programs are here to stay forever.[5]

It may seem that sunset provisions would be a favorite tool of the political right, suggesting they have no realistic prospect of being adopted by progressives. But federal sunset programs first came into vogue as a favorite tool of progressives, as a way to break up the comfortable insider connections between government officials and business lobbyists. Sunset provisions which were included in legislation were pushed strongly by Common Cause. Moreover, as conservatives have noted warily, adding sunset clauses to new legislation makes it politically easier to pass new legislation because it is not necessarily permanent.

Sunset provisions are regularly attached to tax bills, and tax laws enacted during the Trump administration will need to be reauthorized in 2025 if their provisions are to remain law. The PATRIOT Act contained a sunset clause, which permitted strong arguments against its continuation by both the political left and right. The Independent Counsel law required reauthorization and was indeed reauthorized several times. Finally, both political parties— each having been on the receiving end of an independent counsel investigation—allowed the law to lapse. The Voting Rights Act of 1965 contained a sunset clause, and when reauthorized on one occasion expanded the power of the federal government beyond that contained in the original legislation.[6] In short, sunset provisions are not simply a tool to kill legislation. They present opportunities to terminate, to expand or to amend legislation based on experience with its implementation.

Members of Congress are currently considering the termination of war powers granted to the president by Congressional resolutions passed decades ago, resolutions which have little to do with current deployments of U.S. forces in Syria and elsewhere. There is also discussion of placing sunset provisions into future authorizations for the use of military force. Advocates of repealing outdated war powers granted to the president are found in both political parties.

Sunset provisions are not the province of either political party and it is not unrealistic to require them in funding legislation. Sunset provisions would have the virtue of restoring Congress to what should be its central role in domestic policymaking. And they would have the further virtue of providing incentives for executive branch officials to administer programs in the most effective way possible.

It might fairly be argued that unlike most federal funding programs, long-established core programs like Social Security and Medicare should not contain sunset provisions. On one hand, these programs are popular with virtually all legislators and their reauthorization would never be in doubt. But if, as seems likely, these programs are exempted from reauthorization, they should certainly be subject to legislatively required reviews at regular intervals. These reviews should consider funding, eligibility, age, fraud and any other aspect of these programs to ensure they are conducted in the most financially responsible way.

What regular reviews of federal funding programs are likely to demonstrate is that programs can usually be improved, and in ways unrelated to additional funding. But more importantly, they are likely to demonstrate that federal funding programs, no matter how fully funded, cannot produce either social harmony or even satisfied recipients. They cannot moralize people and they cannot produce a broad national base of shared assumptions. Economic assistance does not lead to anything more than the material assistance which it provides. Non-economic components of happiness and shared assumptions must be addressed on their own terms. As we have argued so often in these pages, solving the economic problem does not solve other human problems.

Foreign Policy

We have noted in Chapter Five that development assistance relies on an implicit understanding of the biological term "development." When translated to national economies its use suggests there is a natural progression for socio-economic change. The first step toward effective foreign assistance programs is to give up this notion. There is simply no evidence for this, and at any given moment economic decline is as possible as economic advancement. The "arc of history" is moving nowhere with certainty and even a long-standing series of economic changes can be reversed at any moment.

This suggests that foreign assistance should be provided in a more transactional way. If we wish to achieve a specific outcome in a given country we must do so by making a direct connection between our assistance and that outcome. Measuring success by financial inputs for development assistance is no true measure at all, unless it is a measure of the abstract feeling of "doing good." There is no more connection between providing additional money to recipient countries and positive economic outcomes than in the domestic policies we have just discussed. A hard-eyed look at recipients may strike one as cold, but it is at least honest.

What would this look like? The kinds of commitments required by the Millenium Challenge Corporation are a good start. But more than paper agreements to adopt certain institutions—freedom of the press, settled law, etc.—is required. There will be no "development" unless recipient countries have in place important social norms such as fair play, honesty and a general respect for the basic rules of civil behavior. These can be summed up in one word: trust. The American economy depends on trust between individuals in literally hundreds of ways each day. Actions as simple as writing a check, for example, imply a high degree of social trust in both payers and payees, as well as intermediary banks and authorities which regulate these banks. This elemental kind of social trust is a prerequisite for successful economic growth.

To try to set social norms like these in place from the outside, as it were, is a very difficult task. Neither preaching nor economic assistance can create the bedrock level of social trust necessary for economic growth. This counsels the need for humility on the part of American foreign policymakers. We do not know as much as we pretend to know. Surely our experience in Afghanistan must make this clear. It is true that Afghanistan is perhaps the hardest imaginable case in which to foster economic growth from the outside. But it is also true that there are very few nations in which the United States maintained such complete control over its government for decades.

Foreign assistance programs targeted at specific ends can and do often succeed. The provision of counter-proliferation funds, the counter-narcotic program Plan Colombia and the anti-HIV program in Africa offer good examples.
Each was targeted to a specific, measurable end. Development assistance does
not have this character. If it did, we would not be hearing calls today for an
additional $2.5 trillion to address world poverty. The hundreds of billions
of dollars expended by the United States and other liberal democracies over
the past six or seven decades surely would have brought us to a better point
by now if development assistance had been effective.

The (sad) fact is that we have a limited ability to alter the social norms of
other nations. It would be one thing if this money were merely wasted; but
worse yet, foreign assistance often ends up in the hands of foreign government leaders. Corruption may well exist everywhere, including in economically advanced nations, but if it extends beyond minimal levels it actually
sets back the effort to create the social norms of trust and honesty necessary
for economic growth.

This creates a dilemma for American foreign policymakers. We may wish
to establish a closer relationship with certain foreign rulers for reasons which
have nothing to do with economic advancement. These could include common security interests, such as we have with a number of Middle East nations,
or alignment with U. S. votes at the United Nations or other multilateral
organizations. These two objectives—closer relationships with foreign leaders
and economic growth—are often at cross purposes with one another.

Once again Afghanistan provides a good example. U. S. policymakers
sought to create an Afghanistan which could resist the re-emergence of the
Taliban, and which would not be a haven for Islamic terrorists. This was certainly an understandable hope. But at the same time many officials in the
American-supported Afghan government became quite rich in the process.
Afghan government corruption was to a certain extent understood as a cost
of doing business in Afghanistan. But many Afghans were disgusted by the
blatant corruption which they witnessed, which did not endear the Afghan
government to them.

We may know the kinds of institutions and social norms which are associated with economic growth in foreign nations. But we do not know how to inculcate them into foreign nations. This argues for a substantial reform in foreign assistance programs. A degree of humility is a far more honest way to approach foreign assistance than reliance on abstract economic models of growth which do not consider the variety of political and social factors which shape economic possibilities for foreign nations.

The situation with foreign trade and investment is altogether different. Foreign trade and investment do not occur in order to advance abstract economic goals. They occur because American corporations seek to realize profits in specific situations, such as by locating plants in low-wage countries. Foreign trade and investment do not have noble-sounding goals, but they create economic growth and employment both in the U. S. and in foreign nations as a by-product of the profit motive. Foreign trade and investment have been an engine for American economic growth, but they have also done far more than foreign assistance to alleviate poverty in poor nations.

Foreign trade and investment are not government activities. They are undertaken by the private sector for more immediate ends than the abstract goal of economic growth in foreign nations. As such their results are specific and measurable in a way that development assistance is not. There are surely cases in which the U. S. government has a legitimate interest in restricting foreign trade and investment. Cases include restrictions on certain weapons systems and high technology items as well as the need to maintain a domestic base of certain critical minerals, pharmaceuticals and other items. But the default position should be free and fair trade, a standpoint which today is increasingly coming under political attack. As a general matter, the role of the government here is the same role it has whenever and wherever economic growth occurs, namely, to set out a broad and predictable legal framework within which the private sector can operate.

What shall we do about economic sanctions which, as has been noted, have become a leading tool of American foreign policy? Their use assumes that economic penalties can change the non-economic, political behavior of foreign governments, which is the standard conceit of progressive materialism. Economic sanctions levied against foreign nations for non-economic reasons are almost never successful. The political attraction of economic sanctions, however, is obvious. They provide the happy appearance of doing something effective while doing very little at all.

Because economic sanctions are adopted mainly for political reasons, it is difficult to provide counsel about how to moderate their use, other than to point out their often-negative effects on American businesses. This is not much of a policy recommendation, but here too a degree of humility about what policymakers can and cannot affect with these tools would be welcome.

Finally, foreign policymakers should learn to take the expressed views of foreign leaders seriously. There has grown up a view that foreign leaders often express the views they do for domestic political consumption, whereas in reality they are more aligned with American political and economic views. This is no doubt true in certain cases, but more often it is not. If foreign leaders say they hate the United States, it is wise to believe them. If foreign leaders say they wish to destroy the state of Israel, it is wise to suppose they really do. Going "behind" the statements of foreign leaders to discover their supposed real views, which usually just happen to accord with American political-economic views, is a false and lazy pseudo-sophistication. It is to assume somehow that at bottom all foreign leaders subscribe to the dominant American progressive material view of the world. The same is true in regard to the express statements of terrorists.

Similarly, in assessing the actions of foreign leaders we should not suppose they are making obvious "mistakes." Their actions are "mistakes" only for American foreign policymakers who are steeped in progressive material assumptions. Did Vladimir Putin make a "mistake" in invading Ukraine? Surely so in terms of the ease with which he thought he could accomplish his goals. But did he make a "mistake," as has been said, in not taking actions which would benefit the well-being of the Russian people? The material well-being of the Russian people was no part of Putin's calculation in invading Ukraine. It was in this way no mistake at all. Even today there is no reason to assume he will see the error of his ways and change course. The only way to change Putin's course is to defeat him.

In many such cases, American policymakers busy themselves looking for "exit strategies" for foreign leaders who make what they regard as mistakes. This is a fool's errand. Foreign leaders like Putin are not looking for exit strategies. If they were, it would be easy enough to find so-called exit ramps themselves.

Each of these conclusions reflects what some critics might call a hard-headed realism. It would be fairer to say they reflect a deep degree of humility. Our ability to move foreign nations to economic growth—called development—is limited. So is our ability to end all foreign government corruption. So is our ability to "go behind" foreign leaders to discern their "real" intentions. Each of these policy prejudices reflects a hubris derived from assuming that we know the true (economic) springs of the actions of foreign leaders and peoples.

There is no easy way, no legislative or executive branch proposal, to change this mindset, other than to continually point out its limitations. A strong American foreign policy is not one which counsels withdrawal from the world. But it is one which acts without illusions about what we know and do not know, what we can and cannot accomplish. It is one which sees the world as it is, not as a collection of nations and foreign leaders who are all seeking common and benign policies to bend the arc of history toward economic enrichment.

Intelligence Assessments

Much the same can be recommended to the American intelligence community. To be successful American intelligence assessments must overcome their bias toward material causation. Things that can be counted offer only partial explanations for why events occur or what are their outcomes. Intelligence assessments should require as a matter of routine practice serious consideration of non-material causes. These include non-material motivations such as religious beliefs, the morale of foreign armies, the skill of foreign leaders and deep-seated historical traditions and beliefs. In short, any distinctly human, ideological contribution to the occurrence of future events and their outcomes.

As in the case with foreign policymaking, this means taking foreign leaders at their word. Surely there are cases where foreign leaders dissemble and try to hide their true purposes. But if the intelligence community errs one way or another it is not because they miss these deceptions. The intelligence community's ability to penetrate foreign leaders' conversations is impressive. Assessment failures are more likely due to interpreting the intentions of foreign leaders through the lens of economic causation.

A second bias of the intelligence community derives from its overly economic orientation. That is, the world is seen in broad strokes as one which expresses clear-cut trends which can be known and into which events and decisions can be fitted. There are, however, no observable trends which should be relied upon for any but the shortest of terms. Change does not occur in an incremental linear way but in fits and starts. Relatively calm periods are broken by transformational changes. These changes tend not to be economic changes, which unfold more slowly, but political or military changes. Nor do these changes move in easily predictable directions. In addition to the checklist of factors mentioned above, intelligence assessments should require careful consideration of whether non-linear, transformative changes are possible at any given moment.

Transformative changes do not simply change one aspect of reality; they have consequences which spill over into many areas. When Russia invaded Ukraine and Ukraine successfully resisted this attack, many new factors were introduced. Relations between Russia and China changed in ways never predicted before the invasion. Relations between Russia and Iran, including Iranian military assistance to Russia, have deepened in a way not predicted. Nordic nations which have long stood aside from NATO have surprisingly opted to join. World oil prices have seesawed with every change in western sanctions or Russian responses to them. World food supplies have been threatened in unexpected ways. There is not one bit of economic causation in any of this transformation, a transformation initiated by Putin for non-economic reasons and sustained by Ukraine for non-economic reasons as well. In short, transformations are radical breaks in what are otherwise short-term linear patterns of economic life. Change is not always linear and incremental.

Third, the intelligence community needs to demonstrate more awareness of the speed with which transformational change can and does occur. The examples we have discussed—the fall of the Shah, the implosion of the Soviet Union, the collapse of the Afghan government and Ukrainian resistance to the Russian invasion—offer only a handful of many such cases. The case of Ukraine is instructive. The intelligence community struggled during the first year to reconcile itself to Ukraine's success. When matters finally settled into trench warfare along a long perimeter, both foreign policymakers and intelligence analysts caught up. At each step of the way, policymakers have been predictably cautious about providing advanced weapons systems to Ukraine. An intelligence assessment which ran out ahead of the curve would have emboldened policymakers to do more to help Ukraine, more quickly.

At this moment the intelligence community seems comfortable in its assessments of the Ukraine war because events have settled into a slow-moving war of attrition. But this is the very moment to be alert to the possibility of further transformational change. What would result if Russia breaks through Ukraine lines and moves toward Kyiv? What if Belarus joins Russia and attacks Ukraine from the north? More interestingly, what if Ukraine breaks through Russian lines and seems likely to capture all of Crimea? How would that affect the outcome of the war, Putin's response, or Putin's standing in the Kremlin? Each of these possibilities would generate far-reaching follow-on consequences. Without advance warning events will overtake us very quickly.

The same is true about a possible Chinese invasion of Taiwan. The intelligence community is properly focused on the possibility of an invasion. This is all to the good. There will likely be very clear signs of an impending invasion, just as there were when Russia massed its forces along Ukraine's border. China will doubtless amass forces across the Taiwan Strait and undertake other observable preparatory steps. There will be forewarning of a possible Chinese invasion. But if and when a decision is made in Beijing, there will be no luxury of time to respond to it. Consequences will flow very quickly which will affect the economy of the Pacific region and, for that matter, the entire world. Consequences will quickly spill over to Japan and the Korean peninsula. They will affect worldwide production and availability of computer chips. They will affect stocks of weapons required by the U. S. to respond with a naval and air campaign. And so on. It is not sufficient for the intelligence community to predict an impending Chinese invasion; serious advance reflection on all these possibilities is needed to give policymakers a decent chance to respond intelligently.

All this can be summed up in saying that world events are not only predicated on slow moving economic considerations, that change is not only linear, and that transformational change usually occurs very rapidly. That is what makes it transformational. The intelligence community does a remarkably good job at providing useful information—facts—to American and allied decision-makers. Where it has failed is in its assessments of rapid, non-economically determined changes. Reorienting itself toward these kinds of changes is important.

As we noted in Chapter Six, transformational changes are of course the most difficult to predict and to grasp in their entirety. It is far easier to assume that material, economic factors, which tend to operate in a slower and more linear fashion, shape human events. If the world were like this, it would certainly make intelligence assessments easier. But the human world is less monochrome than the world of economic causation. Successful intelligence assessments must be predicated on the real, more complex and less easily predictable human world.

SOME FURTHER REFLECTIONS

The suggestions above would help to reorient policymaking away from a purely material, economic view of human causation. Each would improve the prospect that American government policies would be more successful in achieving their stated goals. At the same time these proposals might strike the reader as quite modest, as they do the author himself. They would improve policymaking at the margins but would in no way place the underlying progressive material orientation of contemporary America into a richer human context. Nor would they foster a spirit of community or shared values among Americans.

This begs the question whether deeper changes are possible, and if so, what they would look like. Is it possible to reorient American society in a way which gives material considerations their due, but places them in a broader context in which Americans are seen in a fuller, more complete way? Is it possible to inculcate notions of citizen virtue which the Constitution's framers thought were so important to the future of the republic?

On its face this seems unlikely. Progressives continue to find ever new ways to expand federal economic programs and to expand the number of recipients who benefit from them. The ever-expanding list of goods and services to be provided by the federal government seems to have no limit. It seems that progressive materialism is fated to shape our horizon as far as the eye can see. Accordingly, change seems possible only at the margins.

But what if we were to look at this differently? As its name suggests, progressivism is always moving. Is it really possible that such a project has no end? What is the end toward which progressivism is moving? It would presumably be a society replete with individuals who receive the satisfaction of all their material needs. Assuming this is even remotely possible, what then?

It has been the unquestioned faith of progressive materialists that solving the material problem will also satisfy the non-economic aspects of human life. Because material causes are the basis of human conflict and unhappiness, their satisfaction will remove the causes of conflict and produce social harmony. This is the great progressive conceit, founded on the view of man as an essentially economic being.

But a strange and unpredicted thing seems to be occurring. As Americans' economic needs are coming closer to satisfaction, precisely the opposite seems to be occurring. As federal assistance programs grow larger other non-economic issues are coming to the fore. Progressive materialism holds sway, to be sure; but Americans of all political and social views seem increasingly to realize that progressive materialism cannot keep the promise it has made. Americans are no happier than ever, perhaps less so. Americans are no more unified around a set of shared assumptions and values, certainly less so. Political differences seem to run deeper than ever, even to the point of hints of national separation. Why should this be so?

The success of progressive materialism is beginning to display its own limitations. For anyone who cares to look, there are clear signs that this is so. Let me propose four different developments—call them forces if you like—which suggest a growing disaffection with progressive materialism and its promise of human satisfaction.

The first can be found among intellectual conservatives who seek a return to the classical liberal natural rights tradition of the Declaration of Independence and the Constitution. This movement, which progressives dismiss as simple nostalgia, was born in the early 1950's and 1960's. It bubbled briefly into national prominence with the Goldwater presidential campaign in 1964. Following Goldwater's decisive loss, large progressive majorities adopted many left-leaning programs in the 1960's and 1970's. The election of Ronald Reagan embraced an anti-progressive orientation rhetorically but did not reverse progressive programs in any significant way. Neither has any subsequent administration.

What is different today is that the movement to re-establish the classical natural rights tradition is far more broadly based than in its early days. It has grown in scope to include a number of educational institutions, numerous think tanks, churches, and an especially forceful media presence which was not present in the 1960's. In addition, the Federalist Society has been extremely effective in advocating for judges who aim to rein in executive branch governance in favor of returning power to Congress in a manner the framers of the Constitution envisioned. This has begun to have a significant effect in Supreme Court rulings. In short, advocates of a return to the classical liberal natural rights tradition now constitute a far more organic, potent force than at any time since progressivism took hold of American political life in the 1930's.

Alongside these groups there is also a smaller, but somewhat parallel set of groups aiming to re-moralize American society. These groups, which are often but not always founded in a type of Catholic theology, also oppose the dominance of contemporary progressive materialism which they see as a latter-day liberalism. They aim to inculcate a moral order which they call a "common good" order upon which to base American society. While their goals are different than classical liberals (today called conservatives), their presence testifies to a growing dissatisfaction with a society dominated by progressive materialism.

Progressives characterize both groups as retrograde forces which mistakenly hope to return to a society which never existed. It is difficult to say how large a role these groups will play in shaping American culture. But that is not the point here. The point is that opposition to progressive materialism is growing, and this growth reflects less a misplaced nostalgia than the assertion of the non-economic side of human life. It would be a mistake for progressives to assume these groups will diminish in importance with greater economic "progress." The opposite is far more likely the case.

A second and perhaps more powerful factor is the increasing salience of cultural issues. Issues like abortion, parental rights, support for the American flag and religious freedom have come to the fore as concerns which have gained strong support among conservative populists. Progressives have entirely misconstrued the meaning and force of this development. Denouncing these interests as backward and ignorant because they do not represent the "true" (that is, economic) interests of Americans is a fundamental mistake. These cultural issues are not remnants of a disappearing world, but ways in which peoples' lives are fulfilled. Cultural issues have risen in importance in just the past several decades. It should not be surprising that this is precisely the period when the limits of progressive materialism have become ever clearer.

Cultural issues will not gradually wither away with further economic measures because they do not speak to economic problems. It may well be true that necessitous men cannot be free men, but men who are less necessitous do not for that reason cease their concern about non-economic issues. When stated simply, this may seem obvious. But it is the least obvious thing in a society dominated by progressive materialism.

To this point the reader might fairly assume I am talking about cultural and political issues which are important to the political right. Fair enough. But non-economic issues are becoming increasingly important to the political left in America as well. Left-oriented issues like gender fluidity, the fundamental importance of racial identity groups, restrictions on free speech, voting rights for non-citizens, micro-aggressions and a host of other issues have come to the fore. Not one of these issues is economic in nature. Not one of these issues grows organically out of the progressive material project. Not one of these issues was anywhere to be found on the political left as recently as twenty years ago. It seems the political left is in its own way beginning to testify to the limits of an economic-dominated vision of man.

There is perhaps no new non-economic issue on the political left which is more important today than global warming. Global warming is not at bottom an economic issue. To be sure progressives demand resources—money, money, money as John Kerry says—to address global warming. But addressing global warming is not in and of itself an economic issue. It does not aim to expand the economic well-being of either individuals or the nation. It is an altogether different kind of issue, reflecting the relation of human beings to the planet. This has been addressed in a highly intelligent way by the economist Robert Nelson.[7] He argues that combating global warming is a secular religion which is in many ways directly opposed to a progressive material orientation. Addressing global warming requires actions which fly in the face of ever greater economic production and development.

Economists can argue about better ways to address global warming—as, for example, Bjorn Lomborg does—but the goal itself has nothing whatever to do with the increasing satisfaction of material wants. Everyone in America could be well-fed, well-clothed and well-housed and the issue of global warming would not disappear. It speaks to the relation of human beings to the planet which, while having economic consequences, is not resolvable by economic progress. Evidence for this is that global warming is far more important in societies like America, which are rather fully developed economically, than in societies like China or India.

It is interesting and, as Marxists might say, no coincidence that this issue has taken center stage at just the time when economic necessities are increasingly satisfied for Americans. Like the social issues we have mentioned above, global warning has come to prominence as an issue only in the past two or three decades. It is a post-economic preoccupation.

There is one more sign of departure from the progressive-materialist orientation. Here my observations might seem somewhat novel and counterintuitive. The notion of equity is widely understood today as the next step of progressive materialism. But I would argue that the notion of equity, as it is advanced today by the political left, is a new and very different notion than that which has been at the core of progressive materialism.

The fundamental goal of progressive materialism has been to expand production and to share the fruits of production to allow all Americans to benefit. This is the foundation of progressivism's economic transfer programs. Federal economic transfer programs of the type we have discussed throughout this book have had as their goal to provide a minimal standard of economic security for everyone. About this goal, as we have also argued, there may be differences at the margins, but there has been broad political support in principle. Political debates have been less about whether such programs should exist but more about how many programs should exist and what level of support should be provided. The axial question has been how much is enough to achieve a life of basic economic security for everyone.

The notion of equity is very different. It seems like an economic issue on its surface, but it is certainly not the kind of issue which has driven the progressive materialist project. It is essentially a notion of justice, not of economics. It is founded on the recent post-economic notion of identity groups as opposed to the long American historical and economic tradition of individualism. Its feature is equality of outcome, not of opportunity. It is breathtakingly described in planning documents for the Fairfax County, Virginia public school system: the goal is to promote "equal outcomes for every student, without exception." This is a radical departure from what has gone before.

Why must outcomes among groups be equal? It is difficult to say. The ideas of freedom and equal opportunity were founded on the idea of the natural equality of human souls. They were grounded in a widely accepted foundation reaching back centuries. Its theoretical foundations were established by Hobbes, Locke, Spinoza and other philosophers.

What is the foundation for the recent political movement that outcomes, not opportunities, must be the same? Who are today's counterparts to Hobbes, Locke, Spinoza who can explain why equity should be a goal? The notion of equity has nothing to do with the greater satisfaction of human material necessities. As we have seen in statist societies, equity can be realized at any level of material well-being including utter impoverishment or, in the case of education, low standards. The notion of equity seems to be a superficial idea of justice, not an economic notion at all. It by no means grows organically out of progressive materialism but is a radical break from it. This is perhaps why even progressive materialists are somewhat unsettled by the idea.

Each of these developments—the re-emergence of a strong natural rights tradition, the rise of cultural controversies, ecological concerns and especially global warming, and the notion of equity—speaks to the limits of an economic view of man. Each is growing in importance at the very moment that programs to provide economic assistance to Americans have reached their highest point. To put it mildly, this would certainly not be predicted by the adherents of progressive materialism from Marx right up to today's progressives.

This is not to suggest that progressive materialism is creating its successor in an organic, Hegelian way. But it is to suggest that there are signs that progressive materialism is today demonstrating its limits. There will surely be continuing efforts to expand federal economic transfer programs; but Americans of greatly differing views are coming to realize there is more to human life than the satisfaction of material ends, and that economic transfer programs will not and cannot satisfy non-economic human concerns.

This is a repudiation of Marx, Lenin and Mao, to be sure; but it is also a realization of the limits of the liberal tradition of Mill, Veblen, Keynes and modern progressives generally. This explains the otherwise paradoxical result that as more and more Americans are ever more fully the beneficiaries of progressive economic programs, our politics is becoming nastier and more divided than ever. Our politics today increasingly contends less over the economic/technological problem of material well-being and more over the non-economic issues of culture and justice.

Marx said that men who are no longer under the grip of economic necessity would be free to hunt, fish and criticize poetry, as they please. The implication was this would be a world in which there were no longer deep divisions between men (a world requiring only the administration of things, not men). This seems today more and more obviously to promise too much. To stick with this reverie, is hunting, for example, to be regulated or perhaps abolished altogether to suit the tastes of vegans? Is fishing not likely to raise issues related to the depletion of fish stocks and who can fish where? Will everyone favor the same kinds of poetry or should some types of poetry be banned? For that matter, will there be agreement about whether free speech should be permitted? Will there be agreement about when, if at all, abortion should be allowed? Will there be agreement about how to educate our children and who should do it? Will there be agreement about whether God exists and, if so, what God is like and what he expects from us? Not one of these is an economic issue. Not one of these will disappear no matter how fully progressive materialism is able to satisfy the basic material needs of men.

Where then does this leave us? First, it is doubtful we will ever find an agreed sufficient level for federal transfer payments. Economic "needs" seems to grow along with their satisfaction. But apart from this, there is no reason to be surprised that questions of justice will outlast progressive materialism. Only those in thrall to the notion that men are at bottom economic beings will find this surprising. Here and there we see signs that America is gradually relearning this.

But this is no panacea. To the contrary, post-economic men will display all the non-economic passions and desires they ever have. We were fortunate as a people that at our founding we had a commercial society that was embedded in a broader context of agreed morals and shared views. This was certainty in large part due to the prevalence of Christian morality. To some extent it was also due to the happy accidents of geography and a largely homogeneous population.

These advantages are in large part absent today, in part because they were rejected by an ascendant progressive materialism. But progressive materialism promised more than it could deliver. Like Marx, it took the insight that economics is important and made it all-important. Its promise of human happiness and social harmony was more than it could deliver, because these ends of life are not entirely economic in nature. This seems increasingly evident today. Our politics going forward will be fought out less over economic issues and more over cultural political/moral issues.

In this there is both good news and bad news. The bad news is that these struggles will not necessarily be purely benign. They can and perhaps will be deep and vicious. There are fewer guide rails of shared moral assumptions than ever before in our history. As recently as two or three decades ago there was a broad consensus about free speech, American exceptionalism, equality of opportunity as opposed to equality of result, the importance of individuals as opposed to group membership, what is a man and what is a woman, and many other foundational matters. These are now all objects of contention. In such a circumstance it is not difficult to predict deep and continuing political and social tensions. These issues will have to be fought out on their merits and the stakes for what kind of country this will be are very high. Progressive materialism has not and will not lead our nation into a period of harmony and agreement. It seems there is no heaven on earth.

The good news is that it is now possible to see beyond the limited world of progressive materialism. There is some leeway to move beyond the mindless fiction of economic man and its attendant notion of economic causality. As deeper social/cultural/moral ideals are fought out, there is a chance to move toward a fuller view of the springs of human action. There is a chance to move toward government policies which reflect this fuller view. And thus perhaps also a chance to shape a government whose policies are less an object of proper ridicule and scorn and more whose policies are founded on what is true about human beings. This book is a modest attempt to do just that.

ACKNOWLEDGMENTS

There are many people to thank for a project of this scope. Here I can mention only a few of the many who have contributed, including my staff at the State Department and the Senate Foreign Relations Committee, as well as my colleagues and students at the University of Virginia.

I am especially grateful to George Windstrup for his very deep understanding of classical liberalism.

I am grateful to Eric and Kurt Retrum for their many insightful conversations about contemporary American political and social issues.

I am grateful to Jonathan Bergner for reading many sections of the manuscript and for his helpful editorial suggestions.

I am grateful to Jason Bergner for the same, and for helping to craft this book into a finished product.

I am grateful to Steve Kuhn for his technical assistance and for his help in designing the book's cover.

Finally, I am grateful to Susan and the rest of my family. Their support, understanding and forbearance as this book took shape was, as always, invaluable.

NOTES

INTRODUCTION

1. See, for example, Augustine, *On the City of God against the Pagans* (426); Montesquieu, *Considerations on the Causes of the Greatness of the Romans and their Decline* (1734); Edward Gibbon, *The Decline and Fall of the Roman Empire* (1776-1788) and Max Weber, "Die soziale Gruende des Untergangs der antiken Kultur," in *Gesammelte Aufsaetze zur Sozial-und Wirtschaftsgeschichte* (1924).

2. Leo Tolstoy addresses the fullness of this problem in *War and Peace,* Part IX, Chapter I: "In order that the will of Napoleon and Alexander (on whom the whole decision appeared to rest) should be effective, a combination of innumerable circumstances was essential, without any one of which the effect would not have followed."

3. Regression analysis is a tool developed by statisticians and used primarily by economists to identify the strength of correlations between a dependent variable which is to be explained and one or more independent variables. There is no doubt this can be useful in bounded studies, especially ones in which in which there are frequent interactions upon which to plot correlations, and even more so if the relations between the independent and dependent variables are continuous. This approach has not proved very useful in understanding complex social changes which are arguably one of a kind and neither continuous nor repetitive.

4. Daniel Bell, for instance, lists ten qualitatively different categories by which to explain social change in *The End of Ideology* (New York: The Free Press, 1962), pp. 316 ff.

5. The differences between the predictive powers of physical science and social science, however, are often exaggerated. It is true that social science cannot successfully predict discrete events like the outbreak of a war. But without replication the physical sciences cannot predict with complete certainty either. Physical science is so successful because it can eliminate external variables and predict cause and effect in bounded conditions. The exactitude with which gases expand in a tube, for example, is well agreed—unless the tube is broken from the outside.

   This is especially true of evolutionary biology which, in so far as it considers the one-time evolution of the world, is more like history than physics. This is true both of original Darwinism and more modern theories of punctuated equilibrium. The generally agreed formula of natural selection based on random mutation offers no way to predict when, where or how many new species may emerge. Its explanations can go backward, and it can point to gaps in the historical record, but it cannot go forward.

   Milton Friedman spoke to this in his famous 1953 essay *The Methodology of Positive Economics.* He argued that the physical sciences do not always rely on controlled experiments, as the science of astronomy demonstrates. For both the physical sciences and for economic science what is key is the ability to predict a result based on a theory. This prediction need not necessarily be of a future event but could be of a past consequence which has hitherto gone unnoticed until explained by a theory.

6. R. M. MacIver, *Social Causation* (New York: Harper and Row, 1964), p. 392: "The goal of causal knowledge is never attained, though our endeavors can bring us always nearer." One might ask, however, whether an ideologically inspired explanation like that of the 1619 Project is bringing us nearer to the truth. On a deeper level, to know we are coming ever nearer to the truth would require us to know in advance what is the truth. How else could we know we are approaching it? This is the same problem confronted by so-called "negative theologians" who assert they come closer to God by knowing more of what God is not.

7. See Lenin, *What Is To Be Done?* (Mansfield Center, Conn.: Martino Publishers, 2013), p. 152: "*Every* question 'runs in a vicious circle' because the whole of political life is an endless chain consisting of an infinite number of links. The whole art of politics lies in finding the link that can be least torn out of our hands, the one that is most important at the given moment, the one that guarantees the command of the whole chain, and having found it, to cling to that link as tightly as possible."

8. See MacIver, p. 6: "Whenever we set about any task we assume causation."

9. We might consider this book's masthead quotation from Calvin Coolidge, which is a crystal-clear example of ideal causation. In his extended remarks Coolidge acknowledges that the ideas of the Declaration of Independence, whose 150th anniversary he was commemorating, did not arise spontaneously, but had a long gestation. He further notes that the immediate causes of the American Revolution were "largely economic." What he finds new is not the establishment of a new government due to material causes; there are, he says, many examples of this in history. What was new was not that the Declaration simply established a new nation, but rather a nation founded on new principles.

10. Alfred North Whitehead spoke of fundamental assumptions which shape the thought of an epoch. These assumptions, he said, "appear so obvious that people do not know what they are assuming because no other way of putting things has ever occurred to them." Quoted in Robert Nelson, *Economics as Religion: From Samuelson to Chicago and Beyond* (University Park, Pennsylvania: University of Pennsylvania Press, 2014), p. 54 (note).

11. See Patrick Deneen, *Why Liberalism Failed* (New Haven, Conn.: Yale University Press, 2019); *Regime Change: Toward a Postliberal Future* (New York: Penguin Random House, 2023); and *Conserving America: Essays on Present Discontents* (South Bend, Indiana: St. Augustine's Press, 2016).

ONE: MARX ON ECONOMIC DETERMINISM

1. The latter, written in 1845-1846, was not published until 1932 (as Marx later said, it was left "to the gnawing criticism of the mice"). Marx said the purpose of the manuscript was "to settle accounts with our erstwhile philosophical conscience."

2. Marx and Engels, *The German Ideology* (Moscow: Progress Publishers, 1964), pp. 37-38.

3. Marx and Engels, *The Communist Manifesto*, ed. by Samuel H. Beer (Northbrook, Ill.: AHM Publishing Corporation, 1955), pp.29-30.

4. Marx, *A Contribution to the Critique of Political Economy*, quoted in Lewis Feuer, ed., *Marx and Engels: Basic Writings on Politics and Philosophy* (Garden City: Doubleday, 1959), p. 43.

5. Quoted in Feuer, *Marx and Engels: Basic Writings*, p. 396.

6. *Ibid.*, p. 398.

7. *Ibid.*, pp. 399-400.

8. In speaking about historians and evolutionary biologists, Deirdre McCloskey notes their tendency to assume that what happened in the past must have happened. For such people, she says, their "main intellectual tool is hindsight." McCloskey, *Bourgeois Dignity: Why Economics Can't Explain the Modern World*, (Chicago: University of Chicago Press, 2010), p. 376. This could also be said of Marx and Engels.

9. See Engels, *The Peasant War in Germany* and his book *The Origin of the Family, Private Property and the State*, which he produced in part from Marx's notes.

10. Marx and Engels did not compare their interpretation of history head-to-head with other accounts. See MacIver, *Social Causation*, p. 117.

11. The first to use the term "scientific socialism" was the French socialist Pierre Proudhon in 1840. Proudhon was perhaps the best-known early socialist. Perhaps that is why Marx felt obliged to differentiate himself so strongly from Proudhon's *The Philosophy of Poverty* with his *The Poverty of Philosophy*, written in 1846-1847. In his 1890 *Socialism: From Utopia to Science,* Engels credits Saint-Simon, whom he praises highly, with the idea that politics is the science of production.

12. There is perhaps no better evidence of the force of "science" in the 19th century than Mary Baker Eddy. She developed what came to be called "Christian Science" in the 1860's. In 1879, only one year before Engels' pamphlet *Socialism: From Utopia to Science* was published in France, she founded the First Church of Christ, Scientist in Boston. In describing Jesus as a scientist, she meant one who knew and spoke the truth, and in this way she epitomized the power of science in the mid-to-late nineteenth century.

13. Marx, letter of January 16, 1861, quoted from "Marx and Engels Internet Archive," (Gesamtausgabe, International Publishers, 1942).

14. Here we might consider briefly the claims of today's advocates of global warming. Global warming studies the one-time evolution of the world's temperature. In this it aims to be like the scientific gold standard of evolution, namely, evolutionary biology. But unlike evolutionary biology, global warming makes specific predictions that extend far into the future. These predictions, it might be noted, while often referencing other factors, rely heavily on straight line, single factor changes in the amount of carbon dioxide in the atmosphere.

15. See Marx, *Capital,* I (New York: International Publishers, 1967), p. 8. Marx speaks of an "iron necessity" of history.

16. Until a theoretical model can accurately map the past, there is little reason to suppose it will be able to predict the future.

17. Here we might address directly the many efforts which latter day Marxists have made to weaken the claims that Marx and Engels actually made concerning the role of economics in determining men's consciousness. No matter how often and in how many ways this occurs, it is simply not possible to dilute Marx and Engels' claims sufficiently to eliminate the economic basis of human thought. To say economics "conditions" rather than determines human thought, as Marx does in one place, does not do the trick. One cannot deny the role of economics in shaping the deepest character of human thought without removing an essential part of Marx and Engels' doctrine.

18. McCloskey, *Why Liberalism Works: How True Liberal Values Produce a Freer, More Equal, Prosperous World For All* (New Haven: Yale University Press.2019), p. 31.

19. McCloskey, *Bourgeois Dignity*, p. xi and p. 25. See also *Bourgeois Equality: How Ideas, Not Capital or Institutions Enriched the World* (Chicago: University of Chicago Press, 2016), p. xxxi and *Liberalism*, p. 205.

20. McCloskey notes that John Stuart Mill calls this a method of "remainders" or "residues" in his *System of Logic*. She acknowledges what she calls an "inferential gap" in this process, though the same might be said of any kind of inductive knowledge. McCloskey, *Bourgeois Dignity*, p. 33.

21. McCloskey, *Bourgeois Equality*, p. 516.

22. McCloskey, *The Bourgeois Virtues: Ethics for an Age of Commerce* (Chicago: University of Chicago Press, 2006), 410. The quotation is from Mill's *Principles of Political Economy.*

23. McCloskey, *Bourgeois Dignity*, p. 5.

24. McCloskey, *Ibid.* p. 5. For the elaboration concerning wood and coal, see McCloskey, *Bourgeois Equality*, pp. 531 ff.

25. Though McCloskey makes the point that non-material factors like opinions can be studied mathematically as well. She mentions as an example opinion polling.

26. McCloskey, *Bourgeois Dignity*, pp. 31-32. This is much like this book's masthead quotation from Calvin Coolidge. One might also consider the words of John Adams, who was not a latter-day commentator but an active participant in the creation of the United States. He wrote in 1818 "The Revolution was in the minds of the people, and this was effected, from 1760 to 1775, in the course of fifteen years before a drop of blood was shed at Lexington."

27. Friedrich Hayek, T*he Fatal Conceit: The Errors of Socialism*, ed. by W. W. Bartley III (Chicago: University of Chicago Press, 1991) p. 108.

28. Marx, *Capital*, I, p. 8.

29. In his 1866 Preface to *Capital*, I, p. 6, Engels says that Marx thought perhaps England alone of European countries could effect a social revolution "entirely by peaceful and legal means." He says, though, that Marx hardly expected the English ruling classes to submit to this.

30. Marx, *The Poverty of Philosophy* (New York: International Publishers, 1963), p. 174.

31. Eduard Bernstein (1850-1932) was a German socialist who adopted an incremental, legislative approach to the achievement of socialism. An acquaintance of Engels, he served in the German parliament for many terms and sought to grow social democratic party membership to the point that it controlled the parliament.

32. Engels, *Ludwig Feuerbach and the Outcome of Classical German Philosophy* (New York: International Publishers, 1941), p. 39.

33. Marx and Engels, *German Ideology*, p. 50: "All forms of products and consciousness cannot be dissolved by mental criticism … but only by the practical overthrow of the actual social relations which give rise to this idealistic humbug."

34. Engels, Introduction to Marx, *Class Struggles in France, 1848-1850* (New York: International Publishers, 1964), pp. 15-16. See also, Engels, The *Peasant War in Germany* (New York: International Publishers, 1966), p. 136, where Engels makes clear that before capitalism replaced feudalism, the time was not right for the success of socialist-minded Thomas Muenzer.

35. Lenin wrote that six months prior to the Paris Commune Marx said "that an insurrection would be madness." See Lenin, "The Assessment of the Russian Revolution," in *Anarchism and Anarcho-Syndicalism: Selected Writings by Marx, Engels, Lenin* (New York: International Publishers, 1972), p. 218.

36. Marx, *Poverty of Philosophy*, p. 12.

37. Engels, *Anti-Duehring: Herr Eugen Duehring's Revolution in Science* (New York: International Publishers, 1966), p. 292.

38. This was the long implication of Marx's *Civil War in France, 1848-1850*. Engels was forthright to say in 1895 that he and Marx had been overly optimistic in their hopes for the Revolutions of 1848 and the Paris Commune of 1871.

39. Marx, *Capital*, I. p. 8.

40. *Ibid.*, I, p. 8.

41. Marx discusses America toward the end of the first volume of *Capital*, especially pp. 765-774.

42. In *Capital*, I, p. 773 Marx said "the American Civil War brought in its train a colossal national debt, and, with it, pressure of taxes, the rise of the vilest financial aristocracy, the squandering of a huge part of the

public land on speculative companies for the exploitation of railways, mines, etc., in brief, the most rapid centralization of capital."

43. Quoted in Feuer, *Marx and Engels*, p. 457.

44. Engels, *Anti-Duehring*, p. 307.

45. Marx, *Critique of the Gotha Program* (New York: International Publishers, 1966), p. 10: "only then ... can society inscribe on its banners: from each according to his ability, to each according to his needs."

46. Michel Houellebecq, *Serotonin: A Novel* (New York: Farrar, Straus and Giroux, 2019), p. 116 refers to this as a "hollow formula ... an endless source of carping and quibbling if by some misfortune someone tried to put it into practice."

47. This argument was replicated in debates within the International itself, that is, whether the policies of the communists must be generated from the top down in a hierarchical manner or whether they could emerge more organically.

48. Marx and Engels, *The German Ideology*, pp. 44-45.

49. Robert Nelson, *Economics as Religion: From Samuelson to Chicago and Beyond* (University Park, Pa.: Pennsylvania State University Press, 2014) proposes an even earlier precursor in the Biblical idea of a time before the "fall" of man into sin. At that time there was no requirement to work, which came only as a punishment for Adam and Eve's sin. In so far as there were only two individuals in this pre-lapsarian state, however, there was no need for complex administration.

50. This includes the later extended debate about whether there was a "descent of man" from apes, and thus a morally more complex, if not always better form of life.

51. In fairness, Engels suggests in *Anti-Duehring* there will be no end to learning about the inter-connections of the world, that is, science.

TWO: MARXISM IN PRACTICE

1. Sociologist Michael Burawoy observes that "We should not be deceived by Lenin's ability to sound as though he was merely parroting what Marx and Engels said." See "Marxism as Science: Historical Challenges and Theoretical Growth," *American Sociological Review*, Vol. 55, No.6 (Dec,. 1990), pp. 775-93.

2. Among many volumes we might mention the classic biography of Lenin by Robert Service, a more recent biography by Dmitri Volkogonov entitled *Lenin: A New Biography*, *Reminiscences of Lenin* by Lenin's wife Nadezhda Konstaninova Krupskaya, and Trotsky's history of the Soviet revolution.

3. Robert C. Tucker, ed., *The Lenin Anthology* (New York: W. W. Norton and Company, 1975), p. xi.

4. Lenin, *Materialism and Empirio-Criticism: Critical Comments on a Reactionary Philosophy* (New York: International Publishers, 1927), p.106.

5. *Ibid.*, p. 137.

6. Preface, *Anarchism and Anarcho-Syndicalism: Selected Writings by Marx, Engels, Lenin* (New York: International Publishers, 1972), pp. 19-20.

7. Edmund Wilson, *To the Finland Station* (New York: Doubleday, 1953), pp. 467-68 and p. 480.

8. Lenin, "Can the Bolsheviks Retain State Power?" in Tucker, *Anthology*, p. 406.

9. Lenin, "Two Tactics of Social-Democracy in the Democratic Revolution," in Tucker, *Anthology*, p. 143.

10. Lenin, *What is to be Done?*, p.38.

11. *Ibid.*, p. 47.

12. *Ibid.*, p.62.

13. *Ibid.*, p. 40.

14. *Ibid.*, p. 31.

15. Lenin, Impe*rialism: The Highest stage of Capitalism* (New York: International Publishers, 1939), p. 107. Engels had already remarked on this process in England before his death in 1895.

16. *Ibid.*, p. 88.

17. Lenin, "Two Tactics of Social-Democracy," in *Anarchism*, pp. 200-02.

18. Lenin, "Two Tactics of Social-Democracy," in Tucker, *Anthology,* pp. 121-22.

19. *Ibid.*, p. 130. At one point Lenin tried to finesse the question by referring to a "dictatorship of the proletariat and peasants."

20. *Ibid.*, p. 124.

21. Lenin, "Socialism and War," in Tucker, *Anthology,* p.195.

22. Lenin, "Our Revolution," in Tucker, *Anthology,* pp. 704-05.

23. Lenin, "Report on War and Peace," in Tucker, *Anthology*, p. 545.

24. Lenin, "Letter to Sylvia Pankhurst, in *Anarchism*, p. 298. See also Lenin, *What is to be Done?*, p. 21.

25. Lenin, "The Faction of Supporters of Otsovism and God-Building," in *Anarchism*, pp. 236-37.

26. Tucker, *Anthology,* p. xxxiii.

27. Lenin, "The Proletarian Revolution and the Renegade Kautsky," in Tucker, *Anthology*, p. 463.

28. Lenin, "The Immediate Tasks of the Soviet Government," in Tucker, *Anthology,* p.455.

29. Lenin, "The immediate Tasks of the Soviet Government," in *Anarchism*, p. 289.

30. Lenin, *The State and Revolution* (Mansfield Center, Conn.: Martino Publishers, 2011), p.14.

31. Lenin, "Two Tactics of Social-Democracy," in Tucker, *Anthology*, p.142.

32. Lenin, *The State and Revolution*, p.8.

33. *Ibid.*, p. 17.

34. Lenin, "The Immediate Tasks of the Soviet Government," in *Anarchism*, p.289.

35. Lenin, "Better Fewer, But Better," in Tucker, *Anthology,* p. 735.

36. Lenin, *What is to be Done?*, p.76.

37. Lenin, "Report on Party Unity and the Anarcho-Syndicalist Deviation," in *Anarchism*, p. 335.

38. Lenin, "Better Fewer, But Better," in Tucker, *Anthology,* p.735.

39. Lenin, "Introducing the New Economic Policy," in Tucker, *Anthology*, p. 505.

40. Lenin, "How Vera Zasulich Demolishes Liquidationism," in *Anarchism*, p.252.

41. Lenin, *The State and Revolution*, p. 48.

42. Lenin, "Can the Bolsheviks Retain State Power?" in Tucker, *Anthology*, p. 403.

43. Lenin, "Preliminary Draft Resolution of the Tenth Congress of the R.C.P., On the Syndicalist and Anarchist Deviation in Our Party," in *Anarchism*, p.35.

44. Lenin, *The State and Revolution*, in *Anarchism*, p.286.

45. Lenin, "'Left Wing' Communism—An Infantile Disorder," in Tucker, *Anthology*, p. 570. It has been said that one result of World War I was to bring the revolutionary movement to nations where it had not previously existed. However true, it should be noted that it was as a nation state that Russia assumed leadership of the worldwide communist movement. It is difficult to find an instance of Soviet leadership which ran in any way counter to the perceived interests of Russia. As we shall see, the Chinese revolution was founded on a deep sense of nationalism as well.

46. As Vladimir Putin has demonstrated to a certainty, nationalism has outlived communism. Putin has attacked Lenin for policies which led to independence from Russia of Ukraine and other neighbors bordering Russia. We see a similar phenomenon with modern China.

47. Lenin, *The State and Revolution*, p. 74.

48. Lenin, "The Immediate Tasks of the Soviet Government," in Tucker, *Anthology*, p. 449.

49. Lenin, *The State and Revolution*, p. 73.

50. *Ibid.*, p.83.

51. Mao speaks about this in many of his writings. See, for example, "A Single Spark Can Start a Prairie Fire," *Selected Works*, Vol. I (Peking: Foreign Languages Press, 1975), pp. 117-18.

52. Mao, "Strategy in China's Revolutionary War," *Selected Works*, Vol. I, p. 181.

53. Stuart Schram, *Mao-Tse-tung* (Middlesex, England: Penguin Books, 1966,) p. 139.

54. Mao, "The Chinese Revolution and the Chinese Communist Party," *Selected Works*, Vol. II (Peking: Foreign Languages Press, 1967), p. 317.

55. *Ibid.*, p.317.

56. Mao, "The Chinese Revolution and the Chinese Communist Party," *Selected Works*, Vol. II, p. 319.

57. Mao, "On Contradiction," *Selected Works*, Vol. I, p. 336.

58. Schram, *Mao Tse-tung*, p. 127.

59. *Ibid.*, p. 127.

60. Mao, "Socialist Upsurge in China's Countryside," quoted in Schram, *Mao Tse-tung*, pp. 280-81.

61. Mao, "Why is it that Red Power Can Exist in China," *Selected Works*, Vol. I, p. 66.

62. Shram, *Mao Tse-tung*, p. 123.

63. *Ibid.*, p. 125.

64. Mao, "Problems of War and Strategy," *Selected Works*, Vol. II, p. 221.

65. *Ibid.*, p.221.

66. *Ibid.*, p.222.

67. *Ibid.*, p. 222.

68. *Ibid.*, p. 223.

69. Mao, "On New Democracy," *Selected Works*, Vol. II, p. 340 and p. 369.

70. Mao, "Combat Liberalism," *Selected Works*, Vol. II, p. 31.

71. Mao, "On New Democracy," *Selected Works,* Vol. II, p. 382.

72. Mao, "The Chinese Revolution and the Chinese Communist Party," *Selected Works,* Vol. II, p. 332.

73. Again, although the rhetoric is Marxist, the concepts are not. Thomas Jefferson, for example, said in 1787 that "the tree of liberty must be refreshed from time to time with the blood of patriots and tyrants."

74. Schram, *Mao Tse-tung*, p. 337.

75. Mao, "The Tasks of the Chinese Communist Party in the Period of Resistance to Japan," *Selected Works,* Vol. I, p. 263.

76. *Ibid.,* footnote, p. 276.

77. Mao, "Conclusion of the Repulse of the Second Anti-Communist Onslaught," *Selected Works,* Vol. II, p. 467.

78. Mao, "On Tactics Against Japanese Imperialism," *Selected Works*, Vol. I, p. 165.

79. Mao, "On New Democracy," *Selected Works,* Vol. II, pp. 349-50.

80. Harry Harding, *China's Second Revolution: Reform after Mao* (Washington, D.C.: The Brookings Institution, 1987), p. 24.

81. See, for example, Mao. "On New Democracy," *Selected Works,* Vol. II, p. 294.

82. *Ibid.,* pp. 380-81.

83. Quoted in Schram, *Mao Tse-tung*, pp. 220-21.

84. This can be seen very clearly in Mao's Rectificaton Campaign begun in 1942. See Schram, *Mao-Tse-tung*, pp. 220 ff.

85. Mao, "On Policy," *Selected Works*, Vol. II, p. 448.

86. This is so much the case that Harry Harding refers to this period as China's "second revolution" in his book with that title.

87. Quoted in Harding, *Second Revolution,* p.186.

88. Xi Jinping, "Speech on the 100th Anniversary of the Chinese Communist Party," English translation by Xinhua News Agency.

89. Engels, Preface, *Capital,* Vol. II, p. 16.

90. Quoted in Joseph Schumpeter, "Is the History of Economics the History of Ideologies?" in David Braybrooke, *Philosophical Problems of the Social Sciences* (New York: Macmillan, 1965), p. 118.

THREE: THE AMERICAN COMMERCIAL REPUBLIC

1. It was, for example, the purpose of Machiavelli, Spinoza and Hobbes—though they differed in many ways—to consider how government could exist, taking men as they are and not as we wish them to be.

2. Montesquieu, *The Spirit of the Laws*, Book XX (New York: Hafner Publishing Company, 1949), p. 316.

3. Quoted in Albert O. Hirschman, *The Passions and the Interests: Arguments for Capitalism Before Its Triumph* (Princeton: Princeton University Press, 1977), p. 61.

4. *Ibid.*, p. 65.

5. Albert O. Hirschman, *The Passions and the Interests: Arguments for Capitalism Before Its Triumph.*

6. Montesquieu, *The Spirit of the Laws*, Book XX, p. 317.

7. Quoted in Hirschman, *The Passions and the Interests*, p. 107.

8. Adam Smith, *Lectures*, quoted in Hirschman, *The Passions and the Interests*, pp. 106-07.

9. See Harvey C. Mansfield, "Liberty and Virtue in the American Founding," in Peter Berkowitz, ed., *Never a Matter of Indifference* (Stanford, Ca.: Hoover Institution Press, 2003), pp. 21-26. Mansfield observes that despite the importance of a commercial spirit, the American republic still requires the presence of virtues to survive. He mentions energy, ambition and responsibility as virtues which complement the self-interest expressed in commerce.

10. Alexander Hamilton, *The Federalist Papers*, number 12.

11. *Ibid.,* number 6.

12. James Madison, *The Federalist Papers,* number 10.

13. Alexis de Tocqueville, *Democracy in America*, Vol. II (New York: Doubleday, 1969), p. 544.

14. McCloskey, *Bourgeois Dignity*, p. 349.

15. Hirschman, *The Passions and the Interests*, p. 132.

16. Quoted in Robert Wiebe and Grady McWhiney, eds., *Historical Vistas: Readings in United States History,* Vol. II (Boston: Allyn and Bacon, 1964), pp. 223-24.

17. Edwin Seligman, *The Economic Interpretation of History* (New York: Columbia University press, 1917), p. 126.

18. *Ibid.,* p. 105.

19. *Ibid.,* p. 108.

20. *Ibid.,* p. 107.

21. Wilson, *To the Finland Station,* p. 483.

22. See Augusto Del Noce, *The Problem of Atheism.* See also, Francis X. Meier, "How Marxism Won the 'War' of ideas," *The Wall Street Journal,* January 7, 2022.

23. Nelson, *Economics as Religion*, pp. 33-34.

24. This view was also that of the nineteenth century apostle of liberty John Stuart Mill, who was an exact contemporary of Marx.

25. There is an echo of this view in Senator Bernie Sanders' question: why do we need so many different kinds of deodorants? Wouldn't one or two be enough?

26. Quoted in George F. Will, *The Conservative Sensibility* (New York: Hachette, 2019), p. 67.

27. Bryan Caplan, *The Myth of the Rational Voter: Why Democracies Choose Bad Policies* (Princeton: Princeton University Press, 2007), p. 10.

28. In a Speech on June 16, 2022 to the American Constitutional Society, Sonia Sotomayor seems to imply the weakness of theoretical claims concerning the so-called arc of history. She refers to the idea that "the arc of the universe bends toward justice" as "magical words."

29. McCloskey, *The Vices of Economists: The Virtues of the Bourgeoisie* (Amsterdam: Amsterdam University Press, 1996), p. 108.

30. McCloskey, *Bourgeois Virtues*, p. 197. We might think too of Goethe's *Faust* (Part II) where Faust trades his soul for what is essentially a housing development project.

31. Einstein dies and goes to heaven. There St. Peter introduces him to his new colleagues. The first has an IQ of 160. Einstein says, "Excellent. We can do theoretical physics together." The second has an IQ of 120. Einstein says, "Very good. We can play chess together." The third has an IQ of 80. Einstein says, "Which way do you think interest rates will go?"

32. McCloskey, *Why Liberalism Works*, p. 105: "economic science of an orthodox character is good at explaining routine."

33. Quoted in Steven Rhoads, *The Economist's View and the Quest for Well-Being.* 35th Anniversary Edition (Cambridge: Cambridge University press, 2021), p. 189.

34. Quoted in Nelson, *Economics as Religion*, p. 282.

35. Rhoads, *The Economist's View,* p. 123. Consider also the definition of economics in Robert L. Heilbroner and William Milberg, *The Making of Economic Society* (Hoboken, N. J.: Prentice Hall, 1962), p. 1: "In its broadest sense, economics is the study of a process we find in all human societies—*the process of providing for the material well-being of society.* In its simplest terms, economics is the study of how humankind secures its daily bread."

36. An early draft of the Declaration of Independence stated that men's inalienable rights included "life, liberty and property." This was altered to read "life, liberty and the pursuit of happiness." As George Will notes, however, this change was not as significant as it might appear. Following Locke, the framers understood that men had property in themselves, that is, the right to manage their own lives, that is, liberty. This is the very meaning of "property," which is the right to use and dispose of any entity. We will discuss this further in the next chapter.

37. Quoted in Nelson, *Economics as Religion,* p. 53.

38. Nobel prize-winning economist Douglass North offers a straightforward description of Arrow's theorem in *Lives of the Laureates: Twenty-three Nobel Economists,* ed. by William Breit and Barry Hirsch (Cambridge, Mass.: MIT Press, 2009), p. 217: "In effect, one cannot achieve collectively rational choices by aggregating the individual choices of people with diverse values or preferences."

39. Quoted in Nelson, *Economics as Religion,* pp. 122-23.

40. Presentation speech by Professor Ingmar Staehl at the Nobel Prize ceremony, Oslo, 1986.

41. James M. Buchanan and Gordon Tullock, *The Calculus of Consent: Logical Foundations of Constitutional Democracy* (Ann Arbor, Mich.: University of Michigan Press, 1962), p. 12.

42. The author had the privilege of working briefly with him when he testified before the United States Senate about a balanced budget amendment to the Constitution.

43. Caplan, *Myth of the Rational Voter,* p. 206: "In daily life, reality gives us material incentives to restrain our irrationality. But what incentive do we have to think rationally about politics? Almost none … Democracy lets the individual enjoy the psychological benefits at no cost to himself."

44. Robert Kagan, "Our Constitutional Crisis is Already Here," *Washington Post,* September 23, 2021.

45. Mitch Daniels, *Keeping the Republic: Saving America by Trusting Americans* (New York: Penguin Group, 2012), pp. 64 ff. calls today's Americans "shrunken citizens." See also Victor Davis Hanson, *The Dying Citizen* (New York: Hatchette, 2021), pp. 115 ff.

46. Caplan, *Myth of the Rational Voter,* p. 28.

FOUR: DOMESTIC POLICYMAKING

1. John F. Cogan, "Entitlements Always Grow and Grow," *Wall Street Journal,* January 4, 2022.

2. See Cogan, *Ibid.* See also Laura S. Jensen, *The Early American Origins of Entitlements,* online, Cambridge University Press, December 16. 2008.

3. Nicholas Eberstadt, *A Nation of Takers: America's Entitlement Epidemic* (Conshohocken, Pa.: Templeton Press, 2012), pp. 8-9. Alan Blinder and Mark Watson have pointed out that federal deficits in recent years— driven in large part by entitlement programs—have averaged 2.8% of GDP under Republican presidents compared with 2.1% under Democratic presidents. These numbers, however, do not include the vast spending during the Biden presidency, which would skew the numbers back toward Democratic presidents.

4. Joseph Epstein, "Republicans Should Stand for More Than Opposing Democrats," *Wall Street Journal,* August 31, 2022.

5. George Will, *The Conservative Sensibility*, p. 293.

6. Rhoads, *The Economist's View of the World*," p. 123: "In their research, economists usually assume that more income means more goods and services, and thus more satisfaction/happiness."

7. See, among others, Arthur Brooks, *Gross National Happiness.* See also Richard A. Easterlin, "Explaining Happiness," *Proceedings of the National Academy of Sciences,* 2003, 100(19), pp. 11176-11183, and "Does Economic Growth Improve the Human Lot? Some Empirical Evidence," in R. David and R. Reder, eds., *Nations and Households in Economic Growth: Essays in Honor of Morris Abromovitz,* 1974. See also works by Angus Deaton and Daniel Kahneman; Betsy Stevenson and Justin Wolfers; Jane Mayer; Robert Samuelson, *The Good Life and Its Discontents*; Helen Johns and Paul Omerod, *Happiness, Economics and Public Policy;* Jonathan Haidt, *The Righteous Mind: Why Good People are Divided by Politics and Religion*; and various Gallup Poll surveys.

8. Liah Greenfield, "The West's Struggle for Mental Health," *Wall Street Journal,* June 1, 2022.

9. David Mamet, *Recessional: The Death of Free Speech and the Cost of a Free Lunch* (New York: Harper Collins, 2022) p. 131.

10. Engels, *Ludwig Feuerbach and the Outcome of Classical German Philosophy,* p. 39.

11. Arthur Brooks, *Summary: Gross National Happiness* (New York: Business News Publishing, 2022), p. 10.

12. Senator Susan Collins (R, ME), remarks delivered in the United States Senate, September 28, 2021, quoted in the *Wall Street Journal,* October 2, 2021.

13. Nelson, *Economics as Religion*, p. 80.

14. Quoted in Will, *The Conservative Sensibility,* p. 40.

15. William A. Schambra, "Progressive Liberalism and American 'Community,' " *Public Interest,* Summer, 1985, p. 8.

16. See Charles L. Reich, "The New Property," *Yale Law Journal*, April, 1964.

17. These are described in Joseph S. Nye, Jr., Philip D. Zelikow and David B. King, eds., *Why People Don't Trust Government* (Cambridge, Mass.: Harvard University Press, 1997).

18. *Ibid.*, p. 207.

19. *Ibid.*, pp. 91-92.

20. *Ibid.,* p. 149. See also Nelson, *Economics as Religion*, p. 106.

21. Rhoads, *The Economist's View of the World,* p. 122.

22. This occurs frequently with both domestic and defense spending. Much of the final debate over the continuing resolution in December of 2022, for example, concerned the relative percentage increases of domestic and defense spending.

23. Jason L. Riley, "The Biden Administration's New Salvo Against Charter Schools," *Wall Street Journal,* April 27, 2022.

24. Mitch Daniels, "Student Loans and the National Debt," *Wall Street Journal,* September 2, 2022.

25. See the discussion in Rafael Mangual, *Criminal (In)Justice: What the Push for Decarceration and Depolicing Gets Wrong and Who it Hurts Most* (New York: Center Street, 2022). He shows that homicides in New York City fell from 2,200 in 1990 to 300 in 2018. This was a period in which the city's poverty rate increased slightly. He also shows that during the recession of 2007-2009, the unemployment rate for blacks more than doubled, yet murders continued to fall.

26. David von Drehle, "Democrats should ask 'how'—not 'how much,' "*Washington Post,* September 26, 2021. He further says "At times the spending appears symbolic rather than real. Congress signals concern by multiplying numbers. A billion is a thousand times more sincere than a lousy million."

27. Charles Schultze, *The Politics and Economics of Public Spending* (Washington, D. C.: The Brookings Institution, 1968), p. 56.

28. In recent years Congress has adopted an even worse habit. Massive spending bills are written in the offices of the Congressional leadership and called up for a vote with little or no time for members to consider the legislation. In these cases Congressional hearings are absent altogether and even inputs, much less outputs, are haphazard.

29. Von Drehle, "Democrats should ask 'how'—not 'how much,' " *Washington Post,* September 26, 2021.

30. *Ibid.*

31. William Breit and Barry T. Hirsch, *Lives of the Laureates,* p. 261.

32. See George Will, *The Conservative Sensibility,* p. 295.

33. Jonathan Haidt, *The Righteous Mind: Why Good People are Divided by Politics and Religion* (New York: Random House, 2012), p. 215.

34. Thomas Frank, *What's the Matter with Kansas: How Conservatives Won the Heart of America* (New York: Holt and Company, 2004), p. 68.

35. *Ibid.,* p. 121.

36. See, for example, Caplan, *Myth of the Rational Voter,* p. 18.

37. Fareed Zakaria, "Biden needs to score in the culture wars," *Washington Post,* June 26, 2022.

38. Elaine Kamarck and William A. Galston, "Will Democrats Throw It All Away in 2024?" *Wall Street Journal,* February 26-27, 2022.

39. Caplan, *Myth of the Rational Voter,* p. 149.

40. Center for Responsive Politics, on line.

41. Caplan, *Myth of the Rational Voter,* pp. 179-180. Caplan cites studies by Stratmann, Ansolabehere and de Figueiredo.

42. Robert J. Samuelson, *Untruth: Why the Conventional Wisdom is (Almost Always) Wrong* (New York: Random House, 2001), p. 55.

43. *Ibid.,* p. 53.

44. In recent years there has been less focus on the importance of campaign finance reform. Perhaps this reflects in part the fact that Democrats increasingly are raising as much or more money than Republican candidates. This was certainly true in the Obama-McCain election of 2008, the Obama-Romney election of 2012, the Clinton-Trump election of 2016 and the Biden-Trump election of 2020. This was also true of many of the hotly contested Senate races in 2020. Karl Rove notes that "Every winning GOP Senate candidate in a competitive race in 2020 was outspent." See Karl Rove, "Pelosi Tries to Smile Through November," *Wall Street Journal*, October 10, 2022. And in 2022 "Democrats outspent their Republican opponents in 10 of the most competitive Senate races as the midterm campaigns headed into the final stretch before Election Day, new fundraising reports filed with the Federal Election commission show." See "Money Pours Into Senate Campaigns," *Wall Street Journal,* October 17, 2022.

    Perhaps a changing calculation of Democrats' ability to raise money has muted somewhat their traditional support for broad campaign finance reform. Currently Democrats are focused on what they call the problem of "dark money" which both political parties raise. Democrats have demonstrated the ability to raise this kind of money equal to the Republicans. What they seek is transparency, which would permit progressives to "name and shame" Republican donors, a practice which is infrequently undertaken by Republicans.

45. Schultze, *The Politics and Economics of Public Spending*, p. 79.

46. *Ibid.*, p. 79.

47. McCloskey, *Liberalism*, p. 105.

48. Schultze, *The Politics and Economics of Public Spending*, p. 60.

FIVE: FOREIGN ASSISTANCE AND INTERVENTION ABROAD

1. Kori N. Schake, *State of Disrepair: Fixing the Culture and Practices of the State Department* (Stanford, Ca.: Hoover Institution Press, 2012), p. 8.

2. *Ibid.*, p. 12.

3. *Ibid.*, p. 80. Dambisa Moyo argues that every short-term program evaluation gives the impression of success. See *Dead Aid: Why Aid is Not Working and How There is a Better Way for Africa* (New York: Farrar, Straus and Giroux, 2009), p. 43.

4. Moyo, *Dead Aid*, p. 37.

5. Nelson, *Economics as Religion,* p. 1.

6. Diane E. Rennack and Susan G. Chesser, "Foreign Assistance Act of 1961; Authorizations and Corresponding Appropriations," *Congressional Research Service*, July 29, 2011, p. 4.

7. Robert Nisbet, *Social Change and History* (Oxford: Oxford University Press,1985), p. 276.

8. W. W. Rostow, *The Stages of Economic Growth: A Non-Communist Manifesto* (Cambridge: Cambridge University Press, 1965), p. 2. Rostow says that Marx and Engels acknowledged this in their old age.

9. *Ibid.,* p. 139.

10. *Ibid.,* p. 102.

11. *Ibid.*, pp. 143-44.

12. See Moyo, *Dead Aid,* p. 54.

13. Daron Acemoglu and James A. Robinson, *Why Nations Fail: The Origins of Power, Prosperity and Poverty* (New York: Penguin Random House, 2012), p. 42.

14. *Ibid.*, p. 43.

15. Albert Hirschman, *The Strategy of Economic Development* (New Haven, Conn.: Yale University Press, 1958), p. 209.

16. N. Gregory Mankiw, "Outsourcing Redux," online, May 7, 2006.

17. Walter Russell Mead, "Global Free Trade Is In Crisis," *Wall Street Journal*, November 30, 2021.

18. Tim Groser, "The U. S. Has a Way Back to the TPP," *Wall Street Journal*, September 30, 2021.

19. Clifford D. May, "The Fall of the Golden Arch Theory," *Washington Examiner*, March 16, 2022.

20. See Acemoglu and Robinson, *Why Nations Fail*, p. 128. See also Robert Heilbroner, *The Making of Economic Society*, pp. 225-26.

21. Gerald F. Seib, "A Theory About Global Ties Is Tested," *Wall Street Journal*, January 11, 2022.

22. Daniel D. Drezner, "The United States of Sanctions: The Use and Abuse of Economic Sanctions," *Foreign Affairs*, September/October, 2021.

23. See Nicholas Mulder, *The Economic Weapon: The Rise of Sanctions as a Tool of Modern War* (New Haven, Conn.: Yale University Press, 2022). Mulder offers a full account of economic sanctions during the inter-war period.

24. Rueul Marc Gerecht and Ray Takyeh, "Iran's Hard-Liners Believe They're Winning," *Wall Street Journal*, May 13, 2022.

25. Quoted in Georgi Kantchev and Paul Hannon, "Sanctions So Far Are Failing To Blunt Moscow's War Effort," *Wall Street Journal*, June 17, 2022.

26. Aaron MacLean, "What Putin, Xi and Khamenei Want," *Wall Street Journal*, December 28, 2021.

27. Mulder, *The Economic Weapon*, p. 297.

28. Jeryl Bier, "Kerry: Root Cause of Terrorism Is Poverty," *Washington Examiner*, online, January 15, 2014.

29. Alan B. Krueger and Jitka Maleckova, "Education, Poverty and Terrorism: Is There a Causal Connection?" *Journal of Economic Perspectives*, vol. 17, number 4, Fall, 2003, p. 142.

30. Martin Gassebner and Simon Luechinger "Lock, Stock and Barrel: A Comprehensive Assessment of the Determinants of Terror," *CESIFO Working Papers*, number 3550, August, 2011, p. 17.

31. *Ibid.*, p. 17.

32. Michael Jetter, Rafat Mahmood and David Stadelmann, "Income and Terrorism: Insights from Subnational Data," *IZA Institute of Labor Economics*, Discussion Paper Series, December 2021, p. 3.

33. Krueger and Maleckova, "Education, Poverty and Terrorism," p.142.

34. Joshua Muravchik, "Two Cheers: Second Thoughts on the Bush Doctrine," *World Affairs*, Fall, 2008, p. 60.

SIX: INTELLIGENCE FAILURES

1. Angelo Codevilla, *Informing Statecraft: Intelligence for a New Century* (New York: The Free Pres, 1992), p. 125.

2. *Ibid.*, p. 199.

3. McCloskey, *Bourgeois Dignity*, p. 301. See also Codevilla, *Statecraft*, pp. 17-18.

4. Codevilla, *Statecraft*, p. 201.

5. Central Intelligence Agency, "Global Trends 2040," Executive Summary.

6. Much the same could be said about the National Intelligence Strategy which is issued every four years. To be kind, it is very abstract. To be honest, it is less a projection of what should be done than, much like its State Department cousin, a summary of what it is already doing.

7. McCloskey, *Bourgeois Dignity*, p. 354.

8. Quoted in Josh Craddock, "Through a Glass Darkly: How Iranian Revolutionaries Blindsided America's Secular Intelligence Community," *Providence* (emag.com), note #25, November 17, 2016.

9. Malcolm Byrne, "Intelligence Reporting on the Iranian Revolution: A Mixed Record," National Security Archive, George Washington University.

10. The GAO study was titled "Soviet Economy: Assessment of How Well the CIA Has Estimated the Size of the Economy." See also Andrew W. Marshall and Abram N. Shulsky, "Assessing Sustainability of Command Economies and Totalitarian Regimes: The Soviet Case," *Orbis*, 62, #2, Spring, 2018.

11. Michael Allen, "U. S. Spies Didn't Cause Kabul to Fall," *Wall Street Journal*, September 2, 2021.

12. Quoted in Jerry Dunleavy, "CIA Director 'proud' of Afghanistan analysis despite disastrous Taliban take over," *Justice Department Reporter*, July 24, 2022.

13. Joel Brenner, "Counterintelligence Failure in Afghanistan," *Wall Street Journal*, December 6, 2021.

14. See Fareed Zakaria, "Kabul fell one year ago. Here are lessons we should learn," *Washington Post*, August 14, 2022.

15. Quoted in Reuters, "Excerpts of call between Joe Biden and Ashraf Ghani July 23," August 31, 2021.

16. Quoted in Zakaria, "Kabul fell one year ago."

17. Quoted in Sascha Brodsky, "This Is How the U. S. Totally Misjudged the War in Ukraine," *Daily Beast*, November 28, 2022.

18. *Ibid.*

19. Quoted in Jason Beardsley, "Military and intelligence leaders are failing us," *Washington Times*, May 3, 2022.

20. Quoted in Julian Barnes, "Why the U. S. Was Wrong About Ukraine and the Afghan War," *New York Times*, March 24, 2022.

SEVEN: SOME MODEST PROPOSALS

1. Among many judgments to this effect, consider the conservative columnist Gerard Baker, "The ascendant left is the locomotive behind our culture and politics." Quoted in "How the Gas Stove in Your Kitchen Became a Symbol of Freedom," the *Wall Street Journal*, January 17, 2023.

2. Alexandr Solzhenitsyn, "A World Split Apart," speech delivered at Harvard University, June 8, 1978.

3. There is an interesting, though somewhat flawed, discussion of the relation between advocates of free markets and constitutionally guaranteed liberties in Naomi Oreskes and Erik Conway, *The Big Myth: How American Business Taught Us to Loathe Government and Love the Free Market*. Bloomsbury Press, 2023.

4. For state governments see Russell S. Sobel and John A. Dove, "Analyzing the Effectiveness of State Regulatory Review," *Sage Publications*, 2014. The authors conclude that "sunset provisions are the most effective means of reducing state regulatory levels."

5. The author has had experience trying to remove legislation from the books. In 1986 I gathered a list of hundreds of executive branch reports which the foreign affairs committees required to be submitted to Congress. Many were being issued sporadically, others were regularly ignored and some were relics put into law by members of Congress who had long since passed away. In the spirit of accommodation I proposed

that those reports that members or staff still wished to retain would be struck from the list to be eliminated. The remaining list turned out to be very short. Sunset provisions attached to these reports would have required that members argue anew why these reports were still needed. This would have produced an entirely different and longer list.

6. For a very clear and nuanced discussion of sunset laws see Frank H. Esterbrook, William N. Eskridge, Philip H. Howard and Thomas W. Merrill, "Showcase Panel IV: A Federal Sunset Law," *16 Texas Review of Law and Politics 399,* 2012.

7. See Nelson, *Economics as Religion.*